Jenny & Dyke
Keep the faith
"God's got you"

Love
Baye
2023

WHAT YOU CAN BECOME WHEN YOUR FAITH GROWS UP

GAYE LAFOE

Copyright © 2023 Gaye LaFoe.

All rights reserved. No part of this book may be used or reproduced by any means, graphic, electronic, or mechanical, including photocopying, recording, taping or by any information storage retrieval system without the written permission of the author except in the case of brief quotations embodied in critical articles and reviews.

WestBow Press books may be ordered through booksellers or by contacting:

WestBow Press
A Division of Thomas Nelson & Zondervan
1663 Liberty Drive
Bloomington, IN 47403
www.westbowpress.com
844-714-3454

Because of the dynamic nature of the Internet, any web addresses or links contained in this book may have changed since publication and may no longer be valid. The views expressed in this work are solely those of the author and do not necessarily reflect the views of the publisher, and the publisher hereby disclaims any responsibility for them.

Any people depicted in stock imagery provided by Getty Images are models, and such images are being used for illustrative purposes only. Certain stock imagery © Getty Images.

Scripture quotations taken from The Holy Bible, New International Version® NIV® Copyright © 1973 1978 1984 2011 by Biblica, Inc. TM. Used by permission. All rights reserved worldwide.

Scripture quotations are from the ESV® Bible (The Holy Bible, English Standard Version®), copyright © 2001 by Crossway, a publishing ministry of Good News Publishers. Used by permission. All rights reserved.

4233043501@charter.net

ISBN: 978-1-6642-7038-1 (sc)
ISBN: 978-1-6642-7039-8 (hc)
ISBN: 978-1-6642-7037-4 (e)

Library of Congress Control Number: 2022911553

Print information available on the last page.

WestBow Press rev. date: 02/17/2023

gayelafoeauthor@gmail.com

THE STORIES IN THIS BOOK REFLECT THE AUTHOR'S RECOLLECTION OF EVENTS. NAMES, LOCATIONS AND IDENTIFYING CHARACTERISTICS HAVE BEEN CHANGED TO PROTECT THE PRIVACY OF SOME OF THOSE DEPICTED. DIALOGUE HAS BEEN RE-CREATED FROM MEMORY. AND DATES ARE ESTIMATES FROM MEMORY.

DEDICATION

This book is dedicated to my God—my creator, deliverer, and healer. May He receive all the glory.

To Bruce LaFoe, you came along when I needed to feel whole again, and you picked up all the pieces. Sometimes, a girl really does get her fairy tale. Thank you for sharing your life with me. I thank God every day that you are mine.

ACKNOWLEDGMENTS

To my precious children Jonathan and Bethany, you have given me more joy than a mom deserves. Thank you for being my best productions. My love for you is beyond anything imaginable. I pray that every word referenced in the writing of this book will give you hope, direction, and the knowledge that you are not ever alone, God is always there. Keep Him in your life and teach your babies to love Him—that is my greatest wish. Rest in the knowledge that you are valuable to God; you are enough. He loves you more than I ever could, and you must not miss heaven, no matter the cost.

To my grandchildren, I love all of you beyond anything I could have ever thought. My heart's desire is that you know this savior, Jesus Christ, that I have spoken of in this writing. May He take every step of life with you, and, in every decision, you make, may he be your source of reference. I pray that when I have left for Heaven, you will remember Granna with affection and love. Keep your Bible close to your heart to refer to because it gets dark in life sometimes. Do not wonder where to go for help my sweet ones, run to Jesus. Hover close to the cross and let Him give you peace and joy that only He can give.

To Bethany, thank you for helping with the photos for the cover art, and to little Novalee for being so patient while Granna and mommy made them look exactly right.

To my mother, I hope you trusted that I would set the record straight one day. No one ever loved their children more or made more sacrifices than you did. You showed me how to live for God. He was always first in your life. Thank you for my foundation and for telling me about Jesus. I never told you, but you were right every time. I often ask God to slip up beside you and give you a hug. I miss you every single day, Mom.

To my sweet dad, I may not be the famous singer you wanted me to become, but I hope I was not a disappointment to you. I know you felt let down, and that I walked away from something big, but I hope you are proud of me and the choice I made. I learned a lot from you, Dad. You taught me to fight for myself and to have influence when I could. I credit you for my, well some, of my gift of gab. You always authored great short stories. You sacrificed for me. Your love for the country and passion for good live on in me, my brother, and our children. Most of all from your very own proud daughter, thank you for putting cushion into my life the best you knew how so that I would land gently.

An incredibly special thanks to my precious brother. You were the steady one in the family. You never lost direction. Your love and dedication to the Lord is astounding. The sacrifices you, your wife and children have made to plant churches in desolate places do not go unnoticed by God. I love your wife and those boys so much. Thanks for doing life with me. I love you, genius.

To Reverend Don Glenn, thank you for your obedience that day when God healed my back and your counsel after my life-changing event in the cemetery. Your family was a blessing to ours during times when we were hurting. And I will never forget it.

To Pastor Olubunmi Oluwole, you have been my brother for many years. Thank you for being obedient and sending confirmation that it was time to author my story. You know my heart so well. Your love for the master and the work you have done is beyond sacrifice. Your precious family is an inspiration to me. Thank you for everything!

To Pastor James Sears, God showed me that you were the one to come to for encouragement through the writing of this book. I have always had such confidence in your life, and you were there every step of the way through this process to spur me on. I felt your prayers every single day while I was writing. I will always be grateful for your leadership and your faithfulness to the Kingdom. I love your example and how you pour your heart into ministry. Thank you for all you do!

To the reader that happens upon this material, may it encourage you to keep seeking. Do not fight the journey; learn from it, and, no matter what, don't take your eyes off of Him. And always, KEEP THE FAITH!

To Maude, I know you are singing in Heaven. Thank you for seeing potential in a funny little girl.

To Janice, thank you my angel.

For everyone that brought my vision for this book to life, thank you!

He replied, "Because you have so little faith. Truly I tell you, if you have faith as small as a mustard seed, you can say to this mountain, 'Move from here to there,' and it will move. Nothing will be impossible for you."

Matthew 17:20 NIV

SHARED FROM A CLOSE FRIEND

Attestation for Sister Gaye

My family and ministry have known Sister Gaye LaFoe since 2008. She was the Executive President of the organization where I was ordained that year. Ministry brought us together and it united us in other areas as well. Even after she left the organization to do other things, we became inseparable as family friends.

Sister Gaye loves the Lord and people in general; she's a very committed person and dedicated to the core. Whatever she starts, she makes sure she finishes. She is very passionate, relentless, loving and has a caring personality. Her motherhood and godly character has also helped her in her private life.

When she told me she was writing a book titled, What You Can Become When Your Faith Grows Up; I was so excited for her. I cannot wait to have a copy of this book in my hands. I could picture the dexterity in which sister Gaye must have put in the materials, to be a book in our hands now. You and others will surely be tremendously blessed by this book.

Thank you for having given and giving to the world from the wealth of grace and mercy you received from the Lord.

You are loved and appreciated for the strength to work tirelessly, to release this book. Congratulations again my Sister.

Rev. Olubunmi Emmanuel Oluwole
Resident Pastor.
Grace Dunamis Ministries
California.

PREFACE

Every detail of your life becomes more important the longer you live. Your memories become more vivid, and you have the capacity to understand each situation and how it impacted your life. How you envision situations as a child may be fully understood once you become an adult. I guess it is learning to see yourself differently after time. The choices and reactions you make can impact your faith. You may have lived through tough things so you look at everything with a different tilt than you may have in your past.

This is not a project I wanted to take on; it is like an old wool sweater, uncomfortable and scratchy. Reliving moments from my past and my struggle makes me understand even more clearly how dependent I am on Christ now in this season of my life. But my reason for writing is not about me. Far from it. Yes, it is about my journey and how I became the person I am today (good but growing), and still in need of a savior. But it is for everyone who can relate to the battle with faith and a daily walk with God.

When the devil kicks the rug out from under you and you are on the ground with no strength to get back up, learn from me and Get Up! It is a fight until He comes! It is a reminder to keep picking up your cross daily to follow Him no matter what happens. My mother always said, "Heaven is cheap at any cost, and you cannot miss it." Every reference is true and honest, (sometimes brutally honest), for me to share. And, through every difficult page, I describe how God held on to me. My walk with the Lord has not been easy nor has it been easy to understand. Why did we take the long road, Lord? You may have asked yourself the same thing. Through every twist and turn, one thing is sure; Jesus was right beside me. He has always been faithful, whether I felt it at times or not. Sadly, my faith waned, and I lost direction.

I wanted to remove myself from the life I had and, in doing so, I did risky things. The more you feel, the more intense the pain is. So, taking myself to a place of numbness helped as much as it could to remove me from my life situations. Charles R. Swindoll wrote, "Life is 10 percent what happens to you and 90 percent how you react to it." It is a mirror that we can all peer into. The devil magnified the circumstances in my life to torment me. He tried in every way to destroy my life, but I did not fight alone. He failed to remember that. Secret doubt, lacking, as well as wondering if or why we are experiencing something on our journey are normal. God remembers we are dust, and it is OK to question or to ask, *"Why, God?"*

But once you finish questioning, then you must just stand and trust God. Just stand still. I had to learn that I was not always in charge, even when I thumbed my nose at God. Most importantly, I had to learn that God would deliver. The very idea that I, a mere human, would question the ability of God, my creator, makes me feel so ashamed. If He fed thousands with the equivalent of a happy meal, cleared blinded eyes with mud, gave water from a dusty hard ole rock, and flung the stars in the sky, who was I to question his mercy for me or greater yet, his power?

I had to learn tough lessons about just how my response to what I thought was a disaster could affect my outcome. And, most importantly, I needed to learn that God will come through. His mercy for me and the grace he showed towards me when I doubted his ability was more than I deserved. I walked alone for a long time, and he never once lost sight of me. I lost faith, but he was still faithful. I sure have a story to tell, so let's get started, shall we?

FOREWORD

This book is a must read for anyone who has ever questioned where God is, wondered if He listens when people pray, or has grown impatient waiting on Him to respond. Written from real experiences and authentic encounters with God, the story of Gaye's life has often strengthened my faith personally. Her testimony is a reminder of His faithfulness during even the most difficult of circumstances. I pray this book is as much of an encouragement to you as it has been to me!

Pastor James Sears
Lead Pastor
Mt. Olive, Cleveland TN

CHAPTER ONE

My motto has always been, "Leave everything a little better than you found it." It is not just a saying; it was drilled into me as a child. I strive to do my best in whatever I do and that is a direct reflection on my parents and my upbringing. We were raised with values. There was a reason for the ideals we were taught, and with a solid foundation of faith that I credit my mother most with. Our life was molded by discipline, love, and consequences.

I think since this is about my life, I should really start with the people most responsible for me. The only dad I ever knew, and honestly, I really do not know a lot about his life. I have had to learn bits and pieces over time about him. I do not recall my dad ever sharing much about his past, not many stories and, certainly, nothing about the military or the wars he served in. I do know that he was an only child, living in Chattanooga Tennessee at one point, and that his dad had died noticeably young from an infection.

My grandmother, whom he fondly referred to as a little spitfire, then married his stepfather and they went on to have several children together. Dad was the oldest obviously, by I think four years before the first child was born. I know they all loved each other but there was a fine line of family ownership that he seemed to think existed in the early days. It was a disconnect between he and his siblings. It was not talked about, and they all loved each other very much. I know he loved my grandpa, whom we lovingly called papa, but he felt isolated at times and a little like an outsider.

A military man of eighteen years, Dad served proudly in the Sixth Cavalry

What You Can Become When Your Faith Grows Up

in Georgia as a young man. He later went to the Army under General Patton's direction, serving at milestone events like the Battle of the Bulge, where he kept the tanks moving. There were other significant places he served, but he would not speak of the wars. I did receive his metals after many years, and I cherish them. On a few occasions, his Army friends would come for a reunion, and I would overhear stories about my dad and his shenanigans. He was quite a lady's man it appears.

Everyone called him "Bun" and still today I have no idea why. Dad was strong for his smaller stature, but he was someone to be reckoned with. He had taught boxing in the service, and stayed in shape, but oh, he had a temper. You didn't want to cross him. My mother would say before we would arrive at an event, "Now listen, I will cut your tongue out if you say something you shouldn't to these people; be nice!" Dad would wink and smile at my brother and me. He did not pick fights, but he could sure finish one.

Dad was difficult to understand; he was complex. He could be quiet and a little moody. Not extremely outgoing unless he knew you or you made him mad, and you did not want to make him mad. But he had a heart of gold and would give you the last dollar he had. People, (friends or co-workers), would come to our house down on their luck, and Dad would slip them money. He was dark and bouncy, and he walked like he owned the world.

I did not know until much later in life when he retired just how creative he was. He was a master craftsman in leather, and he authored beautiful short stories. Dad smelled like Old Spice and cigarettes. He had his demons though. He smoked from an early age like most kids back then. Later in life, I watched him suffer as the result of tobacco. Those things had a hold on him. There was a war raging in him but not related to the military. I remember when he got saved (not the first time I believe), and he gathered us around the Christmas tree like other Christmas Eves. But, that year, he read the Christmas story from the Bible to us. I still have that photo.

I do not remember how long it lasted, but he had told my mother that if he could not put the cigarettes down, then he truly was not living for God. And he was too weak to stop. I was little and remember the time he left the bedroom for a shower. I sneaked in and took his pack of Camel cigarettes and lighter to the backyard. I tried to get my brother to smoke with me, but he said no, it was a sin. I was not sure about that; up until then, no one had told me it was. But I was curious. So, I began puffing and inhaling every bit of smoke instead of exhaling it. They were small, white, and horrible tasting things, and I had sucked down a few fast, smoke and all. When Dad came looking for them, I had just laid them down on the table. I was too sick to care. Inhaling all that smoke made me so sick the rest of that day. I vowed I would never do it again. Dad smiled, "Well, I think you've learned your lesson, and that's punishment enough." He was so right.

His true demon had been alcohol. He became an alcoholic early and struggled through most of his early life with it and, especially, when he was overseas. He drank to forget, as other soldiers did. Oh, the horrible things they must have seen. I cannot even imagine.

Because he was so serious, he often had difficulties letting anyone into his world. I did not know he had an alcohol problem until he was getting ready to go out to speak at a meeting. I was just a kid and always curious as to what was happening in our house.

I remember asking him where he was going and why. Dad dressed well when he went out and I was so proud of him. Sometimes he and Mom would dress and go to a work event during the holidays. But, this time, he explained to me why he talked to other men about their problems with alcohol. I was fascinated, wanting to know more about what this mysterious elixir did to these men. Of course, with my imagination, I was thinking of some great potion in a big pot like a witch's brew in one of my fairy tales.

Dad was not one to mince words. He did not gloss things over or tell you some concocted story even though thoughts were already swirling in my head. He would explain to me that drinking alcohol offered a little "time to forget about what ails you." That is how he described it. I was certainly let down, expecting a more elaborate description of this mystery stuff, but satisfied with what he told me, and it was not discussed again. He did lean down close to me and whisper, "And I better never hear of you drinking, you understand?" I shivered at the thought of what a horrible thing it would be to taste that liquid sin, but even worse the punishment I would receive from my mother if she ever caught me. And Hell! I would go there for sure. "No Dad! I never will." I whispered back. And he headed out for the evening.

Oh, the things that would go through my mind. There was never any alcohol in our home. Dad's life turned around for the better when he met my mother.

CHAPTER TWO

I will not be referencing many names for sake of privacy; however, I will share my mother's name because of its uniqueness and true description of her. Dorcas, and so appropriate because she truly had a servant's heart. She never went by that name; friends and family called her Dean. When we wanted to tease her, we would call her Dorcas, and she would say, "Why would anyone name their child that?" A kid from the banks of the Allegheny River in Pennsylvania, Mom grew up a little different than Dad. She came from a German and Dutch background and often said she was from the sticks and the river was in her blood. I never knew any of my grandparents except papa, but I would have especially loved to have known my grandmothers. From what I have heard, they were both strong, outspoken individuals, and fitting examples of what a woman could be.

My grandparents carved out a simple life for my mom and her brothers. My grandfather made his living by teaching the locals and visitors that wandered through the area, ice skating on the river. He catered to the wealthier folks who preferred private lessons, and I am guessing locals too that could afford his expertise. He was well known for his extraordinary talent, and, during the summer months, he taught swimming lessons as well. Mom said he was a real charmer and had made a name for himself around those parts. I am sure he did other work to support the family, but she never talked much about him. And he only came up when we would ask questions. Mom was not close to any of her step siblings, only her two brothers.

We did find out that, as a child, her dad had taught her to swim, and she became so accomplished in her craft that the representative from the Olympic Committee came to meet with her and her parents with an offer for her to go with them and train to swim professionally. My grandparents had refused the offer, wanting to keep her home, and mom was stuck in the isolation of the woods and the ole river she grew to hate. Having older brothers was not an asset or company, as they were exploring their own way in the world and did not have time for her.

She would look out into the river of her childhood. Standing there with an almost haunted look on her face, we all wondered what must have been going through her mind, and how she remembered that time in her life. Would it be with regret? Or could there be any thought of good times?

There did not seem to be any great satisfaction on her face, remembering good times or old memories. She shied away from the place where her childhood house once stood.

The woman with the softest and most gentle face looked taunted and sad. We had come to her home place for a brief visit. Our choice had been either Pennsylvania or Niagara Falls. The older kids were interested in seeing where she came from. I wanted to go to Niagara Falls. I could tell it was difficult for her to be there in that place where she had experienced so many grim times. She was quiet and reserved, not our usual mom explaining things or showing us different areas where she played. She was always teaching us something. Everything we experienced was a life lesson we could build on for the future. I remember Dad saying at one point, "Kids, I think it's time to leave, your mom's had about enough."

When mom was eleven or twelve, grandmother became ill with uterine cancer. The only girl of the three, and for many reasons the closest to her mother, Mom took care of her. I asked her once if she was able to get out with friends during that time, and if there were boys. She would laugh a little and say, "Oh, honey, no there were no boys." No one to take her mind off her situation and loneliness. She said, "I was nothing to look at like you are sweetheart. I was a plain girl from the back woods of Pennsylvania." That broke my heart, because, to me, she was the most beautiful woman in the world.

Soon after my grandmother became ill, my grandfather, John, brought another woman and her children into their home to live with him. My poor grandmother. Her name was Barbara Ellen, but she went by Ellie. What she must have gone through. She was fighting for her life and worried about what would happen to her children after her death. She had my mom and her two brothers and there may have been a few children from a previous marriage, I am not certain. My grandfather also had been married prior to marrying my grandmother. All of this occurred when they were noticeably young. This man she had trusted and loved had betrayed her in the worst conceivable way. Mom told us that for many years she hated her dad for not being there for her mother and for being cold and heartless. She would remind him often that once grandmother was gone, she would leave that river she had grown to hate, and all of them behind. My mother, who left home at age fourteen, cared for my grandmother until she passed away.

She packed up what she had, just like she promised, and left, never looking back. She did not speak to my grandfather again from what I know. Mom did talk to her brothers later in life. She could also forgive her dad over time; however, once she accepted Jesus as her savior, she said she had let all the bitterness go. A young naive girl alone in the world, Mom took odd jobs to survive. I know that she was a nanny for a time. Feeling the ultimate betrayal and having no one in her corner, she began to search for answers.

Mom heard of a young woman evangelist known for her healing services and Bible-pounding preaching. Kathryn Kuhlman was touching lives with her ministry and God was moving in her services. But people, the church elite, were turned off by Kuhlman's flamboyant dress and disgraceful lipstick.

Mom said she often wore bright red lip color to the chagrin of the church leaders. In the old church, you did not wear form fitting clothing, and makeup was an absolute no-no. Even as a child in our home, I remember my sisters not being able to wear makeup, sleeveless shirts, sleeveless dresses, and absolutely no pants. I can remember going to school with dress and tights on every day. We did not listen to rock 'n' roll music or have playing cards or liquor in our home, ever. And we certainly were not allowed to go to a movie or drive in. I can remember one time riding with my folks and a drive in was playing across the road. Being a very inquisitive child, I was craning my neck to see behind the mysterious wall. What happened on the huge screen was a mystery to me. I could hear people talking but I could not see anything behind the wall that housed the screen.

"Do not even look over that way; it's sinful!" My mother said very sternly. Yikes! I was terrified. I had looked for a second, oh no! Was I going to hell? That is what they called the fear of God I guess, and she sure put it in us. I did not even see my first movie at a theatre until I was twenty. I had questions that I wanted to ask her, but it was just safer to look the other way that day. I sure did not need a lecture about the repercussions of watching a drive-in movie. Most of the time, we knew the reasons why something was wrong; neither of my folks said *because I said so* or anything to brush us off like that. Mom did stop me on occasion though with "I think I've answered enough questions right now," and that was my cue to take a break, because I had a lot of questions about everything on any given day.

Kathryn Kuhlman's ministry began to take off and she would pack out churches with her message of salvation and healing. It was during this time that my mother became familiar with her and began to attend her meetings. Of course, when something good is happening, you have your elite members and elders of the church that want to put a stop to things. For a lengthy period, many church leaders would not let Kuhlman have meetings and revivals in their churches because she looked worldly. Leave it to good church people to question someone's faith or motives.

Their plan of stopping her from preaching was to no avail. She continued to speak wherever there was an opportunity, and, at one point, they even gave her a small church to pastor. The great church pillars could no longer tolerate her traipsing around from place to place getting congregations worked into a frenzy with her message. So, they devised a plan to give her a church—the idea being that people would come, finally tire of her antics, and then they could shut down her church for lack of attendance.

My mother sat under Kathryn's teaching at a young impressionable age. She witnessed the movement of the Holy Spirit repeatedly. Mom credited Kuhlman many times for teaching her about the Lord and giving her direction. She had been nurtured from a lonely bitter young woman to the strong Godly woman I knew and loved. Knowing this as part of my mother's early life means so much to me. I listened to her stories about God's goodness, and how her life had changed because of it, and I saw an unwavering faith in her.

I am not sure when it occurred or how their story began, but my mother became involved with a young man. His family was well-known and well-off financially. They were known in parts of Pennsylvania because of their real estate holdings and other business endeavors. Mom later married this man, and they started a family. Since she had been tormented by loneliness and isolation as a child, mom longed for children of her own. "I was determined to give my kids the life I didn't have," she once told me. She had moved to Pittsburgh to start her new life, and for a time things were good. A daughter was born, and soon after a son. It is at that point that her marriage began to deteriorate.

Being a young naive woman from the river, she began to see him in a new light. He was a party boy, spoiled and used to having what he wanted. He always got his own way. He began to stay out at night. My mother had just had another little baby girl and was struggling physically to take care of everyone. Of course, when she needed help, her gadabout husband was nowhere to be found. From what I learned; he had been on his best behavior until he won my mother's heart. And, she did not know about his past not having lived in that area.

Drinking, fighting, and women were his vices, and he would find himself in jail on any given night, but his family would rush to bail him out so that their name would not be tarnished. My mother trusted his pleas of wanting to change, and she had given him more than enough chances.

A young Christian mother, she was determined to make her marriage work. Another son was born, and things were fine for a time. Mom knew that he may never change, but she had these children to care for. She could never reach out to his family because they had made it clear from the beginning that she was an outsider and not good enough for them. There was no one to turn to.

What You Can Become When Your Faith Grows Up

Mom left her church and what few friends she had made to move to this town to be with the man she loved. She had mentioned to me on one occasion, that she hadn't wanted to ever be dependent on a man for anything, "But there I was, these little babies to care for and me with no secondary education. I was totally dependent on this man." Winter months were approaching and, once again, the playboy was nowhere to be found. It was freezing in the house, with only a small amount of food left to share among her little hungry children.

Knowing my mother like I did, I know she would go without so her children could eat, if put in that position. It was in one of those desperate times that she did break down and contact his family to see if they knew where he was. She was met with judgment and with no regard for her children or the condition they were living in.

They advised her that they could not contact him and there was no offer of money. Mom had kept a small amount of money back for an emergency and she had not wanted to use it.

My mother had read often about a school of nursing in Detroit Michigan and had tossed around the idea of becoming a nurse one day when her life improved and the children were older. She had become angry when the family refused any information about her husband's whereabouts. How could they constantly protect him from his own family? Why would they justify his behavior and let his children suffer?

Sadly, she realized that her life was never going to change if she stayed there. So, when there was no sign of him returning, mom packed up what she could carry with her little children and left for the Greyhound Bus terminal, headed for Detroit, and a new life.

"It became apparent to me that I, alone, was responsible for my children's wellbeing." I had asked her once why his family did not help her, and she smiled at me with regret on her face, "I was from the wrong side of the tracks, and I was a plain girl." That broke my heart. Everyone loved my mom. She was caring and loving, and it was awful to think someone would hurt her.

How could anyone reject her, not my mom? She would go on to say, "God was everything to me, and He kept me and the children. Without Him, I don't know what I would have done. Had I not learned to trust Him, I wouldn't have made it." But, in my mind, I was thinking, why would God cause you to suffer like that? This petite powerhouse was thin with brown hair and gray eyes that changed like a chameleon. I would say, "Mommy, your hair is soft" and she would laugh and say, "Oh, it's mousy brown and thin honey." I wondered if my mother ever received compliments in her early life because she was never comfortable hearing them about her looks, abilities, her fabulous cooking, or any other talents she demonstrated. And, I would wonder how I had been as a baby during all of this.

In those days, the Young Woman's Christian Association, YWCA, was popular for young women to come to and stay. It provided shelter and a room or bed for them while they worked, or until they found a permanent residence. It was no frills, but safe and clean.

This night, Mom showed up with her little ones in toe. Because she did not meet the guidelines of being single, nor did she meet the *no children* policy, they first denied her entry. I can imagine what everyone must have looked like after a long bus ride—little tired looking kids and my mom worn down to a frazzle, standing before them. So, with compassion, something from their bylaws that stated *do not turn the helpless away*, I am guessing, they made an exception and let her stay.

Determined to make a new life for herself and children, my mother signed up and was accepted into nursing school. She had great people that God had sent to help with the children, and she was able to work for food and extras. After a brief time, she was able to leave the YWCA and find a small apartment to settle into. Her life was on track and thoughts of returning to her past were long forgotten. Sadly, her ex never paid one penny of child support for the children, ever.

With her nursing studies over, Mom became a Licensed Practical Nurse, and worked in one of the larger hospitals in Detroit. As part of her training, she would volunteer at the local mission from time to time. And it is there where she met my dad.

CHAPTER THREE

Oh Dad, you were something else. He was someone that was serious and could talk the stars down from the sky. He had a job. Dad was an expert mechanic and could tell you what was wrong with any vehicle just by listening to the sounds it made. He often had people come by the house when I was little, and he would say, "Start it up and let me hear it." Dad would immediately diagnose the problem and they would be on their way. He drank. He did not just drink; he was an alcoholic. So, sometimes he would be at the mission drying out. He would not remember coming in. He would find his way there, sleep it off and then go back to work. His employer kept him on because he was so great at his job.

At one point, the drinking got so bad he gave up. It took over his life and he gave into it. Having been a military man, he had seen things, horrible things he did not want to talk about. War changes men often and Dad was no exception. He drank his troubles away. Alcohol was his weapon of choice. He had turned to it to forget.

Neither of my parents ever gave us the details of their romance. I knew that dad had been a bachelor for a long time when they met and that he came to the mission even after he started turning his life around, just to see my mother. Of course, she did not give him the time of day. My dad was falling hard for her. He told me once that my mother represented everything good in this world. He said she made him smile and he did not do that often. She gave him a sense of belonging. And he was not about to let her get away. One day, he had come to the mission to see her, and they told him Mom had not been there. He learned from someone on staff that my mother and children were quarantined at home due to polio.

Dad begged for her address (using that charm), and went there as quickly as he could. My poor mom said that it was one of the most challenging times in her life. All the children had it and she alone was the one who would need to care for them. There was a sign placed on the door stating they were under quarantine, and no one could come in or out of that home.

Dad was around forty years old at the time. I imagine the thought of taking on a wife and sick children surely must have come to his mind on more than one occasion, as he pursued my mother. He had to have thought about the great responsibility looming over him. Mom said later that Dad nearly broke the door down before she could get to it. She would smile and say, "There he was, and I tried to get him to leave." She said, "You cannot come in or you could get sick, go away." She did not understand she was dealing with someone as determined as herself. Dad told her, "I'm not going anywhere; you need me, and I need you. And those kids need a dad. So, just open the door and tell me what to do."

Since Mom was a nurse, she became solely responsible for my siblings' care during the polio. But Dad helped. They had to have hot baths and exercises and I could just imagine how worn down she was doing all of this. But they survived by God's grace, Dad, and my mother's determination. Not one suffered from any side effects later from polio. When she talked of this time, she never mentioned me, but once she did say, I hadn't had the disease.

My mother's ex tried to make trouble for her on a few occasions. He came to Detroit to win her back, but that ship had sailed, and she would have nothing to do with him when he would come into town. My dad was very protective of my mother and us kids. Because of his own feelings of insecurity, he did not want that for us. I developed Spinal Meningitis in 1960. My mother told me much later that it was one of her scariest times. I could not move my head or neck and my fever had spiked to a dangerous level. For several weeks, I was in isolation, and it was touch and go. She could not hold me, but she would come and pray and as she described it to me with a laugh and shaking her head, "With God's healing and your determination to fight, you made it."

She had shared that for many months after I left the hospital, I would not let a man near me. If one entered the room, I would scream. And people wearing white would cause the same effect. I assume my reaction was from all the doctors and nurses dressed in their stark white uniforms that I associated with pain.

I didn't know much about how I fit in the family then, she had only shared little tidbits from time to time about me as a baby. And I didn't ask much. I guess I wouldn't have known what to ask. My parents were as different as night and day. Mom was so dedicated in her belief in the Lord and determined to make everyone happy and content. And Dad, irreverent and outspoken, neither ashamed of his beliefs or strong opinions, yet they worked together as a well-oiled machine both bringing their best gifts to our family. They were not the best at being married all the time. There were disagreements and loud reasoning that you could hear from what seemed like a few houses down the street, but, once they aired their grievances with each other, things went quickly back to normal. One thing they both had were big hearts.

I will say something and laugh to myself now thinking, that is something Dad would have said. Or I am quick to give money to someone in need and know he would be proud. And there are times I feel humbled after overseeing an event or I do something like Mom would have done, something that touches my heart to the core, and I think of her. I will always remember with pride my mother's sincerity, grace, and love of service. I am grateful to both and the sacrifices they made to give us a good life—and Mom especially, for introducing me to Jesus at an early age. That is the best gift you can give your child. Not just the knowledge of the Lord, but to encourage a daily relationship with Him that she coveted and became as natural to us as breathing. I heard her prayers; I watched her live her life and saw her faith through some horrible and heartbreaking times. And she trudged through life never taking the time to complain or whine at her circumstances. She fought the devil daily for us and fanned sinful influence away until we were old enough to have a solid foundation.

We were all dad's kids; there was never a difference made between any of us, we were all treated fairly, and he loved us. Nobody was a favorite. I felt at times that I did not fully belong though. I was the odd kid out (I imagined), and even with my dad's family when we would visit, my siblings had each other, my cousins had each other, but then there was me. I did not feel like I truly belonged anywhere. There was a disconnect that I could not for the life of me understand that started early. One evening I was sitting on the front porch and my middle sister told me I was adopted. My parents got home a brief time later and I was in a bundle in my room with my cat, sobbing. She got in serious trouble that day. But it would have made sense to me had I been adopted; maybe that would have explained how I felt at times when everyone was interacting and together.

Everyone meant well and treated me good. My siblings were wonderful to me and treated me like a little princess. As the baby in the family, I was sheltered. But it was down deep inside that I experienced feelings not only did I not understand but I could have never put into words to ask. I connected with my parents, but I felt different with everyone else. All those strange feelings as a child, the chasm of a void or separation was there and as clear to me as anything. I felt fragmented and that they all had a bond I did not share. After my sister told me that I was adopted, it was like yes! That is why I am different. But my parents had sworn I was not adopted so there had to be something else. I loved some of Dad's family more than others, but even with some of them I felt isolated. Like wanting to play a game but all the teams were full. That is how I felt. And I did not know why. I was a funny kid, wore a large red felt floppy hat, kept candy stashed in my pockets and I had a love for animals more than anything else. Mom said I had a heart of gold, and she loved my passion for everything.

We visited Tennessee for a week at a time in the summer or more if there was a funeral. And a couple times Dad's family members would say, "You look just like your daddy" and I would think to myself, what is happening? Did they know my daddy? Everyone knew this was our stepdad, didn't they? We did not talk about our real dad in our house. My siblings did not mention him and neither did my mother. I did not want to ask anyone what was going on. I just thought I would get "You are too little to understand," like I often did when I had too many questions for my older sisters. We shared the same last name, and I often felt guilt from even questioning anything.

Once, my middle sister yelled at Dad that he was not her real dad, and he could not tell her what to do. They had been having words about her usual unruly behavior and she had blurted it out in anger. I had thought at the time, this is not nice, he is a good man, and he takes loving care of us.

We had come to Tennessee for a funeral once in the summer. We were visiting the family, and my cousin's wife was sitting beside me on the couch at my aunt's house. I had mixed feelings for my aunt; she and dad had tempers. And sometimes they had words over how she took care of papa. Dad had let her live in a house he owned with the explicit understanding that she would take loving care of papa. However, he often felt that this was not happening. I know he was grateful when papa moved to my other aunt's house, and he thrived there. It was a load off my dad to know he was doing well.

We were sitting on the couch, and she said to me, "You look like you feel uncomfortable here, like you do not belong." I had that uncomfortable laugh you get when you do not know what to say or how to feel and said, "I guess sometimes." She said, "Yeah, they do not want me here (meaning my aunt), but I do not care; I am comfortable in my skin, and I am not leaving." I shook my head to show I was listening. But I could relate to her.

During my childhood, I believed there was some man out there that was my dad whom I had never seen. It is like a twin who has another twin out in the world. They have emotions and feelings like something is missing, until they meet that other twin, and it all becomes clear.

I was loved by everyone and never lacked attention or affirmation. But something did not click inside me. I loved this man that lived with us, and I called him Dad, we all did. He was funny and I know he loved all of us. But I knew that the other kids remembered Dad and, when I asked them questions about him, they changed the subject or told me to go play. So, I was never able to put the pieces together. There were two men, but I did not understand why.

My earliest recollection was being around age three and living on Ferdinand Street in Detroit. But really streets all blended like people back then. It was a mix of hot concrete, row-type housing structures and a variety of ethnic groups all mingled together. I was too little to care, I was just a happy little kid. It was a black and white existence, long before color took over. Much different than today. Closest to my brothers, I wanted to be with them all the time.

My oldest brother wore his hair slicked back and he dressed in tight black jeans. He even started wearing a black leather jacket with the collar pushed up, making him look so handsome. That was the look back then. It was James Dean and Elvis Presley, and that rebel gang type vibe. All the guys looked that way, or at least the ones we knew.

Mom did not approve, and there were many discussions about the way my brother dressed. I would hear them talk about it, and the conversations would get elevated and heated at times. It would scare me. She pulled one way and my brother another. Mom told him he was not going to dress like a thug, and he would rebel and say he would do what he wanted to do. Dad only stepped in when my brother became disrespectful to my mom. He would say, "Now listen, son, you aren't talking to your mom that way. She is only trying to protect you. If you dress like a thug, people will think you are one." I would run off and cry somewhere, I hated to see him get into trouble.

I liked his look; I thought he looked like Elvis! My middle sister had photos of Elvis plastered on her walls and my brother did favor him. He had that dark hair and high cheekbones. I was so proud of him. He could do no wrong in my eyes; I adored him. He taught me how to dance. That is when my Mom was not home, and he and my sisters had to watch me and my other brother. They would turn up rock 'n' roll music loud on the radio, and we would dance. He said I had gotten good at the twist and a few other dances. I just wanted to be with him, and I would have done anything to get his approval.

Later, I still had dancing fever and I wanted to take tap dancing lessons. Of course, I did not get any encouragement from my mother. Dad picked his battles, so he stayed quiet when things like that came up. When my sweet aunt purchased me new tap shoes, they were promptly returned to her with my mom saying something like mind your business and take these shoes back where you got them, but, in a more Christian tone of convincing, of course. My sweet mother could cut you to the quick. You did not mess with her children or overstep your boundaries where we were concerned. I hated her that day. I was so tired of hearing that God did not approve, or God would not be happy. I know she meant well in her relationship with the lord, but there were times when I just got sick of hearing it.

CHAPTER FOUR

There were five of us kids. My brother, the one closest, is five years older than me. He was and is still like a best friend. Then there was my middle sister who was eight years older, a brother nine years older, and my oldest sister is ten years older than me. My brother and I would play outside until the streetlights came on and we were called into dinner. One day, I was maybe three or four years of age at the time, and I found a little fabric clown in the trash can. I loved toys and animals. Everything had feelings to me whether it was a scrap of material that resembled a stuffed toy, or something with a heartbeat. It did not matter what it was, I loved it. My imagination was insatiable and only added to the joy of the things around me.

I took the little clown into the house with every intention of taking care of it and treasuring it. Of course, when I showed Mom, she told me I must go next door and show the little girl and ask if it was placed in the trash by mistake. And only then could I have it. I refused, and so she marched me over to her house. The mother answered and said, "Oh, it's fine, it was in the trash; Gaye can surely keep it." But that little hateful girl said no she wanted to keep it. Anyway, after much deliberation with them, my mother agreed to purchase the girl a new clown and I would keep the little one. I named him Don Ameche, an actor from a show we watched on television, and I still have him today, some sixty years later.

My mother was really involved in volunteerism back then, and she involved all of us. She had heard that the Salvation Army had a terrific community outreach. So, we began to attend services at the church. The women wore very tailored dark suits and hats with fabric bows that tied under their necks. Everyone looked alike. The first time I saw Mom in one, I thought she looked like an old paper doll I had seen. I saw no earthly purpose for that silly hat. But to laugh would have not been wise. So, I just kept that to myself. They were gathering funds for the League of Mercy. It was a division of the church that focused on reaching out to the community and giving to the poor. That is one wonderful thing about the Salvation Army; they do so much for the poor and help in times of disaster. I listened when the minister had spoken on giving and the impact it had. And I wanted to be part of the League of Mercy. I was about four at the time. But I had sat in church, and I knew what was going on. So, the church goal was set, and they had designated a time when all funds would need to be brought in.

The congregation was challenged to gather as much money as possible. So, my work began. I started collecting pennies from any place I could find them. I asked people for spare change; I picked up pennies on the sidewalks and I even put some of my allowance into the container. My goal was to bring it to church on the assigned day.

The Sunday arrived and I could not wait to get to church. The service had started and there was no mention of the offering. Well into the service, the pastor came to the pulpit and said they would be taking the special offering at that time. I guess, as a child, I was expecting fan fair or something big to happen but there was nothing. The minister then stated that since this offering was for the League of Mercy, those that were part of that ministry should bring their offerings to the front. Women and much older girls began to go down to the front of the church.

Mom and my sisters went with their offerings. There I sat with this big, crumpled paper sack that stored my penny candy from last week's purchase, and it was now full of money. I had twisted the top so the money would not fall out. What was I going to do? I wanted to give too but he clearly stated you had to be a member of that group. I eased out of the pew as members were finally tucking themselves back into their seats, and I made my way down front. Mom said every person in that huge church watched as this little girl headed for the altar with a brown paper bag in her hands.

The bag was so heavy I had to carry it with both hands, but I was determined to give my offering. I stopped at the altar and placed the wrinkled bag there with all the offering plates then headed back to my seat.

Before I got far, the pastor and a lady dressed in the same drab uniform my mother wore came down and called me over to them. The pastor asked me about my offering, and he said, "You are so young and not yet old enough to be part of the League of Mercy, but yet you have brought this generous offering today." He asked my name and the lady smiled and said, "One day, you will be a fine cadet." I did not know what she was talking about. She meant I could be like what my sisters were at the time.

She was apparently the head of the organization because she said something about little children in the Kingdom then she continued, "Because of your sacrifice today, we realize that children also play a big part in ministry. As you are too young to become a member of the League, we would like to start the Junior League of Mercy in your honor." The crowd clapped, and my mother smiled so big.

People came up to me and said how brave I was for going down alone to the altar, me being such a little girl. I do not know why I was not scared. In fact, I was only scared of two things. One was water and the other snakes. My mother was a talented swimmer as I have mentioned, but my dad was terrified of the water. So, no matter how much my mother pleaded with him, he would not let us take swimming lessons.

I had gotten lost in the reptile house at the Detroit Zoo not long before this day at church and I could not find my family. I was screaming to the top of my lungs, when the police saw that I was in distress and came running. About that time, my family flew into the building as well having heard my screams. My parents got on to me for wandering off and then hugged me until I could not breathe. It was beyond me how they could be happy and mad at me at the same time, but I was just relieved to see them.

I did not sleep for many nights after that, and I could never watch a movie or anything on TV that had a snake in it, or I would have horrible dreams. That has carried through my entire life. Even in college, I could not be in a biology lab with snakes, in aquariums; they had to be removed or I could not stay in the room. My professor tried to assure me that desensitization would take the fear away, but I refused to touch the snake he offered as part of the process. One ruined a perfectly good trip to Cypress Gardens in Florida too. It crawled out in front of us on one of the paths, and I went screaming back to the front gate, ready to leave. I was sweating and having trouble breathing. So much for their tranquil walking paths. Not that day!

So, after this service and my offering, I became involved in the ministry known as the Junior League of Mercy. There was a big write-up about me in the church's global newspaper. I still have it somewhere. I took cookies to the elderly as part of my work. Mom and I would make batches of cookies to take, and the people were always glad to see me. The little ladies stroked my long hair and told me I was precious. Or, I wore pigtails and they would pull them gently and laugh. The men shook my hand which felt awkward, but I would just smile at them. I loved meeting people and taking things to them, or doing anything that made them happy. Since everyone liked cookies, it was a win-win.

I was only around my grandfather (papa), twice a year when we would come to Tennessee. So, being around older people made me uncomfortable. I did enjoy their excitement though, and I felt good doing things for others.

My parents purchased a home on the other side of town. A quiet street lined with trees and decent sized homes. Lawns were mowed, and we did finally have a backyard to play in. It was Pittsburgh Street, in what was known as the Polish section of Detroit.

After a few years, the different areas of Detroit became more defined. This neighborhood had brick homes with A-frame fronts and small porches. No one had a garage; so, you parked on the street. We had sidewalks and a corner store that I loved to frequent.

All of us kids would go to the little store with its screened door that bounced back quickly on your heels if you did not hurry in. There was a strong smell of meats curing and cheeses displayed in the open coolers. Crackers and bread were stacked or heaped in large barrels and wooden crates stacked in numerous ways held other products. Cokes and grape pop in glass bottles would be bobbing in big metal containers with ice so cold you could hardly reach in to get one without feeling like your fingers were going to fall off like icicles. And the candy, oh the glorious penny candy. There was every kind imaginable. The little man that owned the store was a character. There was always a small worn-down pencil hanging from his mouth like a cigar that made him drool when he talked, or should I say when he yelled at you as you placed an order.

He would take the pencil out of his mouth, lick it, and then write on a little book of paper everything my mother wanted to get. His white apron was always smudged with mustard or sauce of some kind and my oldest sister swore that he could not hear a thing without looking right at you. But he sure knew when we came in without our parents and he watched us like a hawk until we produced money for our purchases. Later when he got to know us better, he would yell hello when we came in and would just go on with what he was doing while we looked around.

My folks had planned with him that they would have a running tab. Others in the neighborhood also had that arrangement, so it had been a good idea. They would not take anything for free, not my folks. But, in case we needed something while they were at work, we could run over and pick it up. They would take care of the bill at the end of the week. One day, we were home from school for a holiday. And we all got the brilliant idea to go to the store and get a few things and put it on the tab. My sisters, brother and I headed over and proceeded with our shopping spree.

We came home with our loot, and nothing was said until the weekend when my mom happened to stop in, and the little man asked for the tab to be paid. Oh, she was so mad when she realized what we had done. Four kids having a heyday in a store buying snacks added up to a lot of money and even more punishment. Punishment plus working off what all we bought taught us a good lesson.

My oldest brother had left for Pennsylvania by now. He had begun to run around with a young man that had no direction in life. His mother was an alcoholic and he got into trouble at every turn. My parents loved this young man, we all did. But he was a bad influence on my brother. My parents had sat my brother down and tried to make him see that if he did not stop hanging out with this kid, he would get into trouble. So, the decision was made for my brother to go for a brief time to be with an aunt in Pennsylvania. This was the sister of my mom's ex.

She had not apologized for her brother's actions, nor how she and others in the family had treated my mother and her children. But I guess she and mom had a good heart-to-heart before she was comfortable sending my brother there. I do not really know the story of how he ended up there, but I guess Mom had her reasons.

My folks explored other places, but he would be unsupervised most of the time, and, at least in Pennsylvania, he would be with family. Again, he would be staying just a brief time until things settled.

The goal was to get him away from the crowd he was hanging out with as soon as possible. Both of my parents were very worried about my brother. When we had a family meeting about the plan for him to leave, I was devastated. I would miss him terribly. And I remember crying for days after he'd left us. But we knew he would return soon for a visit and then again for Christmas. I tried to be brave, but my heart was broken. I had been given a cat that I named Candy. That cat became everything to me. She went everywhere with me like a dog. I grabbed her up and went to my room just heaving and crying uncontrollably.

My other brother had a little toy pool table set and Candy would come up and push all the balls into the pockets with her paws while he and I tried to play. I found a photo of her doing that not long ago and it was a sweet memory but made me sad. I would tell her my secrets, and she would try and protect me when I got into trouble. My mother had a drying rack in the utility room where she would hang her hosiery for work to dry. Candy would gently climb the rack until she was perched on the very top and do it so gently that she never touched the stockings. She was so smart and unlike any cat I have ever seen.

Mom and Dad kept track of the young man who had become like a son after my brother had left. They tried to get him to come live with us where he could be supervised. But he would laugh and say he was fine. My folks talked about bringing my brother home, but they were afraid he would get back together with this friend and others, so he stayed longer in Pennsylvania. His friend had met someone, married young, and then his wife had become pregnant soon after. He had gone off to jail for some more trouble and had stayed there for a brief time. Unfortunately, once released, he was in the wrong place one night and was shot between the eyes and killed. We were all heartbroken. He was so young and had a little family. His mother, still a struggling alcoholic, never recovered from his death. My folks had to tell my brother what happened, but his attitude about leaving home had not changed. He was bitter.

When we had moved to Pittsburgh Street, we were too far from the Salvation Army and my sisters were becoming old enough for more youth activities. So, we started attending Berea Tabernacle Assemblies of God on Schaefer Road in Detroit.

Pastor Kenneth Norcross was a sweet man who wore black and white spat shoes and sharply tailored suits. He had the biggest smile I had ever seen. His wife was sweet, and they had a son a little older than me named Kenny. The pastor was serious about order and worship. So much so that you were not allowed to talk in the sanctuary for any reason. Any conversations or visits were conducted in the vestibule of the church. He would often go to the pulpit and tell people to take their conversations outside the sanctuary before service. He called down the youth if there was any talking during the service, right from the pulpit.

One Sunday, my sisters were sitting at the front with the youth and there was some laughing and talking. Pastor Norcross was at the pulpit preaching and stopped to remind them that they were in God's house. Mom was furious since one of the culprits was my middle sister. She had been craning her neck to see what was happening in the first few pews. Mom stood up with a few other parents and went to the front to escort my sister to the vestibule. I remember my sister walking from the front at least three stages of red covering her face. They came back to the pew later and she plopped down having been visibly in tears and a little deflated. She was a victim of my mother's sternness and her total nonacceptance of any shenanigans in the sanctuary. I had felt so sorry for my sister that day.

We would either ride public transportation or the church bus to church. So, we always left home early for church. Mom refused to drive. So, to keep the peace, we took the bus. Dad did not attend church unless it was Easter or when I would sing much later in life. He would drive us off and on, but he wanted my mother to drive so it was his way of trying to get her to be uncomfortable enough to get her license. His attempts to get her a car as bribery were met with little interest and a lot of resistance. My mother was not one to be influenced, nor did she care about new or fine things. Dad, on the other hand, traded cars as soon as the new smell was gone, or so it seemed.

I remember when he started receiving calls from the dealership advising him of a new model or color in the showroom and he would get the fever. We had great times in his candy apple red Barracuda.

There were four children (with my brother gone), he and my mother, so this car was the least practical of cars for us. Mom would remind him of it when, after dinner, some nights he would load my brother and me in the car to make our pilgrimage to the Dairy Queen. I guess the only advantage of having had a parent that had once been an alcoholic was that he loved sweets and we benefited from it.

One day, during the summer, we were riding in his prized little car, and I had gum in my mouth. They were the best gumballs ever. Sour grape, wrapped in little pieces of cellophane. I usually kept two or three in my pockets. Dad was never a fan of gum of any kind. He would say girls that chewed it looked cheap, and there was no earthly reason to chew it anyway. He hated when it got stuck on the bottoms of his good shoes. But I loved my bubble gum. So, on this day, I had tired of the large amount I had in my mouth. My logic was if one was good, two was better. I had been chewing and decided to open the window and throw it out. It was always great for the first minute or two, a little crunchy from the sugar coating and the combination of sour and sweet taste would be so satisfying. But shortly after, it became like a piece of wax in my mouth, and I wouldn't want it any longer.

It was extremely hot outside that day. When I started to throw the gum out it got caught in the bottom rim of the window. I thought I had thrown it farther, why had I not paid more attention? Why did I even throw it out in the first place? I panicked and tried to roll the window up and down to get it out, but it only made it much worse. There were sticky streaks of the purple goo in long sections on the window. I did not know what to do. So, I looked at my brother who had his mouth open in shock at what I had done. He touched the back of Mom's seat in front, and she turned around and saw what I had done, and mouthed, "Oh no." I guess Dad had realized something was happening, and Mom started with her usual request of him not to be mad; however, no conditioning of my dad's temper would soothe him.

He pulled over and got out to look at the window. I could hear him cursing. Mom yelled over from the passenger side to stop talking like that in front of us, but I could tell he was furious at me and the more he looked at the window caused him to say a few more choice words while I cringed in my seat. He looked in the window at me and said, "Why did you have gum in your mouth in the first place?" He did not give me time to respond; he was trying to scrape it and only making it worse. While he was spewing words about kids not minding, I was feeling dejected and ready to burst into tears. I glanced at my mom who was looking back from the front of the car with a reassuring smile, "You did not mean to do it, dear; it is just one of those things. Daddy will get over it."

On the way home, he lectured me about how I was going to pay for the mess, and if he ever caught me with gum again, I was going to get it. He did not know I had more in my pocket, but he would never know that if I could help it. He took the car and got it all cleaned out and never said another thing about it except do not eat or drink in the cars again. Nothing!

But that would always change on trips to Tennessee. We would leave late at night to miss traffic. I would jump up in the place above the back seat and ride lying down. Dad would drive until mom would threaten him to stop soon so we could use the restroom and stretch our legs. He hated to stop worse than anything. I had a little box I took in the restroom to make things a little cleaner. It was filled with spray cleaner, paper towels, and soap. In case I needed it to make things more sanitary. My sisters would laugh at me, but I did not care. I was not a fan of using public restrooms, even as a kid. I was an old soul. When we would finally get close to Tennessee, we would always stop for snacks and gas. We quickly rolled out of the big car (Dad always took it on trips), relieved to get out and move around.

The Big Best Western, (or something with a Western in the name), was clean and had a nice restaurant and gift shop. There was a gas station close by. We would head straight to the gift shop, and my brother and I would get the largest round suckers on big thick wooden sticks that they had displayed on a stand. They had a good variety. Some long ones in swirl shapes, small round ones, and large round ones that were almost as large as a dinner place. My sisters would get snacks, but we always got those, and the selection of flavors made it difficult to choose from. They would tease us for getting them and say we were babies, but once back in the car they begged for a piece of the hard candy we loved so much. Dad would moan and yell that we better not get one thing in the car, or we were going to get it. And, once we were settled back in, we knew there would be no more stops until we got to Chattanooga. It was all about making time. And I hated trips with Dad because of it.

CHAPTER FIVE

We ate wonderful balanced meals at home, but there was also junk food around our house. Mom did not approve, but she would give in, or Dad would buy it. Some nights when we loaded into the barracuda and headed to the Dairy Queen, Dad would rev up the engine and take off down the street. He did it to get my mom worked up and it always happened. She would say, "One day, you are going to kill these children in this car." Dad, my brother, and I would laugh and laugh, but she did not think it was funny. Sometimes after we were ready for bed in our pajamas, Dad would want ice-cream and load us in the car.

We would laugh and have the best time. Mom would say it was past our bedtime and we shouldn't have ice cream before bed, but Dad would say we needed adventure. And that it was always time for ice cream. My parents had a playful relationship. Dad was mischievous and funny around her. It was true; Mom did bring out something great in my dad. And she would get a twinkle in her eyes and laugh at him. He would say something about the way she looked or compliment her hair and it would embarrass her. She would swear to cut his tongue out if he did not stop. All of us kids would laugh at them.

Our house was a chaotic place much of the time with everyone going in all directions, but it was always filled with love. I remember when JFK was assassinated. We were sent home from school and teachers and parents were crying. It was like a funeral at our house. We watched every minute of the news and the coverage about it. I was in kindergarten, and I remember being huddled around the small black and white TV to watch coverage of his funeral. The teacher would ease her handkerchief to her face to blot her eyes from time to time. JFK's photo was displayed on our wall at home and had been for some time. In the entryway, we had a picture of Jesus and then a large painting depicting the last supper over our buffet in the dining room.

My parents were both patriotic and my mom a believer. So, all the bases were covered in our house. I will never forget the first time I voted many years later. Dad was sure I had voted along with his party and was mortified that I had not after pressuring me to find how I had voted. My mother had told him, "We have raised her to be a good citizen and weigh her reasons for voting both pro and con. She voted how she sees fit." Mom especially prepared us for life. Dad, in all fairness, also contributed a lot to mold our lives. It was a different time then, men were different. Dads worked, and they were not always as involved in the day-to-day activities. My mother was extremely independent and poured her heart into raising us, even though she worked to help provide for us.

She also worked for her own independence and to never get caught again without being able to support herself and us.

She would say, "Dad and I will always love you, kids, but there is a world out there that doesn't have to. You must be prepared to be a friend, a partner, a citizen, and worker when you go out on your own." I was little so that seemed forever away. When we did family things or had talks or gathered around the little black and white TV, I longed for my oldest brother to be home so that everyone was together.

I walked to the altar of the large sanctuary in Berea Tabernacle one Sunday morning and gave my heart to the lord at five years of age. I went alone before anyone saw me and I was not scared to step out. I always sat at the end of the pew if I could, so that I could see better. I would get frustrated when we had big events at the church because that meant more people, and often I got scrunched in the middle and invariably behind a very tall person. I fully understood what I was doing that Sunday morning. I do not remember what I said, whatever version of the sinner's prayer a five year old can produce, I guess. But, at some point, I went to a different place. Some of what I share in these writings has been gently tucked away, wrapped tightly so the memory would not escape, and kept safe in my mind.

I had never thought of ever sharing, until I had the urging from the Lord to write everything down. I certainly do not understand my experiences, but they did happen to me. I remember the altar was quiet, if there were those praying or crying, I could not hear them. And there was a type of haze or covering that surrounded me. I noticed it right before this experience took place. As I closed my eyes, I found myself standing in front of a very ornate gate that was partially open. I was wearing the same clothes I was in when I came to church that morning. I thought it was strange that the gate made no noise. My neighbors' gate squeaked when you opened or closed it.

I entered a garden. I lived in a mostly black and white world with television, but as I began to walk into this place, everything turned from black and white to colors right before my eyes. With each step I took, beautiful colors and combinations of colors appeared, each more brilliant than the next. Soon, I realized I was there alone and became alarmed. I felt that I should not be in such a wonderful place, and that I was intruding in some private spot.

Ever so gently, someone placed their hand on my shoulder and, when I looked up, a man was standing there. He was draped in white and what looked to be a cream or natural color. The draping had no seams or buttons and no signs of being sewed together. It just flowed over his body. But it was his eyes, I got lost in his eyes. Eyes that changed from gray to darker shades and colors and they were as vivid and deep as I could see. I was not scared, as he began to lead me beside the river that flowed nearby. The water was clear and running freely and I could hear little frogs and small fish splashing about. My hearing was heightened there, and I could hear the slightest noises.

There was so much to see, but my eyes never drifted far from the man's face and especially his eyes. He led me to a large rock and, as he leaned against it, I sat down at his feet.

We talked, and this is where I cannot remember anything from that conversation. I so wish I could remember. My mind easily remembers past conversations and events, but not this one. My mother told me later that I was at the altar for a few hours and that people were coming to the front of the church and getting as close to where I was as possible or kneeling nearby. The women would pull their dress skirts away from what they called the holy ground that surrounded me. They would remain there and pray silently or watch me. She told me that I was having a conversation with someone and that I would say "Yes, sir or yes Lord." Once, she said that I had tilted my head to the right and put my left hand to my face as if covering someone's hand. I remember him touching my cheek. I am not sure how much time went by, but we moved from the large boulder.

We walked through the gardens, and I remember him pointing out things to me. I could smell the flowers and if I had eaten something in that place, I know it would have tasted wonderful. The air was light and smelled like fresh green grass and florals. He was not demanding but his very presence demanded my attention. He took such care that I was a child. Never startling me or scaring me. He knew my name. There was no one else there that I could see and as we walked, he touched the top of my head affectionately.

I had no thoughts of my life or missing home. I was so contented there. After we walked a good distance, we were at the gate again. I had no idea how we had arrived back there. He leaned down and hugged me, and I walked back through the gate. I was sad to leave. It closed behind me, and I was back inside the large church at the altar like nothing had ever happened. I do not know how much time went by it seemed only seconds. When I opened my eyes, Mom said I had a glazed look as if I was trying to comprehend returning from some distant place. My oldest sister, a true Bible scholar at fifteen, was quizzing me on the way home about what I saw. I was still in somewhat of a fog and couldn't give details right then.

The pastor and a few elders came later that afternoon to our house to meet with me and my parents. Dad was not happy about it. He had commented to my mother that it seemed like a personal experience and not for others to question. And I was a child not to be grilled for information. Dad threatened that if things got out of hand, or if they got too pushy with me, they would have to leave. When they arrived, I recognized the pastor, and a few of the men from church. There were five or six. They had many questions about what I had encountered. Pressing me with everything from, "Did he wear sandals?" to "Was he handsome?" I would try and respond. He was not necessarily strikingly handsome but nice-looking like Dad, he was tall, but he was gentle looking. It was his eyes I remembered the most and the most difficult to describe. I was being bombarded by questions from these men and my sister. What did this look like? Who else was there?

They asked me what we talked about, and I could not tell them. Sadly, it was blotted from my memory. I could not understand what the big deal was; didn't everyone experience this when they got saved? It was as if they had completely forgotten about the step, I had taken that day—a five-year-old making the decision to serve the Lord. I knew early what I believed. I sat in every church service, attended every revival and Wednesday night prayer meeting, and heard every message. I was not allowed to attend children's church. We sat in the sanctuary, and we better be listening when the sermon started.

I saw little girls my age with toys and snacks spread out on the pew and I thought I had the worst mother ever because I could not bring anything except my Bible to church. I knew what salvation meant. But what I did not know was why what I had experienced caused so much discussion. Even at church, people would come up and touch me or try and hug me. My mother tried to explain that my encounter with the Lord was a special one, and that everyone needed to remember I was a child. I was thankful for her protection, and soon, everything went back to normal.

The Holy Spirit moved in our church. It was powerful. There were so many things we could not do, no dancing unless in the spirit, no talking, no this, or that. It was even wrong for a man to sing a duet with another woman unless they were married. There were just a lot of rules and restrictions that we had at home and at church. But our services were filled with freedom to worship.

My brother came home to visit finally after what seemed an eternity. We were all so excited to see him. He still played with me and jousted my brother around. And, my sisters, especially the middle one, had been closer to him, so they laughed, and he teased them throughout his visit. We laughed at his accent; his thick Dutch accent was prevalent in several words. It had not been that long since he had been home, but he had adapted and thrived very well in Pennsylvania it seemed. Mom made every effort to impress with his favorite foods and Dad talked to him about how when he came home for Christmas, we could have most of the work done upstairs for a little private oasis for him. We were already looking to his next and final visit; he would be coming home next time for good.

All too soon, the time had come for him to leave. He assured Mom he could not take one more thing with him when they were gathering his suitcases. A few moments of goodbyes and the door closed. He was gone again. I cried hard and was inconsolable, I loved him so dearly. My mom pretended to tidy up the kitchen and Dad found something to do. None of us liked this, but it was for his protection only and my mother's heart broke every time his name was mentioned. She struggled with the decision she and Dad had made, but so much of Detroit was becoming infested with this gang like behavior and my brother gravitated towards it and could easily find trouble if he had the chance. There was no other choice.

Oral Roberts would come for services at Detroit's Cobo Hall. It was a huge arena that I think held around 12,000 people. It opened in 1960 and was home to the Detroit Pistons. Big name entertainers held concerts there as well.

I do not know how many people attended the Oral Roberts crusades, but I can attest from the best seats in the house, that there were thousands, and it was always packed at service time. My mother was part of the Detroit team, and she worked in counseling services or altar work during the meetings. We would get there early, and she would be prepped for her part in the evening's activities. I was a child, five at the time of my first meeting, and I attended a lot of services. It was a well-oiled machine. There were teams for the platform, area ministers, singers, and musicians.

Teams were prepped early for counseling or altar work so they would understand how the service would flow, and that they could be ready to go. There were hundreds of people in the altars each night. Mom was always rushing around; her talents were well utilized explaining and instructing and Reverend Roberts' staff came to assure things went smoothly. Nothing was left to chance. Once during mom's preparation meeting, I asked the woman that ran activities if I could be an altar worker. She looked at me through the bottom of her black-rimmed glasses and said, "Well, of course, I know your mother, so I'd be tempted to, but you are very young." I pleaded with her, and she said I was persistent and much more mature than my age. "I will give you a series of questions and if you answer and can explain some of your answers, I will think about a spot for you," She offered.

After a few minutes and a couple lengthy responses from me, she looked surprised and even pleased. "Your mother would be so proud. And yes, you will be an altar worker for tonight's service." I was so excited the first night of the

What You Can Become When Your Faith Grows Up

crusade. There was great anticipation. As a little girl sitting in this huge arena and watching it slowly fill to capacity was impressive. It was usually extremely hot even with whatever air they had piped in, and it could get uncomfortable at capacity.

Reverend Roberts, who I got to meet, and it was a great honor, was always so grateful for the people who worked in the crusades. Volunteers were crucial to the success of the meetings. My Mom would always say, please pray a special prayer for him because some people are not pleased, he is here. I would think that was so strange. This man would pour out his heart during a message and thousands of people would respond to his plea for their salvation. But I understood much later that he was not interested in bringing segregation into his services. He would say something like, anyone that wants to attend can, and we will worship side by side. This night, he had preached a long sermon and was dripping wet in his long sleeved white shirt. At the end of the service, there was an altar call. Hundreds of people went down to the front and were escorted to the large rooms first for prayer and then on to counseling where any questions were answered, and materials were given to assist in their new commitment to Christ.

I must admit I was scared. I was a kid, and I always wanted to do something I was either too young for or too short for. But the kind lady had confidence in me, and I was not going to let her down. I would do my best to help others find the Lord. There were benches set up if I remember correctly for kneeling if people preferred, and I began to see people come through all the doors like ants hurrying to a picnic. Before long, a young man was brought to my spot. He was tall and seemed just as nervous as me, and he did give me an odd look at first like are you playing church little girl? But I took what I did seriously and began to ask him some questions. And I offered to say the sinner's prayer with him. I can still see him standing there with big tears dropping onto his shirt as he bowed his head. He would be the first person I helped lead to Christ, and I have never forgotten him or the joy I felt that night.

My favorite part of the crusade was the prayer line; it was also called the healing line. Reverend Roberts and pastors from across the area would begin to gather at the floor in front of the platform with an open space between, leaving a place for people to walk through. The reverend would take oil and then touch each person on the forehead and pray. He never seemed to be in any hurry. Then the people would continue down the line while pastors would lay hands on them and pray. I do not think anyone ever went through that prayer line without feeling a touch.

And if you wanted prayer, the line continued if people kept coming to go through it. I would always step to a good spot so that I could see everything that transpired. There would be shouts and hands lifted and running. People would leap from wheelchairs or throw down crutches. There were things that happened that I could not explain but it was real. Reverend Roberts would shout something like, "Go to the doctor and bring us a report."

We would not leave those meetings until extremely late at night, but I always left with joy in my heart. It saddens me so much to see churches now compared to what I experienced as a young person.

I am troubled by how fancy talking TV preachers manipulate people today with their pay for blessing teaching and lust for money. I believe and know firsthand that God is still the healer and changes people's lives freely, and I am so grateful that I got to witness wonderful things in my childhood that were real and beyond the understanding of the world and non-believers. In those days, people would stay at the altar, and would tarry there for hours or until they were filled with the Holy Ghost. It was not uncommon to see people groaning in the spirit both young and old. Some believers joined them, others sat on the front pews praying and no one was in a hurry. People would come and hold their arms up while they waited on the things of God. I saw it more than once when a person was seeking for the Holy Ghost.

I have been in services where the pastor would jump to the pulpit and grab the oil to lay hands on those that needed a touch or needed healing. My mother had a heart attack, and she was anointed with oil once in service. She washed around that spot on her forehead to keep from removing the oil. We had anointing cloths that the elders and pastor would pray over, and they were made available to the church. In fact, my brother recently sent me one and it remains under my pillow. The Bible clearly speaks of the oil and gathering the elders to pray. James 5:14-15 NIV says: "Is anyone among you sick? Let them call the elders of the church to pray over them and anoint them with oil in the name of the Lord. And the prayer offered in faith will make the sick person well; the Lord will raise them up. If they have sinned, they will be forgiven."

I can remember being in a regular Sunday night service. I say regular instead of normal because there was nothing normal about our services. Our pastor would say, "What did God do for you this past week? Do you have a testimony?" People would begin to pop up like popcorn all over the sanctuary talking about God's goodness. A wind of worship would saturate the air and blow over that room and you would hear the shouting begin. The organ and the piano would take off on a blended sound that would get stronger with a song about deliverance.

Oh, how I miss the organ sometimes. I miss old music and worship songs. The songs today are not the same. Some nights you could hear a little high-pitched scream or noise, I don't even know how to describe it. But my mother would head down the aisle spinning like a top with her eyes closed and speaking in tongues. Like a beautiful skater on ice, round and round she would spin her feet never tangling as she spun. She never lost her balance or fell. I never saw anything like it. I could hear that sound and know from anywhere in the sanctuary that it was mom, just delighting in the Lord.

One night, she was slain in the spirit and melted like butter down to the floor right between the pews. Never touched the pew in front or back. It was not uncommon to see people slain in the spirit when the Holy Spirit began to move in a service. I have witnessed large men fall out in the spirit, and there was no one to protect them as they fell, hitting the floor like they were landing on a soft mattress. It was not fake, and certainly not charged with smoke and other devices used today to keep people interested. Back then, God was enough! We never used silly things like little blankets or coverings preachers use today. They have someone follow them with these little cloths. It is so orchestrated. The power of God is never out of line or embarrassing. One time, I saw a man get angry at an evangelist who was trying to push him down when I was much older.

The evangelist brought his wife along. She was covered in heavy makeup and gaudy costume jewelry. And he was flashy and ran his hands through his hair. He stretched on the platform like he was going to exercise and was limbering up. I was scheduled to sing, and after I sang, he sprinted to the pulpit. The outside appearance had turned me off from the beginning and I knew deep in my spirit that something was wrong, but the crowd loved him.

Through his message about love and extremely basic teachings, I began to see him differently than the audience did apparently. I was seated on the platform, and I became so uncomfortable; the more he spoke, the more the crowd bought the baby food he was feeding them. I was used to the meat of God's Word both at church and at home. And I was honestly alarmed for the many I saw in the audience who could not see through his facade. He finally finished, and I went to sing for the altar service. While he was instructing everyone on how he wanted the altar service to proceed, people began to swarm the altars.

The wife came to the front with a little stack of towels that they brought because we never needed anything like that in our services. She walked behind her husband as he prayed for people, and he would try and push them down. If they did not go willingly, he would get excited and push harder until they gave in, stopped resisting and fell to the floor. She would scurry behind him, grab one of her towels and would lay them over the people. Mostly, the women. I had a tough time sitting on the platform because I saw some odd things and there were times, I honestly had to close my eyes and pretend I was praying because I would want to burst out laughing. I would never have laughed at the Holy Spirit, not ever. But the antics people tried to do under the guise of being in the spirit often alarmed me for them. The Holy Spirit would never do anything unless it was in decency and order.

Toward the end of the altar service, I was just waiting for something to happen, I could feel it. Everything about this man was fake. I was a young girl, but I understood when there was a problem with someone and I could not explain it,

I just knew. About the time I had repeated what seemed like the one hundredth verse of the altar call song, the preacher made his way to a very tall man I had never seen before in our services. He towered over this little evangelist, and his wife by now had taken off her shoes and was down to three towels in her arms. The evangelist laid hands on the man, and he did not budge. The man kept praying and I had to stop singing because I could feel the tension from the platform. When the preacher went in for the next hit the man pushed right back in what looked like a duel for the stronger will.

The man was agitated, and I do not know what may have occurred after the service or if he ever returned, but he moved away to pray on his own, while the deflated evangelist jumped to the pulpit and turned the service over to the pastor. I knew from that and a few other early experiences that I could discern people. I could tell when I entered a room, and our eyes would meet, or I would be introduced to someone whether they were real or not. When I shake someone's hand, I can tell a lot about them even now. And it would really be made clear later in my life in a more dramatic way.

CHAPTER SIX

I pulled out some old photos of me while I was growing up. Even though I was full of insecurities and self-doubt that started incredibly early, I was filled with the love for books and music. I was so confident when I had my mind set on something right or wrong, super curious, and when I did anything, I did it full throttle, one hundred percent.

My imagination was insatiable, and I loved the holidays as a child. My mother started us out early, learning to help with events and holiday preparations. I had to laugh at one photo I remembered well. It was one of my very first visits to J. L. Hudson's Department Store in Detroit, around the holidays. If you are not familiar with this store, you missed something great! It was a huge brick building at 1206 Woodward Avenue, downtown Detroit. Towering over the city at 410 feet, it was the tallest department store in the world in the early 1960's. Its massive 2,124,316 square feet was only slightly smaller than Macy's in New York City. Hudson's had 32 floors, 51 passenger elevators, and 48 escalators. There were a world record number of fitting rooms at 705! So, when I say this place was the greatest store ever it was.

I was about three or four years old, and we were going to the twelfth floor at Hudson's. This was the children's floor that was totally transformed into a winter wonderland of imagination and fun. Nothing relating to Christmas started until after Santa arrived on Thanksgiving Day during the Detroit Christmas parade. After that, it was free game, and people kicked into high gear to shop and prepare for Christmas. This day, I had worn a hideous fur hat. Mom always wrapped us in layers because of the cold, and there were always hats and mittens or gloves.

We left early in the morning to take the bus downtown. Even though I was incredibly young, I can still remember most of that day. We had hot donuts and cocoa at a restaurant across from the massive store, and I could see the people pass by through the large glass windows at the front of the restaurant. It was a tradition, and Mom and my brother had gone there before they saw Santa at Hudson's before I was old enough to go. Later, she would always take us out of school for a day so that we could go and spend the day downtown and see Santa. Mom always told our teachers what the plan was so they knew ahead when we would not be at school.

I do remember getting off the elevator on the twelfth floor that first time. I remember it being a magical place. It was a child's world for sure. Full of clouds, and snow and musical creations. There were exhibits and decor that covered this large floor and it entertained you as you wrapped around the roped-off lines inching closer to seeing the man, Santa. That was always my goal even when I got older, I hated the lines. Standing in line was a waste of time, I had a plan and I needed to get to my destination, I needed to get to Santa. Mom would say, "Honey, just enjoy the time here, and don't try and hurry." But that was not in my nature. After we saw Santa in later years, we shopped in the children's only shop. They placed your money in an envelope on your shirt with a pin and you shopped for gifts with no adults allowed.

This little girl with the goofy hat needed to get to Santa quickly but I could not get past all of the children in line. My mom said I was so restless that day and she knew I was on a mission. I had dragged the Sears catalog that had come in early November with me. We all took turns carrying that large heavy book. Finally, my brother and I got to where Santa was, and the Detroit News cameras were there capturing sweet moments with kids as they saw Santa.

It was finally time for me to sit on his lap and the cameras were rolling apparently. I handed him the big catalog. He looked quizzingly and asked me what I wanted for Christmas. "Well, how would Santa know all of the things you would like?" Mom said I gave him a look like listen the real Santa would not ask dumb questions. "Well, it's all marked," I answered. It caused an uproar. The tv cameras caught all of it, and, at one point, I got so close to one of the cameras I put my face right into it. They told my mom to watch the news that night, we would be on television.

We gathered around the black and white TV that night and watched as they played the film about a little girl who was not taking chances with her Christmas list this year. Dad laughed, shook his head, and called me a little mess. We did have big Christmases and I loved it. I did not know till much later in life that Mom and Dad had begun shopping for all of us early in the summer so that we had things we needed, but more importantly that we wanted under the tree. My parents were not rich, but we had everything we needed and more.

As I got a little older, I loved everything about being outdoors. My brother and

I would play for hours in our yard or in the alley behind our house. We loved the game statues and jumping in the fall leaves. We played dodge ball and hopscotch. I would play cars or cowboys with him. We would have friends over and play for hours, just enjoying being outside.

My chore was setting the table for meals. Not just setting the table, but doing it right, with silverware in the appropriate places and the plates and bowls evenly across the table. If I did not get it right, I had to do it again. I once devised a plan to make it easy on myself (or so I thought), by lumping all the silverware together on the table and stacking the plates neatly on top of each other so you could just take what you needed and move on. That was not the hit I had envisioned. Not only did I have to set the table the correct way, but I also had to hear about making bad choices and doing things like unto the Lord the rest of the evening from Mom. That was a night I was ready to go to bed to finally have peace from my great idea gone bad. In our house, there was no easy ways out of things and very few shortcuts.

To say my mom was strict was an understatement. There were more Noes than Yeses. One time, we had gone to the little store, and I bought Jolly Ranchers. They only had the sour apple and the grape back then, but I loved them and so did my middle sister. I was running in the house, and Mom called after me to stop because I would choke on what I had in my mouth. She leaned in, which I thought was strange and smelled the Jolly Rancher (green apple), on my breath. "Where did you get that?" she asked. I told her from the store, and since I had candy or bubble gum in my pocket all the time, I had offered her one. "Absolutely not! They smell like wine, and you are not to have them anymore," she said sternly. So, we would laugh when we got older that Mom was afraid we were going to hell over a Jolly Rancher, or as she called it forevermore, wine candy.

Every Saturday morning, we were up by at least by 7:00 a.m., dressed, fed, and ready to clean the house from top to bottom with my mother. My job was dusting, and I hated it. It was of the devil, and it still is. We all had assigned jobs so there was never a surprise at what needed to be done and by whom. We worked until we were finished and that was it, no questions, no excuses. However, my oldest sister was messy, and my middle sister was mouthy. Neither good attributes to have early on Saturday morning before the sun came up.

They knew every week what was going to take place, and every week Mom had to deal with them. There would be whining and yelling, and she would take their messy dresser drawers and dump them in the middle of their room for them to sort. She really got livid when she found things under the bed, and you better never have food in your room.

It was finally time for my oldest brother to come home and stay and I was so excited. My parents were happier than they had been in an awfully long time. I guess if I counted, it was when my brother last visited that they were this happy. I was going on six I believe. Mom had worked getting everything exactly right for his arrival. We all helped clean and bake, and it was my first attempt at baking cookies which became one of my many passions. Dad had gone to get him, and we were all waiting. I was beside myself with excitement. My dad walked in first and he did not look happy. My brother came in behind him with a little bag, and I ran to meet him.

There was no picking me up and spinning me, only tight arms that I felt tense up when I touched him. He patted me in a strange way. But no hug, no dancing. Mom, always kind and hopeful said, "Honey, brother's tired from his trip, let's let him rest tonight." It felt like all the balloons at a party just deflating at once.

There was something wrong. But I did not know what. I could not figure out what was so different or what had changed about this visit. I do know this, I felt horrible, isolated, and alone. I grabbed my cat and went to my room. My bedroom was right off the dining room, and I could hear everything taking place.

My brother had gone to freshen up, and I heard my dad say something like, "I'd like to whip him for acting like this." But Mom as usual, was making every excuse she could make for him to calm my dad down. My other brother sneaked into my room so we could hear everything that went on together. He knew something was up and we had my cat and his dog Nikki with us as we spied on the dining room. My brother returned to the room and informed my parents that he would be going out. Dad asked where he wanted to go, and he mumbled something. I could tell Dad was trying to stay calm. I do not recall where my sisters were; they probably picked up on the tone of the night like we did and made themselves scarce.

Dad said something like, "There isn't anything good out there for you this time of night, son." My brother said he just wanted to go out. So, my dad said, "Well, let me get my keys and I will take you anywhere you want to go." I do not know what happened that night, maybe he waited until my parents went to bed and then snuck out, but Dad had laid the law down heavy on him. I do know one thing, Mom may have slept well for the first time in a long time, knowing all five of her children were under the same roof, safe and together. That had been a dream of hers.

The next day, nothing was right. Everyone was on edge. And I remember my brother leaving the breakfast table and returning with the little bag he had brought. He said, "I'm leaving." I ran to him and held his leg as he was much taller than I was. "No, please stay, don't leave," I cried. My mother tried to reason with him, and my dad was silent. My sisters were crying, and my other brother was quiet, and I am sure he shed some tears. But as my mother talked to him, my brother became like someone we did not know. He did not like the rules, people telling him what to do, he didn't want to be around us anymore. And there it was. We were not good enough any longer. He had been plied with money and lies and he bought it all. Bought the lies that his family did not want him and had sent him away.

"Oh! I love you so much, please don't leave me," I pleaded. I was crying and my heart was breaking. He pushed me away and I leapt for him and caught him by the leg again, begging him to stay. That memory is still so vivid and raw in my mind.

I promised whatever a little girl could promise in desperation. I was reasoning with him that everything was wonderful, and we needed him home with us. And I held on to his leg as if my life depended on it. I was not going to let go until he changed his mind. But he shook his leg, dragging me towards the front door when I would not let go, and then pushed me away like dirt on the bottom of his shoe. As I screamed "No, No!" My mother was sobbing and said in her sad broken voice, "Oh, son, what will I tell her when she is older, how will I explain this to her?" He had the coldest eyes, and simply said to her, "Tell her she never had a brother." He walked out and slammed the door behind him, and I ran to my room, gathered up my cat, and cried until I had no more tears left. We never saw him again.

My mom grieved for him. She wanted so much for him and seeing the guilt and longing on her face, over time made me hate him. It took a long time, but bitterness had set in. I would sit on my bed with that cat and sing hymns and try and forget that day. It would come to me in the night mostly. He did not love you, did not want you. You are not good enough or he would have wanted you to go with him. It was hard to think badly of him and love him at the same time and that was difficult for me. I had heard in church that hating people was wrong, but I could not suppress those feelings. And they went so nicely with my already multitude of insecurities. That is a lot for a kid to carry around but that would be just the beginning of my nightmares.

Sometimes my parents would get angry with each other. Dad kept a little apartment across town. When he was in the doghouse, he would go and stay there for a few days. The man he rented from was named Jack. He was loud and abrasive and used terrible language, but my brother and I grew to love him and his sweet wife. Years later, Edith Bunker reminded me so much of her. She was quiet and always had an apron on when she answered the door. When we came in, she would try and touch her hair to make it look tidier, smile at us, and then trot off to the kitchen. We would be visiting for the weekend on those few occasions Dad stayed there.

When we arrived, he always took us to say hi to Jack. Jack would always be at the dining room table in the same seat as if he were a king presiding over his court. There were always papers strewn all over the table. And he was always puffing on a cigar that would dangle from his mouth as he talked. I would just envision that at any moment that thing was going to fall out of his mouth onto the table, but it never did. He laughed big, and his big belly would jiggle.

They always had cookies that were shaped like triangles but had a consistency of waxy pastry, fried, and they were coated with powdered sugar. I could never explain what they were, but I would eat them until I could not eat any more. They were delicious, and there was always plenty of them. Jack wore a hat all the time even in the house and looked like someone in organized crime. He knew some tough-looking people. Dad did too. They could make a call and get anything handled. Dad knew everyone it seemed. My parents always assured us that, even when they argued, they loved each other, and it never really caused us much concern as kids because Dad always came home after a few days.

We went to church every time the doors were open. Every Sunday morning, back for Sunday night service, Wednesday night, and every night of revival or other unique services. Dad would not attend, but he made sure we were there. One such special event was when the missionaries came. It was always a husband and wife team, and very seldom did they have children. They would set up the front of the sanctuary with tables draped in colorful blankets and display the things they brought back from the country they served. The part I liked was the slides of places and people, thousands of miles from where I was. When you are a child, your world is small. It is places and things you see every day. This opened a different world I had never thought about. Places I did not even know existed at the time. Names of places and people whose names I could not pronounce, or spell, touched my heart.

And there was the clicking sound of the slide cartridge as it advanced the little cardboard piece with a tiny negative inside. You could hold them up to the light and see the tiny image, but when you placed it in the cartridge and flashed it on a big screen, it became larger than life.

The missionaries would explain each slide (always black and white), and then click again to the next one. I must admit that with the lights low and the methodical clicking of the slides, it would cause me to doze off on occasion. That was until I got a pinch from my mom who we were sure had eyes everywhere. We would tease her about having eyes in the back of her head. Because she could see us everywhere. And that when she got angry her nose got pointy. She would laugh and say it was not so.

Once the missionary stood before the church and held up a piece of paper, we called them tracts. Back then, and even occasionally now, I will see one somewhere. It usually had one topic like salvation, basic information, and people passed them out as a way of witnessing to the lost. Way before the Internet, this was a great outreach to people on the streets or in public places to pick up a tract and read it. Anyway, on this night, he talked at the end of the service about giving to the mission field. He put up a photo of an elderly man and one of a young man on the screen. He then asked with tears running down his face, which should receive the last tract. "The elderly man, who has limited time left here on Earth or the young man whose life has just started?"

He pulled out a handkerchief and blotted his eyes about the same time I had reached for a tear of my own. He went on to say, "There are times when we are far away, and the funds run out and we are down to our last materials. We must make tough decisions, sometimes heartbreaking decisions." I remember processing that information. I would lie in bed at night and think, *I would give the tract to the elderly man so that he does not die lost. No, I would give it to the young man, because he could reach more people throughout his life.*

It was at a discussion at the dinner table that I was talking about this, and my mother had shared her heart for missions. She told us with big tears streaming down her face that she had been called to the mission field as a young girl, but that life had taken her another direction and she was never able to get over it. I never knew my mother had received a calling in her life until that day.

Mom said, "It was a piece of my heart that has never mended. I disobeyed God." I had continued to talk about the missionaries' other nights; they fascinated me. One night I said, "Well if you ask me, they can probably find bad sinners right here and not have to go far away." I never learned. My mouth got me into trouble often. I was instructed that night before bed that there is an entire world that needed Jesus. But I still thought there was work to do right here and I did not want to leave to go anywhere else like the missionaries. In fact, I had made the decision to just not grow up and stay with my parents for the rest of my life.

There was a little woman named Maude that came to our house and did small jobs like ironing or cooking. She was usually there every day during the week, and we all grew to love her dearly. Mom would have a list of things for her to do, and most days, she came before we left for school.

Dad insisted on picking her up at the bus stop, but she never allowed him to. They would be in the kitchen and Mom would go over the list and finish and Maude would say, "Well, I'm not planning on getting to those today; I have other things in mind to do." We loved it when she and Mom would banter, and Mom would finally laugh and say, "Whatever, Maude." I could hear her singing in the utility room when I would come home from school and she had such a beautiful voice, soulful and deep like the perfectly tuned instrument.

When my brother and I had chicken pox, another lady came. She always seemed to come when any of us kids were sick. My parents were too concerned to have Maude exposed to anything since she was older. But this woman had zero personality, she liked to stay in the kitchen. Invariably, no matter what the occasion for her being there she would make us fish and chips. My brother and I detested it, and, when you are sick, the last thing you want is something smelly and fried. We did not like it when she came; it always seemed that we bothered her. On one of her visits, I had the measles. She brought me that horrible fish, and I asked her if she could make something else. She replied that I could eat it or starve. "It makes no difference to me," she said in passing to the kitchen. That night I told my mother about it and how every time she came, she made the same thing, and had told me I could eat it or starve. We never saw that lady again.

It got to be a habit. I would hurry home, drop my things, and run out to the utility room where Maude was. I would jump on the counter and kick my heels on the cabinet while we sang old hymns. She would say, "Gaye Elizabeth, I swear, child, you are going to be a singer one day. Now listen to me, before you get up in front of any crowd to share that beautiful voice, you make sure your heart is right." When she talked, she often sung her words and her voice would go up and down. "Music is a ministry like preaching. People are going to believe what you sing. Make sure you are not faking it, and make sure God is in your heart." I would say, "Maude, I will, I promise." And my long braids tickled the sides of my face as I shook my head up and down in agreement. If Maude said it, I believed it.

Maude said to me as I got a little older, "Girl, that's some smooth singing," and we would laugh. I did not know then what impact music would have on my life. She obviously saw something in me, and she could sing, oh could she sing. She would say, "When you sing, and you will sing, honey, you don't have to get all jiggly or silly, your voice, and the words about Jesus are more than enough."

One day, when I was much younger and long before she and I began to sing, I said, "Maude, I love you so much." "Well, baby what is this all about. I love you too?" "Why are you different than me?" That had bothered me for a while, but I did not know how to ask her. She smiled with that big smile that covered her precious face and pulled on my long pigtails. "Well, you see one day God was baking cookies and he just left me in the oven a little longer." She always said she could tell when my eyes would start dancing that I was either up to something or thinking. That was all I needed to know, and she often reminded me of that day as I grew older, and we would laugh together.

I would say later, "Oh Maude, I'm so sorry, I should have never asked you that." She would laugh and say, "Gaye Elizabeth, no telling what was going to come out of your mouth at any time. I'm never surprised at you, child."

Often, she would lay her hands on my head and pray. Oh, she prayed for my brother too. He would say, "Maude, you know, I'm going to be a preacher." And she would say, "Oh, boy you are going to be great." At night while Mom prepared dinner, my sisters and I would be in the kitchen and sometimes Mom would start a hymn. She, and my oldest sister had beautiful soprano voices. My middle sister would sing the alto part and I would lead. Occasionally, we switched parts, but we had a wonderful time singing. Mom and I would sing a little song: *"The devil is a sly old fox, I would like to catch him and put him in a box, close the door and lose the key, for all the tricks he's played on me. Glad I got salvation, glad I got salvation, glad I got salvation, I'm trusting in the Lord."*

My brother was such a joy and so gifted. His room was like walking into a large toolbox. There were wires crossing the floor that you had to step over, and they were taped all along the tops of his walls. His desk and any available space were full of parts or pieces that he "tinkered with" as Dad would say. He would bring him home a box of old parts and my brother would take off to his room to make something or enhance a project already in the making. One time we heard someone speaking in a foreign language and it sounded like it came from his room. Dad and I headed in to see what was going on. There my brother sat with what looked like a handmade Hamm radio. He had picked up some people talking. He proceeded to go to another channel, and we talked to someone in some foreign country. Dad was always so enamored with what my brother could do. He is so talented in mechanical things and electronics. He never said a mean word to anyone, never got into trouble (unless he was influenced by me), and he was and still is the kindest and most intelligent person you will ever know. Bruce asked him once if he was part of Mensa, a society of extremely high IQs. He said, "Yes, I had a membership card, and I attended a meeting, but they were all a bunch of nerds." We laughed about that. Bethany, our sweet girl, wrote her first article for Mensa at the age of fifteen. It was published in their magazine.

We would get our allowance on Friday. Oh, that was a wonderful day! I would run to the little corner store and buy penny candy. The selection of the various candies was so bountiful and tempting, and each piece was a penny. I would take out ten cents because that was my tithe.

Then I would spend a lot of what was left on candy. The little store owner would put it all in a little paper bag that overflowed, but I would be so happy. Usually, by Sunday, my allowance was gone, and on a few occasions, I would ask my brother for a loan. I hated to, and the first few times he refused. He would say, "Now, Gaye, I'm going to be a poor preacher, and I need to learn to take care of money now." It would aggravate me so. Finally, one day, he agreed to give me a loan, but he called me into his room. He had written down on a piece of paper my name, how much I wanted, and when I was supposed to pay it back. And there was a place for me to put my name.

Dad took me shopping with him sometimes, and I would pick out something. We would get to the counter, and he would say, "OK, get your money out to pay for you toy" and I would say, "But, Dad, you told me to save my money." That usually worked on him, because he was soft and because he would be too embarrassed to make the clerk wait. My mother, on the other hand, was not drawn into my scheme, and I would have to put the toy back or pay up.

My brother warned me that this was an agreement, and I could not back out once he gave me the money. So, thinking I would be fine, and he would never come after me his little sister, I signed my name. I never thought another thing about it, but he confronted me one day with that paper. I asked him what he had, and he said, "I have the paper you signed saying you would give me my money today with interest, and I am here for it." He was as serious as I had ever seen him, and I had to pay him back. I did not borrow from him again after his little lecture about watching my money. My brother, the loan shark, who would have ever believed it.

CHAPTER SEVEN

There were people that came by our house frequently, salesmen. The Good Humor man was one, he rode a bicycle with a little box on the front and it held different ice creams and treats. He wore solid white clothes and there was music coming from somewhere I could never figure out where, as he rode along. He would stop in front of our house and take his hat off to me, which always made me laugh. And when he opened that box, you could see the chilly air escape. He later came in a little truck instead of the bicycle and gave us treats from the side opening.

The other man that came quite often was the Jewel Tea man. He wore a suit and carried a satchel and a large book. The pages had all the items he sold, and they were covered in plastic. We all sat down when he came to watch him try and sell my mom things like food items or cleaning products. She would buy things from him, and she enjoyed things that came in sturdy containers. She collected containers because we had all kinds of plastic ones. When we would get ready for a trip, Mom would gather all these containers and fill them with food and put them on ice in the cooler to take with us. Most times, she did not mark them so opening them was always a mystery.

We had picnics beside the road at tables that were placed every few miles and, no matter how things were packed, the bread always got a little soggy. Even much later, when we went on a trip with Mom, she would bring her electric skillet and cook in the room. My mother would say that convenience food would kill us all someday.

Anyway, the Jewel Tea man would give my mom some of the things she wanted if he had them on his truck or he would order them and bring them back another day. He was smooth; he knew kids needed immediate satisfaction—well, I did—, so he would remind Mom that he had a certain kind of candy or cookie on the truck, and she would give in at times and get it for us. Great marketing tool even back then—get the kid hooked and win over the parent.

I have mentioned before that our church was run with extremely strict instructions from the pulpit. There was no talking in the sanctuary before, during, or after services. And the service never concluded until the last person seeking at the altar was finished. On Easter weekend, my mother made sugared eggs with little scenes in them, like the cross, or a lamb, and they were always beautiful. Our house smelled of ham and hot cross buns. She decorated like every holiday, over the top with everything she crafted herself or bought and remade to her liking, and every holiday was beautiful. We would wake up to big baskets on Easter morning filled with candy and small toys we had seen in the stores. And they would appear the same way at Christmas under the tree. I always wondered how my folks remembered all of that for us.

My sisters received baskets too, but, since they were much older, they got things that teenagers enjoyed. On Good Friday, in the afternoon our house shut down. We prayed, had family devotions and then were to do quiet reading during the hours of Christ's death on the cross. It was a time of reflection. I could hear my mother praying aloud and her crying out to God her thanks for the gift of Jesus.

And, of course, it was about the outfits. Those dreaded Easter outfits. Mom and Dad made sure we had everything new from underwear to shoes for that day. Mom would say, "Only give your best to the Lord." We shopped weeks ahead well the selection was good, and the prices were right. My oldest sister always picked a plain outfit befitting the solemness of the holiday. My middle sister picked the most outrageous patterns and was often sent back to the dressing room for something with a little more taste, more fabric, and a more muted color. It was Easter, for crying out loud.

My brother had a nice new suit, and even Dad looked handsome in his suit. The same one he wore all the time to events it seemed. He thought it was not necessary to have a new suit even though my mom would get on to him for being lax in his outfit choice. Then there was me. Mom picked out little dresses with bouncy skirts and tops that itched. I had shiny patent leather shoes that made me slip until Dad got out the sandpaper and brushed it along the bottoms so I would not fall. We had gloves for reasons I will never understand, and my mom wore a big hat. I was always worried about what my mother wore on Easter. She was most concerned about all of us, and she would say things like, "My clothes are perfectly fine to wear," or "I don't think I need anything new this year." My parents wanted to be sure we had what they thought we needed before ever thinking about themselves.

There was a tradition back then that the ladies who reached a certain age would wear a lily corsage. Usually, my mom and sisters' flowers arrived on Saturday so they would be fresh for Sunday. They came in little paper boxes with a little clear place on top so you could see inside and were immediately placed in the refrigerator. And God forbid you opened the refrigerator door or dwelled too long with it open because you would get yelled at.

Do not ruin the flowers!!! Dad always got Mom this huge ugly lily a few days prior to Easter. It looked like it would suck you inside. It had a hideous paper bow tied on the bottom with tinfoil-colored paper. She displayed it on the dining room table proudly with all the Easter decor.

It was off to church before the crack of dawn for the Sunrise Service and breakfast afterward in the large fellowship hall. I would sit there half asleep and make faces at my siblings because not only did I not want to be awake, but I did not want to eat that early in the morning. We sang *"He Arose"* and *"He Lives"* in service and my mother's beautiful soprano voice world mingle with all the other voices making a beautiful melody. I was young, but I knew what all of this meant; it was a somber weekend, but sometimes it was difficult to be serious when your mind took you so many places, and church was always so serious. And we were always there it seemed.

The ladies of the church tried to outdo each other with the best-looking dress or ensemble. Our church was a mix of poor to extremely wealthy families. I knew one of the families who was in the steel business along with many other ventures and my sister had read an article about them that stated they were one of the ten richest families in the country at that time. Even though I was little, I had my mom's back, and I would pester her about her Easter outfit. I wanted to know what she was wearing, and I would ask my sisters what they knew. They always thought I was a little weird anyway because I had an imaginary friend named Montine LaPoor, I had made up with my best friend Carol in the yard playing one day. So, I would get the brush off from them. Carol had told me that she had a friend that no one could see that she told her secrets to. Of course, I wanted one too. So, she explained that you had to decide if you wanted a male or female friend, and you had to give it a wonderful name or the friend wouldn't show up. So, me being the gullible child I was, I sought out a name day and night. It had to be perfect and something that would surely bring my new friend to me. I do not remember if I saw Montine on a label, or how I came up with that, but LaPoor just came out of the blue. It was just how my mind worked. Montine LaPoor came into my life and became a great comfort to me.

So, this Easter Sunday, Mom came out in a well-tailored dress, but nothing like I wanted for her. I wanted bows and bright colors like the church ladies wore on my mother because she deserved the best. And I secretly wanted her to outshine the others. But that was not my mother. She was not one to be like everyone else. She was not flashy, nor did she draw attention to herself. She was complex though, because where she was so confident in some ways, she was not as confident when you praised her. I believe this all stemmed from her childhood and her previous marriage.

She felt inadequate. I am so my mother's daughter. I was raised to be independent, to speak my mind and to get out there and grab life. But I am more introverted than I ever realized. When groups gather, I often seek a place to myself. And I am completely comfortable just being at home. I have always been in the spotlight with my singing and work and my love for event planning. But when it is just me alone, or it is just Bruce and me, I am happiest and the most content.

I genuinely love people like my mother did, but feelings of inadequacy can hover over me at times even now, and I am content to be alone. Now, I look back and see that her outfits did not make her better or more of anything. She reminded me of this one Easter when I was a teenager, and I wore a black midi outfit to church on Easter. It was a black vest, white blouse and black midi skirt that went below my knees. I was a girl who knew her options and was not afraid to explore them. Anyway, that Easter I had to ask God to forgive me that night in my prayers for wanting her to outshine everyone else. She did in my heart, and that is all that mattered. "You can never go to sleep with any bad feelings in your heart," my mom would say. "You need a clean slate before the Lord when you go off to sleep."

Our pastor did a nice thing on Mother's Day as well. Everyone would be seated, and he would have all the ladies come in last to show them off. I had sat at the edge of the pew this Sunday, so I could see better with my brother while my sisters and Mom were to parade in. Mother's Day was also a day the women wore flowers. In this case, it was tradition that if you had a deceased mother, you wore a white flower and if your mother was alive you wore a red or pink flower. They came down the aisle all smiles to music and took their seats, and I began to play a game. It was a lot of women and seemed like it took forever, and I was getting bored.

Here is one! Her mom is alive I thought to myself. Next, next, I saw my sisters come and they had on flowers which I could not understand why I never got. "When you are older," Mom would say. They headed up to the choir loft. My game continued, *hers is alive* and then I shouted excitedly while watching them file down the aisle and without thinking, "Hers is dead!!!" blurted out of my mouth for all to hear. The room hushed in silence as our pastor began to look down from the platform to see where the outburst had come from. My brother pulled me down under the seat, but it was too late; my mother saw and heard it all. She was coming down the aisle looking less than pleased and pushed me over in the seat to sit down.

She leaned over and I got that whisper in my ear that I had before, "We will discuss this when we get home." Didn't we always?

I was given my very first solo part at Berea Tabernacle Assemblies of God around that time, at age six. *Away In a Manger,* third verse. I came home from church so excited to tell Dad. He was always watching Rex Humbard when we got home, that was his church, I guess. I did not like to hear him; he talked like he was crying all the time. The music was nasally and twangy and Dad turned the TV up loud when they were on. Unless you went outside, you could hear it all over the house. On the way home though, I began to wonder why I did not get the entire song, all the verses. Of course, Dad was excited for me when I told him during lunch around the table, but they must have seen the wheels turning in my head.

My siblings were happy for me. And my sisters had given me encouragement saying they would be right behind me on the big night. They both sang in the adult choir. Mom kept giving me that side look like she always did when she knew I had something to say. "Gaye, how do you feel about singing in the big sanctuary?" she asked, not looking at me, just passing a food dish around the table. "Well, it's OK. But why didn't I get the whole song, all the verses?" My sisters laughed.

Mom told me lovingly and looking disapprovingly at my sisters, "Well, honey everyone needs a chance to sing." That did not hold water with me, and I continued, "Mommy, I know all the verses and the lady said my voice was great for a little girl." Everyone began eating because they knew what was coming. She went on to tell me that other children needed to be a blessing and that their parents would want to hear them. I looked to my dad who was quiet and said, "Dad what do you think?" "Well, hon your mom may be right, other parents will be there and want to watch their child sing." My mother gave Dad that look like you better support me in this.

Dad said, "I don't know, her voice is really good, I'd love to hear her sing the whole song, but we have to do what was asked, I guess." And, looking at my mother's expression, he gave me a smile and a wink. The night of the Christmas program had arrived. I had practiced that verse in my mind after I went to bed, during church practice, on the way home from school and during bath time. I sang it to Maude, while she worked, to my imaginary friend Montine LaPoor, and in the backyard as loud as I could sing. I was ready. My middle sister fussed over me and did my long hair with a nice thin ribbon that crossed over the top of my head and tied under my heavy hair. I had a blue puffy cotton candy dress that had a little shimmer when I walked and, once again, new black patent leather shoes that Dad had brushed the bottoms of with sandpaper so I would not fall.

There was a significant difference between my parents' approach to encourage you. My mother would say something like "Oh, Honey, God is going to anoint you and you are going to be a blessing to everyone there tonight." My dad in contrast would say something like, "Listen, I bet none of those people have a voice like yours, so you get up there and show them what you got. Don't you be afraid, I'll be out there."

The choir came in first. We had a lot of people that sang in the choir, so it took a few minutes to get them all in place. Then all the children marched in with their new outfits while cameras flashed from proud parents in the audience. I could not see where my parents were sitting, and the bright lights were blinding from the front.

My brother was nowhere near me; he had a part in the play, and I felt a little nervous not seeing him. But I did look behind me and see my middle sister smile from the risers which boosted my confidence. My song had started. I got just a twinge of nerves, but I was determined to sing my part and give one hundred percent to Jesus because Mom had always said, "Give your very best to the Lord," and this would be my best, all I had to give him. The hot spotlight flashed on me, and I began to sing. Shortly into my verse, the big boxy microphone began to shrink down on the stand. Suddenly, a man came from nowhere and started fixing it. I rolled my eyes like the dumbest thing ever had happened, but I never stopped singing my verse. There was laughter and applause as we were coming down from the low risers to sit in the front pews. I was so embarrassed, that dumb microphone ruined my verse I had worked so hard on.

The pastor jumped to the pulpit like he always did. He was so animated. As the crowd still laughed and cheered, he said, "Well friends, I think we have witnessed the making of a star tonight. Not only did Gaye touch us with her beautiful voice but she pressed on in a tricky situation and was a true showman as well." What was a showman? Oh well, it must have been something good; I got many compliments that night after the program.

CHAPTER EIGHT

Many years later, when I was a teenager my dad heard a song, *"Why Me Lord"* by Kris Kristofferson, one of the biggest country singers of that period in the 1970's. He had written it during a challenging time in his life. Dad would say, "I've got the perfect song for you to sing; it's going to get to people." It had not been out long, and he would say "When it comes on the radio, you are going to love it." He yelled one day from the other room, "Come on, Gaye, hurry, that song is playing." I listened to it and told him it was a great song, but it was not for me. I sang songs that God laid on my heart. He did not really understand that, but, after time when I got better at the piano, I would give him little mini concerts. He loved those. I would be at the piano, and I would say, "Dad, what do you want to hear?" I could sing all day as far as he was concerned, but he had two favorites, *"Why Me Lord"* and *"In the Valley He Restoreth My Soul."* This song was written by one of the greatest gospel music writers of all time, Dottie Rambo, in 1970. It would be one that I sang on many occasions in services. I sang several of Dottie Rambo's songs; I loved her music so much. And I was so touched by the words that often related to my own life.

I met my best friend Carol when I was about six. She lived on the other side of the alley behind our house, and she watched as my brother, his friends and I played in the alley one day. We were not in any real danger playing back there. Only a few cars were parked in back and only on occasion do I remember having to move out of the way to let people drive by.

I called her over to play. She was thin with short brown hair and a sweet round face. My mother later called her a little pixie face. She was shy, but, once we became friends, she quickly opened up and enjoyed being at our house.

We came back and forth from her house to mine one summer. When I went there, her mother would be lying on the couch as if she had a terrible headache and would tell us to be quiet or to get what we wanted and leave. Her brother and sisters were much older, and they would be heading off in their own directions and Carol would be on her own. She was only slightly older than I was and, at dinner time, when she was still at our house after a day of playing, my mother would ask her if her parents would be worried about her still being there. She would shake her head no, no one would be worried. Mom or Dad and I would often walk her home to an empty house. We would wait until we were sure she was inside safely and then head back across the alley.

One day, I came home from school and said that Carol had joined the school crossing guard with me. If you were a good student, you got to try out for the crossing guard. You would get a little badge and a brightly colored belt and stand on the corner watching for kids to cross the street before and after school. We had talked about joining and I had asked her why she wanted to. Her reply was that she wanted the hot chocolate. That seemed like an odd reason to me, so when I got home that day I talked to Maude and she said, "Mention that to your folks, that poor baby is skin and bones anyway." That night at dinner, I did. Mom was worried and my dad wanted to know more about her family. Especially if I was spending any time over there.

After dinner, Mom and I walked over to her house to meet her parents. I remember her mother on the couch again, but, this time, there was a terrible smell and a few bottles I did not recognize scattered around.

Carol was nervous, and I could see she kept her head down like she was either afraid or embarrassed. My mom had the ability to make people talk easily and feel comfortable. Someone was always bending her ear about their problems, and she was eager to offer help or to point them in the direction of God. I felt for my friend; we had become so close, and I loved her with my whole heart. Mom had asked us to run and get Carol's pajamas since she was spending the night with me.

On the walk home that night, my mother was quiet, but not long after she had told us at mealtime that Carol's dad had left long before, and her mother was an alcoholic. Her oldest sister was married and gone, and the other sister and brother stayed away as much as possible, leaving Carol to her own devices. I think once we had gone to Tennessee for a funeral. When we returned, the first thing I did was run over to my friend's house. It was horribly cold inside the house; no one seemed to be there, and the door was unlocked. It was dangerous. We lived two houses from a little factory, and about a block from a busy street. So, people would come and go. As I entered the house, I called to Carol. I headed up the stairs and called again. She responded in a quiet weak voice. There she was terribly sick and all alone.

I told her I would be right back and ran home and told my mother and she came back with me quickly, wrapped Carol in blankets and grabbed a few of her things and we headed back to our house. She stayed with us for several days and was too sick to go to school. I would leave in the morning hating to leave her, but I knew she was safe at my house with Maude. And, only after a few days did her mother come to our house asking if we had seen Carol. She had been gone on one of her drunken benders and, when we finally saw her, she was bruised and had a black eye. My mother was horrified that she was in this condition and especially around us girls, and my brother.

She had assured my folks this would never happen again, and insisted Carol go home with her. I could see my friend's eyes tear up leaving our house that evening and I took my cat, ran to my room, and prayed hard for her that Jesus would watch over her. She was at our house at dawn the next day with only a small light jacket on and quickly sat down, made herself at home and had breakfast. Dad was furious I could tell. He did not say anything, but I knew he was upset. He made us his famous chocolate oatmeal that day with toast, juice, and milk. That was our go to meal on a chilly morning.

That afternoon, there was a new heavy coat waiting for Carol when she stopped at our house before heading across the alley.

Since she was at our house so much, she began getting an allowance like the rest of us. Nothing had changed at her house; her mother would make promises to my parents, and they never trusted her. My oldest sister had a bracelet with a little glass ball, and inside was a tiny mustard seed. Mom had told me that if my faith was only as big as a mustard seed, God would answer my prayers according to his will. I would wait until after she said my prayers with me, "Now I lay me down to sleep, I pray the Lord my soul to keep. If I should die before I wake, I pray the Lord my soul to take, if I should live another day, I pray the Lord to guide my ways. Amen."

She would kiss me and leave the room, and I would be in the dark. Many nights I would whisper, *Jesus, are you still there?* And I would pray, "Wherever my brother is, please keep him safe and bring him home and be with Carol in her house. It is scary over there Jesus, please help my friend." Some nights, I felt good about my prayers, and I could drift off to sleep. Other nights were not so easy. I would lie there in the dark with my cat and quietly sing those songs like *In the Garden*, or *No One Ever Cared for Me Like Jesus* that Maude had taught me, and tears would stream down my face and onto my cat. I had fears of loss, like I was waiting on something bad to happen, and I could see my brother and hear my screams for him to stay.

When I started first grade, I had a teacher that was a young woman with long

What You Can Become When Your Faith Grows Up

hair. She dressed nicely but had allergies and constantly blew her nose. When a child would do something wrong, she made the entire class stand the rest of the day with our arms straight in the air. If we tried to put them down or move, she would come over and rub the inside of your hand and hit it hard with a ruler. I was terrified of her. Every morning, I got sick to my stomach just thinking about Miss. Dokes room. She had what looked like a little compact or mirror in her drawer and was always looking into it while we did assignments. One day, right after we got to school, she thought someone had talked out of turn. The bell had not even rung yet as a reminder to get in your seats and begin your day.

Immediately, she yelled for all of us to stand up and put our hands in the air. We had a brief respite for lunch and continued with our hands in the air until time to go home that day.

When I arrived home, I was so sore I could hardly move. I did not want to tell on her because I knew she would take it out on me, so I did not say anything. Only my brother knew because I had told him on the walk home. I tried to set the table, but my arms hurt so bad that night and it did not go unnoticed by my mother. Once we were seated, she began to question us about our day, and she began asking me about mine. "Everything's fine," I replied. She knew me too well. "Gaye, tell Daddy and me what happened at school today," she said.

My mom always went to the school for things like helping give vaccine shots or bake sales. She was familiar with everyone. "I am going to ask you again, what happened at school today?" her voice a little stern. I began to cry and told them about us standing all day and that we were all punished when one person did something the teacher thought was bad. My dad shot straight up. He jumped out of his chair and was calling her every name he could think of. Mom was trying to calm him down and talk to me at the same time. Dad would not calm down and said he and mom would handle it in the morning.

So, the next morning, the three of us went to school. They met the principal. She was an exceptionally large-built woman. Quite manly as I recall; with big shoulders and large glasses. Her hair was in a big knot on the top of her head and her mostly beige dresses hung off her long body and lingered below her knees. We always thought she wore combat shoes. They were no-nonsense black shoes with soft soles so you could not hear her coming, I suppose. My mother began, but Dad quickly took over and said to get that (I cannot say the word he used), down to the office. Miss. Dokes came down to the first-floor office and when she entered, my dad jumped up not even letting the principal start the conversation. My mother could not even speak and sat with a look of horror on her face. Dad told her exactly what she was in no uncertain terms and that if she ever made me do anything again, he would handle her.

She was to do the basics with me, and he would have me reassigned to another class and report her to the school board. Dad had spoken. The principal looked speechless, and Miss. Dokes left the room in tears. Mom and the principal sat there stunned while my dad was still pacing around the room like an injured lion.

He told the principal that she would get me into the other class as soon as possible and that he would be contacting all the parents in my class to be sure they knew about this teacher. The principal tried to calm my dad but not even my mother spoke; it was no use. I was told to go to my class and that if anything was said to leave and come straight down to her office immediately. When I arrived, Miss. Dokes was still crying and never said another word to me, nor did she ever look at me. I was transferred to another class in the next day or so. My dad did not play. I do not know if my mother and he had words after that day, but I doubt it, Mom knew my dad's temper and even though he could have managed the situation in a better way, she knew he was right. Anytime, one of us kids was involved he fought hard for us, and mom appreciated that.

My oldest sister had a friend, a guy friend. He really liked her, and she liked him as well but not in a romantic kind of way. He was a little older than her and quite handsome. He would have done anything for my sister and often his parents would come over for a visit. Dad called his dad a little weasel and that always made my mother upset. She would tell him to be nice and try and talk to the dad. But dad said when the guy talked it was so softly, he had to ask him to repeat everything. His mother was a large woman and she never stopped talking. When she talked, her chins, as in plural, shook like jelly. And I could hardly keep from laughing. She had big, teased hair, that fit around her face like a clown, and large dark rimmed glasses. And I do not even know what she did to her eyebrows. When they came over, my parents would always tell us after dinner to do something while my sister, her friend and all the parents visited.

Once we were headed out to eat one afternoon. For some reason, they were riding with us in our car, and my two sisters were riding with the young man in his car. I had a special place I liked to sit in the car and the Mrs. was taking far too long to get in so that I could not get my favorite seat. Mom was at the sidewalk and told me to get in the car! "I will if she would get her fat butt in!" I yelled. It was as if everything stopped right at that moment. The birds in the sky I am sure even froze in place. I realized what I had said, and about that time my mother flew from where she was standing, grabbed me up, and practically drug me into the house. "Gaye Elizabeth, I should wash your mouth out with soap. Whatever made you say something like that to her? You are to go outside and apologize immediately and I will deal with you later."

Mom was another person you did not push. So, after I got a good tongue lashing, I went back to the car and had to tell the lady I was deeply sorry for what I had said. She would not take my apology and kept on and on about it, finally, my mom told her I had apologized and that we needed to get on with the evening. It was going to be a long night for sure.

I had to sit in another place but was right where Dad could see me from the rearview mirror. He did not look happy with me and having both of my parents disappointed in me hurt worse than any punishment.

I never once meant to be hurtful or disrespectful but, sometimes, I would get frustrated or impatient and I wanted things done a certain way. It had to be done right, and no matter how hard I would need to work, if I was going to do it, it was going to be at one hundred percent. My mother would tell me, "Honey, you put too many expectations on yourself and others. You're too young to worry like that."

My sisters began dating. Well, I should say my oldest sister began dating. My middle sister went out in groups of friends. She liked a crowd. When my brother did not come back home, Dad had the upstairs remodeled for my two sisters. We still had a big attic space, but their room consumed most of the upstairs. You got to that space by going through the kitchen, and the stairway was in the utility room. They had quite different personalities and it showed in their room decor. My oldest sister had motivational sayings and Bible verses on her walls and other things with mute colors. My middle sister had paintings and some of her own work displayed with bright and brilliant colors. My oldest sister was a Bible scholar and studied that and her schoolwork all the time. My middle sister was rebellious, never cracked a book and would try and draw my oldest sister into arguments. She was an instigator. Unless everyone was mad or upset, she was not happy. She did have good moments and I loved her, but she did make it difficult.

My oldest sister was going on a first real date, and she had been upstairs with my mom and other sister for what seemed like forever getting ready. When she came into the living room, she wanted Dad's approval.

He told her she looked beautiful and asked where she was going dressed like that. By then, we had all gathered in the living room or the (front room) as my parents referred to it. My sister asked my dad what he meant, and he said, "Well, you won't be leaving this house in that outfit unless you go back up and put on an undershirt." She looked desperately at my mom who had started trying to reason with my dad. Dad said quietly but firmly, "Well, I am not your mom, and you are not leaving like that. So, if you want to go you better go up and change." My sister ran through the house with my mom and other sister following her and soon after we heard beeping outside. Dad jumped up and yelled, "This better not be what I think it is." My brother and I knew there was going to be trouble and we wanted to sit back and watch.

He threw open the front door leading to the porch and sure enough this young man was beeping his horn for my sister to come out. My dad bounded down those stairs and went to the driver's side and the young man rolled down the window. He got a stern and quick lesson in etiquette and followed my dad into the house with his head down and sat in one of the chairs. When my sister came down, Dad explained that no one would be beeping the horn for one of his daughters and that if the young man was too lazy to come to the door like a man, he wasn't mature enough to be dating. Of course, I was sitting right there by the poor guy watching him wilt down into the chair. After asking the fellow what seemed like a lot of questions, he walked with them outside and reminded him to open the door for my sister.

The next afternoon, Dad sat the older girls down and called for me to join them. I never got invited to these sessions, and it was usually Mom going over personal things with the older girls. So, I was excited to know what we were going to discuss and to be included for once in adult family business. When there was a family meeting or family devotions, I was included, but never something like this. Dad called this **Rules for Girls**.

1. There will be no beeping for you from the car horn. If he cannot come up to the door and get you or meet us if he has not yet, then you will not be going anywhere that night.
2. Undershirts were not optional. You will not leave the house with sleeveless dresses, nor will you show any undergarments.
3. Leave a little mystery. A man wants to be curious about you. Do not put your business on display.
4. No cussing! It makes you look cheap. I think that one was really for my middle sister.
5. Not too much makeup or perfume; you are not a clown.
6. Eat before you go; he may be too cheap to buy you anything.
7. Take One dollar and a dime. That way you can get a ride, eat something, and make a call home, because we will be up until you get home.
8. Don't sit in his car long once you get back home; it makes the neighbors think you are doing bad things and you better not be!

None of this made sense to me at the time, but I was proud that Dad had let me participate.

My parents had people to dinner often, but no one got the treatment our pastor and his family received. It was like we were having royalty visit. Everything was perfect, the house, the food, us. I could not understand dressing up for a meal at home. But we would all be on our best behavior. One night when I was in the kitchen and Mom was rushing about finishing before they came, I said "Mommy, why are you fussing; he only works on Sunday, right?" Why? Why didn't I keep things to myself? Why did I blurt out whatever came into my head? I was lectured on all the pastor does until they arrived, and again after they left for home that night. I was asked a few times to speak on Pastor Appreciation Day many years later, and I talked about this. I would try and refrain from asking questions in the future for sure, well, if I could.

What You Can Become When Your Faith Grows Up

The winter before my seventh birthday had been a harsh one. Along with the chilly air that cut through to your bones, the sun hid most of the daylight hours. It was dreary and depressing. It is strange though that life can be moving along so smoothly one minute, and your very foundation is shattered when tragedy strikes suddenly. And that is just what occurred.

I witnessed something no child should ever experience or see, and it not only affected me, but it devastated my family as well for a time. My parents tried to navigate their way through it the best way they could and tried to help us kids understand. But we did not; none of us did. I thought when my brother rejected us, it would break my mother's heart and crack her foundation of faith in God, but this was so much worse. I dreaded the darkness at night. It traumatized me although we did not discuss it. I am sure everyone felt that way too.

I would wake in a cold sweat replaying those awful images in my head. How could this have happened? Why weren't there signs or warnings? The dynamic of our family changed. Where there had been laughter, and everyone talking over each other at the dinner table was now quiet and subdued. Home wasn't the same. Nothing was the same, we were all just surviving, trying to navigate through the long frigid days.

It was as if the air had left our home. Our safe place. Dad was quiet and always seemed troubled and in deep thought. Both my parents looked vulnerable and tired. Oh, they went through the motions and tried to make things as normal as possible for us, but we all knew our normal had changed. I would hear my mother in her quiet space praying and crying out to God to get us through this time. If mom hadn't given up on God, there was hope. And that brought me comfort. I was not responsible for what I had witnessed. We were not responsible, but it still hurt to my very soul.

It was watching someone you love go through a dark time. However, I had deep guilt that I could have done something to change that night, reset the course. But life is filled with what ifs. It didn't matter now, I could not rewrite that day, that moment. It had happened and we would need to come to grips with it. It was quite some time that my family was in the throes of this nightmare. It broke my heart and left me unsettled. Our little world on Pittsburgh Street had been shaken to the core. We never heard of this occurring back then, and if it did people kept quiet about it, but it would be an awfully long time before we moved past it and the pain it had caused all of us. I would never share the full details for privacy reasons but suffice it to say it was extremely difficult.

I decided I wanted to play an instrument in second grade. I would hear them practicing around my lunch time and I thought that would be fun to do. So, I went and asked Mr. Stacey, the band director, if I could play an instrument. He was a tall man with gray and silver curly hair and glasses. He always wore a tweed suit and I thought he looked just like Don Ameche. He said I was young for the band.

It was made up of fifth graders and middle school students. I stopped in to talk with him after lunch a few times. I would eat quickly and take off next door to the band room. One day, he gave in to my persistence and gave me a little recorder to bring home. He told me that if I learned a couple of songs on that recorder by Monday (this was Friday), he would think about something for me in the band.

Happy with my recorder, I practiced all afternoon, all day Saturday and after church Sunday. Everyone was happy when I took that recorder back to him. Since I was serious, he smiled big and asked me to perform. I aced both of those songs and he seemed pleased. He explained to me what was required from band members. You had to keep up your regular school assignments, be at practice on time every day, and know your material. I promised that if he gave me a chance, I would not disappoint him.

We talked about an instrument, and I settled on a clarinet. It was an old used one that he kept as a spare, but to me it was beautiful. I loved the reeds you used to blow into the mouthpiece that helped make the smooth sounds. And I loved the silver keys and the wood smell when I opened the case.

I got some looks because I was only in second grade at the time. Kids wondered why I was in the band room at all, let alone having an instrument. But I did exactly what he required. I practiced hard, never missed a practice and had been on the honor role since first grade so my schoolwork was taken care of.

When he realized I was serious about the clarinet, he came to our home one Friday evening. I was surprised to see him when he and Dad walked into the living room. He told my parents that I had the ability to play with the older kids but that I would need my own instrument. They were expensive and I guess I had not thought about that. My folks asked what they cost, and he told them, and I could see my mom especially cringe a little. I wanted to jump up and say it's OK, I do not need to be in the band. But you never talked when adults were talking in our house. That was not acceptable. I had to sit there quietly while they discussed it.

When we went to someone's house, we had strict rules to follow. We filed in and sat on the couch until we were asked to get up and move around. You certainly better never open someone's refrigerator, or you would be punished. You did not move; it was that simple. My Dad's family always joked with my parents that they drugged us before we went anywhere. We were taught respect and to honor people's privacy.

Mr. Stacey had a little box with him, and he pulled it out from beside his chair. He said he could give us a particularly good deal on this clarinet if we were interested and pulled the clarinet out of the box. Whatever he told my parents made them smile and shake their heads. They even looked less strained and enjoyed the rest of his visit. That night before I went to bed, I looked at my shiny clarinet. I was as gentle with it as if it were a valuable piece of art, and I grew to love it.

What made it even more special was that my teacher had faith in me, and my parents trusted me enough that they sacrificed something else for me to have this gift and I would not let them down.

I played in all the concerts we had, and then was moved up to the senior band that summer during break. I was with the teenagers now, and I would have to do duets with another girl in front of crowds of students, teachers, and families. The worst thing that could happen was if your horn squeaked. So, I tried hard to keep that from happening. But I had developed a problem though. I could not read notes. I could not read music. Early on I was feeling terrible and guilty, and I went to this man who had given me such a fantastic opportunity and I had to explain that I could not read the music.

Mr. Stacey asked how I had managed to know when to come in and the timing and other questions. I explained that I could hear the song once, and know what keys to hit, but I could not explain how I did it, or how I knew what to do. He would tell me that I played so flawlessly, and that he did not understand how I did it, and I assured him I did not know either. And so, from then on out, I played by ear. He would play the song once for the band before practice and I would get it in my head and then go from there. I grew to love that man. I learned so much from him. And I played in that senior band until we left Detroit.

I tried so hard to do some things, and other things like music came so easily to me. Later in life, I was able to play most instruments I picked up, by ear. I still faced fears that something else dreadful would happen, that the family I knew would go away. I had thoughts that someone would die. Those thoughts lingered in my head. Especially at night. We had not received any counseling after that tragic night, so I do not think any of us including my parents, dealt with it all.

I had my brother, my best friend Carol, and my big old cat that I could not live without, and then there was Montine LaPoor. She stayed near the swing set. Writing this, I asked my husband why kids had imaginary friends and he said he was not sure and that I should look it up. That was odd because I thought he knew everything. Easy enough though, I googled it. It said something like a child that was dealing with stress, loss, or insecurities would invent a friend that they could share these feelings with without judgment. That was me. I told her things I could tell no one else. She never responded, but at least I had an outlet. Oh, I did pray, and I tried to have faith that Jesus would take these feelings away, but it was a struggle that I did not understand, nor could I ever explain it to an adult. Not even my mom.

I was afraid I would hurt my parents' feelings if I told them I did not feel like I belonged at times. I loved my brother and sisters, but I did not feel that I totally connected with them. I was not worried about being judged or anything of that nature, but I was tied to these feelings, and nothing would remove them, not even telling the people I loved the most. I struggled with an alliance I was building with this great man that lived with us. But I wondered if I had a real dad out there that would come back and question my devotion to someone else.

It did not help much that we were scheduled for testing at school soon. I had been on the honor roll until now. I had difficulties with math so I was sure that would change things. The day arrived and I dreaded it. It took all day for the testing and the next day would be the results. I was nervous going to school that day. I was getting used to expecting the worst and that is what happened a lot these days. The teacher stood at the front of the classroom and said that the results were finalized, and she proceeded to give us instruction on what to do when our name was called.

If you did well on the testing, you stayed where you were. But if you assessed poorly, you moved to the other side of the room. Oh, I was sick inside. I prayed, please do not make me move, please do not make me move. Names were called and children stayed where they were and then one or two began to make the shameful walk to the other side of the room to take a seat. And then it happened; she called my name, and I was told to go to the other side of the room. I could not look at anyone; I was so embarrassed and near tears. The children that had not moved began to snicker and make faces at the ones of us on the other side of the room. I wanted to run, to run as fast as I could, far from that place. I closed my eyes and tried not to cry but tears were waiting to fall.

The teacher was so matter of fact; there was no comfort for us on the dumb side, just move here or stay there. When she was finished, she took off her glasses and said to the children who had not moved, "You will be in advanced math and will be learning new and exciting things." And then as an afterthought, she told us that we would be in remedial math, whatever that was, she did not say, and that we would do only basic math. There was no encouragement, no I am sorry you are dumb, nothing to close the divide between the now separated groups. I could see new alliances already start with friends that had been mine, now clicking with other smart kids. I hated school, I hated math and I hated that teacher with all my being.

She sent a note home to my parents who immediately set me up with a math tutor. It was an older lady that lived in a house with blankets and afghans over her furniture. It smelled like old perfume and there were flowers in random containers all over the house. We would work on times tables and math problems, and I would bring my homework for her to help me with. She played little forty five records to help me memorize times tables and I shut it out, I shut her out. Every time I visited; she had some great dessert for me to have as a treat for my challenging work. She encouraged me and tried to help me, but I had built another wall. I associated math with rejection, and I knew those feelings all too well. I knew how they made my stomach hurt and made it difficult to sleep. I struggled with those feelings all the time, and I was not having any part of it.

Math was always an obstacle for me. To this day, I do not like dealing with math of any kind. You must use math every day of course, but it is still a battle, and I still remember at times that dreaded day when, I did not measure up.

CHAPTER NINE

I was accident-prone all my life, and it caused me to have some serious injuries. A proud tomboy, who preferred to play with boys over silly girls, I would try anything once.

So, when my mother found out about the Search for Cinderella contest in Detroit, I was shocked she had entered me. We went downtown on the bus to a large meeting place where many girls my age waited for this opportunity they had heard about on the news and radio. If your foot fit the glass slipper you would win an abundance of prizes along with a college scholarship. I had no desire to go, but Mom had thought it would be fun.

The line inched around the building, and we stood for what seemed like forever waiting for our turn. Then it was my chance. We were instructed to wear slip-on shoes so that it made the process move more quickly. The place was decorated with a throne, and elaborate decor in gold and silver. There was a cute young man dressed like a prince, and a lady that was in charge, spewing orders to everyone. I was instructed to go up the steps onto the stage and try and face the crowd, where I was able to see my mother eagerly watching everything transpire. There were bright lights and some type of royal organ music playing. I was so far from being in my element. And, I was extremely uncomfortable in the dress Mom had selected for me to wear. The lady was pushy and kept instructing me to hurry as I climbed onto the platform. But between the lights shining on me and camera flashes from all sides, I had difficulty seeing where I was going. Finally, the prince who wore a hat like the Jiffy Pop pan bursting with hot popcorn asked me my name. He had a big smile when he placed the slipper on my foot. He looked surprised as he yelled to the woman, "We have a winner!" No! Not me? The lady looked shocked. "Yes," he told her, "Her foot fits perfectly." "It can't be," the lady said. And of course, I was looking off the stage for my mother, and squinting because of the lights. The two were now arguing. I just wanted to go home. I was upset and tired. Finally, she flung a bride doll in a plastic container at me and pushed me down the stairs to where my mother was waiting. The boy called out to me, "You did win; this isn't fair." Mom gave me a pep talk on the way home, and I pretended to listen, but it figured. I wasn't surprised at what had occurred.

I had a series of disappointments close together. I never got over my brother leaving the way he did, and at night I could hear myself screaming for him to stay. It would wake me up. We had also faced that night that rocked our world and left our family scarred and hurt. And I had won but lost that dumb Cinderella event. Dad had said it was rigged. But my birthday was close, and so we planned a party. I was seven at the time. For some reason, I had not wanted a party before, but this year would be different. My mother worked tirelessly making everything look beautiful as only she could, and I was dressed in a nice but comfortable dress waiting for my guests to arrive. Time went by and my sisters peeked in as they headed out for the day. My brother was attending the party, so he waited with me forever it seemed, and no one came. I went to my room, got my cat, and sat on my bed holding her with big tears flowing down my face.

I heard the doorbell, but I did not care. Mom came into my room and said, "You have a party guest." I had only really wanted one boy to attend, and his name was Johnny. He was so funny in school and would laugh so hard that his face would turn as red as his hair. He was one of my two best friends, he, and Carol, and we had so much fun together. He had been on vacation late that summer with his parents and had drowned in a swimming accident. His parents were too heartbroken to come to our class to tell us, so the teacher told us one day before we were dismissed, and I cried all the way home. So even though I wanted a party, I missed my friend. I was missing my brother, and Carol couldn't attend at the last minute, so, I refused to come out of my room. My mother became stern with me and declared, "You have invited guests and this guest has arrived. You will fix yourself and come to your party. We do not treat guests like this in our home."

My brother was in the dining room with this boy dressed in a navy blue suit with his light-colored hair, all slicked back. He had a big smile on his face and had brought me another doll in a plastic container like I had received at the Cinderella event. His name was Jerry. He was quiet in school and never talked. He was so shy. But today, he was all smiles and very polite.

I explained that no one had come to my party so if he wanted to leave, he could. I can still see him standing there with great posture saying, "Gaye, it does not matter if they did not come, we will have a wonderful time and it is just more cake for us." My mother gave a "That's the spirit" as the cheerleader she was, and he, my brother and I had a fun time that day.

On more than one occasion I had come home from school with my long hair messed up. Some days, I wore it down as it was very long. On other days, I wore it in two braids or a ponytail. But I always had to wear a dress and tights. No pants in our house not even for school. Maude would see me coming because I would stop and say hi on my way to change into my play clothes. She would shake her head, "Gaye, how do you get so dirty and get your tights torn so much?" "Oh, I don't know," I would say, "Just playing, I guess." I made my brother keep my secret. I did not want my parents, and especially my dad, to know that some little boys in my class were kicking me and pulling my hair. I was not a snitch, and I was not telling.

I thought it through for a few days, and then I set a plan in motion. Never again would I be bothered by Roland, the worst of the two boys. He was a little taller than me, a little heavy with a bald head and glasses. I always wanted to call him rollie Roland, but it was not nice to make fun of someone's weight even if they were the meanest person you knew.

He did not look like he could do anything to anyone, but he was strong, and he became empowered when he was around other boys. I worked everything out with my brother—my accomplice, and someone that no one would suspect in helping me. My brother was a saint. He never got into trouble, never asked dumb questions and he was so kind and gentle. But not this time. We would take down Roland and make him pay for causing me trouble. Our plan was calculated. My brother was to hurry out after school as quickly as he could and hide behind the big tree that was near the door I was dismissed from. I would already be out there because we got out earlier than the older kids. That morning on the way to school my poor brother was nervous. He tried to get me to call it off, but I was determined.

I wore my hair in big, long pig tails that morning and chose to wear one of my older dresses and thicker tights for what was near summer weather. No one that morning at breakfast had a clue as to what I had planned and that was a good thing. No stopping and no regrets. I reminded my brother of what we were doing immediately after school, and we separated on our way to class. At recess, I stayed close to the teacher instead of wandering off to play like I always did. I did not want those boys to come around. I was getting my nerve up for the afternoon. They jeered at me and laughed while I was close to the teacher, but I only thought to myself, we will see who is laughing later today.

After school, we were dismissed by rows, and I always got to the outside near the playground before Roland's row did. Besides, it took him a little time to get down all the stairs. And, after a couple of minutes, I saw my brother running towards me and jumping behind the tree. He was as white as a sheet and so nervous. He tried to tell me that God would not be happy with me for doing this, but I did not want to hear that now. I had convinced myself that God would understand that I needed to stick up for myself this one time. And so, we waited.

A couple minutes later Roland came out with two of his friends. He was always meaner with other people around to back him up. But today, they walked on ahead, and he straggled behind, which was perfect. My brother ran from behind the tree and grabbed Roland from behind and pulled him back behind the bushes so he would not be seen easily by those passing by. And he held him there while I tore into him. I kicked him and hit him in the face and when I was finished his glasses were askew and his face was a little bloody. A nosebleed. Yep, it looked good on him. I told him that if he ever touched me again, I would beat him up worse than today. My brother let him go and he grabbed his book bag and ran crying. I was a little worse for wear too, I got home with my dress torn and one of my pigtails had come apart at the top with a pulled place that stood high on my head. Maude knew I had been into something, but I just kept moving to my room to change.

Sometime in the evening, my parents received a call from the principal, and they were to meet with her in the morning as soon as possible with me in attendance. Great, I knew it would not take long for him to go home and tattle to his mom about what I did. But I was not scared. He had bothered me one time too many and he got what he had coming. The next morning, we were off to Hannerman Elementary.

It was a huge brick building with separate floors that housed kindergarten through seventh grade. I was in second grade and my brother was in seventh, his last year in the same place as me. From our house, when you approached the school, it was the backside you saw where a huge chain link fence loomed over everything protecting the innocents from the evil outside. The playground was also on that side and it was concrete, gravel with maybe a few trees that framed the school along with some tall bushes and green spots around the area we were dismissed from. To say it was bland would be an understatement. It looked like a prison. Inside it had no color, just more brick and long concrete stairs we had to climb every day. A huge bulletin board hung inside displaying outdated events. It was overall just a drab place.

My dad insisted on going with us this day. Usually, my mom managed things, but dad insisted. When we got into the principal's office, she gave me a look like I was a regular in her office. But I had not been called to her office for anything except for the situation with Miss. Dokes. And would not again, if Roland was smart.

She smiled as Roland and his parents came into the room and took their seats. He would not look at me, but I was staring him down. The principal began to ask me questions and I tried to respond honestly. "You had to have had help so who was with you?" she asked. I looked at Roland as if to say you rat my brother out and I will get you. She kept pushing me, but I would not tell. Better to keep silent than lie, maybe?

Then my dad had sat there enough and started to speak. "You need to teach your son how to treat little girls," he said to Roland's dad.

"Gaye has come home time and again with her tights torn or her clothes torn, and your son has bullied her." I had admitted everything that previous evening and Maude and my brother had backed me up.

Of course, they acted like their child could do no wrong. The principal told my parents that fighting would not be tolerated on school grounds and my dad spoke up, "OK, but self-defense is necessary when you are being hurt. So, if he does it again, I will encourage her to take care of herself and that is how WE will handle it." And he told his parents that if it happened again, it was on them.

I never told on my brother, and no one ever asked me again. I had sat right there and told the principal that I handled it myself. They would have never believed me that my brother had helped in this plot, anyway. But I had some explaining to do to God when I went to bed that night.

CHAPTER TEN

I do not know why, but there were families at church that always wanted to take one of us home after church with their family to spend the afternoon, and then bring us back for the evening service. For some reason, that very wealthy lady gave me a lot of attention. People would always comment to my mother how well behaved we were in their homes. Mom and I were heavily engaged in volunteer work, so it appealed to this rich lady. Her husband was an incredibly quiet man, very understated and he wore the same brown suit every Sunday, it seemed. You would have never dreamed he was so wealthy. She, on the other hand, wore dresses or suits with animal fur around her neck and big expensive jewelry. When I found out that her coats were real fur it made me think less of her, but I never told anyone.

She had invited my parents and all of us to eat after church on occasion at one of their restaurants in town. I was a simple eater; hamburgers and fries are what I lived on, and they always had fancy things I did not want to try. She would talk to me and my mom about volunteering and even had little fancy bags of cookies made up for me to pass out at some place for the elderly they gave money to.

I really did not understand, I thought my little tissue bags of cookies drawn together with a thin piece of string made people just as happy.

One day, she asked my mom if I could come to their home to visit for the weekend, and that her little granddaughter would be visiting. So, their fancy car picked me up and took me to St. Clair Shores, which was a nicer area than most I guess back then. They lived in a complex of nice condominiums. My sister had told me before I went that they had sold their exceptionally large mansion because it got too much for them to manage. I did not know why she thought I needed to know that, but I had guessed she had her reasons. My sisters knew everything about everyone it seemed.

We had a play date the next day and I tried to play with the granddaughter, but she was so mean. Everything I played with she wanted, and it was like that the entire weekend. I was so glad to get back home. However, the lady and my mom had made plans for the next weekend as well. I was so upset to think I had to spend another weekend with this girl. Anyway, when I arrived there that weekend, the girl had brought her bicycle and there was an old beat up bicycle that had seen better days, there for me.

I never saw the man he was always on the phone or reading the newspaper, but the lady was jumping up and down like she had bought me some expensive bicycle. She was excited that she had found this used dilapidated bike in the complex and had got it for me. Again, it was another day of having a miserable time with this girl. And finally, at one point, she began to cry telling her grandmother she wanted me to go home.

My parents had always told us that if we were visiting someone's home and they left the bedroom or whatever room we were playing in, to go to a common place like the living room and not be alone in their personal space.

So, I went and sat in the living room on a chair near the kitchen. I heard the girl say she did not want a new friend, that I was boring and other things just as untrue, and just as hurtful. I would have never got away with speaking to an adult like she was to her grandmother. The lady was trying to console her by bribing her with things. I heard the girl mumbling at times, but I could hear the lady clearly.

She told the girl that I did not have the things she had, my family was a little bit poor (whatever that meant), and that they needed to be extra nice to me. She pleaded, "You go to the best school and live in a beautiful home, you have so much to be grateful for and we need to help this little girl."

I felt like someone had hit me in the stomach. They felt sorry for me!! Wanted to help me!! I sat there holding back tears and all I wanted to do was leave. Just leave that place and these awful people and go home. I kept thinking to myself, your husband has the money. You do not deserve it because you want to try and make yourself feel good by using a child to teach your ungrateful granddaughter how to behave. You will never be half the people my parents are no matter how much money you have. And that bratty girl will never know the sacrifices my parents make, or the love they give to me. I had everything I wanted or needed. I did not need their sympathy. I felt sorry for them.

After a few minutes, the lady came into the room and was shocked that I had been sitting there the entire time. "Oh dear, you didn't hear that conversation did you, Oh, I'm so sorry," she said. I could not even look at her or that horrible girl. "If you would call my parents, please, I think I would like to go home." She begged me to stay, but I felt hurt and that I did not measure up to their lives. And I honestly did not want too ever be around them again. She even tried to have me take that ratty old bike home and I said, "No thank you, I do not want it."

I remember going home that day and was grateful everyone was busy. No one asked about my visit or why I was home early until bedtime. I told my mom when she inquired that I just missed home. And I did. I never ever told my parents or my siblings what had taken place. I would have not hurt them for the world. But I was determined to never let anyone ever make me feel that way again.

Money and security are wonderful, but it does not take the place of family or love. It does not give you the right to think less of someone. And I could never look at that woman again at church. I did not hate her, but she made me feel less than I was and inferior. And, for a kid that was dealing with insecurities already, it caused me to doubt people even more. Her riches and the things they were teaching that child were nothing like what I was learning. The riches I had were my family, an old cat that I carried everywhere and a little woman that sang with me and told me I was special. I had a mother that prayed over me and a dad that protected me. Oh, I was rich all right.

I was a kid that sought out people or animals that I felt were hurting or needed a friend. In the neighborhood we lived in, it was mostly adults.

Next door was an elderly man that kept to himself. On holidays, we would take him goodies. The other side of us was a single man that stayed gone a lot, and two doors down lived a couple with no children.

The man was never out an about, but the lady would be in her yard in the morning tending to her flower beds and I would be sure to run out before leaving for school and say hello to her from across the fence. She always ignored me. Always acted like I was invisible. It bothered me and I was determined to win her over. I was the human version of a therapy dog. If I thought you needed a smile, I gave you mine. If I knew you and you were upset, I would want to make it better some way. I so enjoyed visiting the elderly or helping make food for the needy. I had learned at home and at Sunday school that we were to show love to people, to spread the love of Jesus, and to appreciate what we had.

After school on our walk home, this lady would be outside in her front yard, and I would wonder what her life was like. She had dark hair that she had cut short and dark rimmed glasses. I think everyone did back then, except my mom who had glasses that went up on the sides in an almond shape that reminded me of cat eyes. I had even worn glasses for a brief time when I was little, and I still have them. They were pale blue cat eyes, and I would walk around the house like I was really something. Somebody should have told me how hideous they were. At dinner time around the table, Mom or Dad would say, "Well, did she say good morning back to you today?" And I would reply, "Nope, not yet." But they encouraged me not to give up.

One day, I was extra bold and had been watching her in her yard for a few minutes. Finally, I blurted out, "I know you can hear me when I say good morning, so I will not stop until you say it back. I want to be your friend." Nothing, no response. So, I left for school. On the way home that day as my brother and I walked past her house, she still did not say anything. I told my parents at dinner, "I might as well give up she is just a mean lady, and I am not wasting my time anymore." "This is where faith comes in. When you pray for someone, you ask God to take care of it, to change them, and then you believe like you never have before that he will. That's what faith is honey," my mother said.

I prayed that night after our regular bedtime prayer, asking God to help me and to help her. The next day, I ran outside before breakfast and, sure enough, she was working in her yard. I yelled, "Good Morning!" And without even looking at me, she yelled back, "Good Morning!"

We had a dear elderly Polish lady that lived directly across the street from us. She would sit on her porch in the morning, and in the afternoon when we came home from school. We always waved at her. And she would wave and say something we seldom understood because of her broken English. I wanted a grandmother and often wondered about what we would do together if I had one. Many of my friends had grandparents and they were always talking about them or visiting them. I would pretend that she was my grandmother some days while I played in the front yard. One day, we were walking home, and she motioned for us to come over. We could not take our time getting home from school even though it was a short walk from home. Although it was not a bad neighborhood, we were expected home as soon as we could get there.

This day, we ran inside, dumped our things, and told our sisters where we were. When we got to her house, it was the first time I had seen her close; we always waved from across the street. She had a gentle smile and lines that formed around her mouth and eyes. She wore a little scarf around her hair and a lose fitting soft dress that had lost most of its color from being washed.

Her apron looked like the one the man wore at the little corner store; it was stained but clean. I loved the smell of her house; it was lemon pledge and some amazing aroma floating through the house. She ushered us into the kitchen where she had set her small table for three. On the table were plain looking plates, I do not remember if they even matched. Cloth napkins were at each setting, and I was starting to feel special and a little fancy. In the center of the table was a huge cheesecake covered in either cherries or strawberries, I just remember it being red on top, and a large pan bubbling on the stove with stuffed cabbages that she had just taken out of the oven. You could see the steam making its way in big puffs towards the ceiling.

We ate with her that day, so much food, we could hardly walk home. I wondered why she made so much; I think she had a son, but she never had much company. From then on, we became great friends and I visited her quite often. Most days we sat on the porch, or she would show me photos of her past. I was finally able after time to understand her better and grew to love her.

I mentioned that holidays were the best at our house, especially the three main ones, Christmas, Easter, and Halloween. Now, you might be surprised that a mother that was as strict as ours would even think about Halloween, but she did. We did not decorate much for Halloween, but we did get out early to get costumes. My parents took us shopping and we would pick out the costume we wanted. There were rules, no devil or anything scary. They came in cardboard boxes with a clear window on the front and that is where the mask would show through. The costumes were made of nylon type material that was scratchy and most often fit over your clothes and would tie in the back. The mask was a hot piece of plastic decorated with some macabre face with tiny slits for your eyes and mouth that you could neither see nor breathe out of. The thin rubber band that held the mask on your face would always get caught in my hair or snap off ten minutes into trick or treating.

Mom and Dad would start early in the evening with Mom making a big pot of chili or some other hot tummy stuffer that would keep us warm to our toes at least until we left our block. And Dad would get out his big pan and everyone would take the little wrappers off all the caramels for melting down. Because Dad made the best caramel apples ever. Mom would make popcorn balls and those and the caramel apples were the talk of the neighborhood. They always shared with the neighborhood kids but made sure we had plenty of both when we returned with our loot. We did not use those silly little bags for trick or treating, no, we used pillowcases. Yes, the biggest pillowcases we could find. They were sturdy, never ripped and held all our goodies until we got home. When we were adventurous, we would come home dump out our stash and go out again in a different direction. Those times did not occur often but on occasionally warmer fall nights. Even then, we would have our regular clothes on, then the costume and about every year either a sweater or a coat over our costume.

My sisters would take us while my parents handed out treats at home, and we would meet up with friends and go in groups. Lights would be on everywhere, and only seldom would a porch light be turned off, meaning they were not participating in giving out treats. A few times we were tricked with lights out and we would hear a noise, approach the porch gingerly and hear a loud Boo! by the owner, who then handed out treats after scaring us.

Often, we would see a large bowl placed on a table outside the front door and it was filled with candy or pennies. A little sign read, *Take one*. And that is exactly what we would do. We would never have thought of taking more or emptying the entire bowl into our bag. You just did not do it, we knew better.

We were invited in to use the restroom or get a drink or even visit a few minutes with people. Especially older people. They wanted to know your name and where you lived. Oh, there were some weird people even then, and we would hear about people putting things in treats like needles or some other terrible thing. We were never allowed to eat our candy until we were home, and everything was inspected by my parents. Any loose items like apples, or homemade bags of cookies were thrown in the trashcan. And things like jaw breakers and round candy were taken from me because I was prone to choke. Even my parents only gave apples and popcorn balls to our neighborhood kids who knew us. They gave out wrapped candy to everyone else.

One night, we had walked quite far from our neighborhood, and nothing really looked familiar. I saw this place and could hear music from inside. It was a dingy old storefront with a half lit up open sign flashing in neon. My always wonderful brother must have known what I was thinking, and he was not having it. "We are not going in there," he scolded me. I told my sisters I wanted to go in as I was sure they would give us something. They could have cared less what we did, both in a little rebellious stage getting something over on our parents was OK with them. I told my brother I was going in. I noticed the smell right away. It was a mix of tobacco and cheap cologne. The sticky smelling liquor that found its way from the top of the bar counter onto the floor grabbed at my shoes like glue.

There were women inside, and that surprised me. For some reason, I would not have expected to see women at the bar. I compared every woman to my mother. Of course, not ever being in an establishment like this before I was curious to see everything. We had passed places like this riding with our parents, and I always wondered what was going on inside. People were drinking, and the music was much louder than from the muffled sound we heard from outside.

When the bartender saw me, and then my brother who had come in to protect me I guess, I said "Trick or Treat!" Although some were shocked, we had come inside, most everyone gave us loose change and seemed happy to do so. We did go into a few much nicer places that night but were not met with the nicest people. And they were stingy. Maybe they did not get as happy when they drank, who knew. That proved not to look at the outside and judge it. I remember getting home and dumping all my loot onto my bed. My brother did the same thing and we had mounds of candy and money. My sisters, too cool to trick or treat, always wanted to bum candy from us after the fact when all the work was done. But we had to share; we did that in our family.

My mother was especially curious as to how we had obtained so much money. Dad always called me whizzy bits, but Mom used my full name Gaye Elizabeth when I was in trouble. And I knew I was in trouble. So, she asked again, and I knew it would be worse on me if I did not confess. I said "Well, we went into some places where they sell drinks." This piqued her interest, and her nose was starting to come to a point. It could have just been my imagination, but her anger was becoming clear and that was not my imagination. She said, "You mean to tell me you went into bars?" It was always at those moments when you had two choices, you just blurted out what you did and waited for your swift punishment, or you drug it out, making things only worse for yourself because the result was going to be bad either way. So, I said, "Well, yes I went into bars." Mom looked at my brother and said, "And you went into the bars with your sister?" "I was trying to protect her." My brother said. And, in fact, that is exactly what he was trying to do.

"But I can explain," I blurted out, trying to think fast, "They gave us money, and if they gave us money, they didn't have any to buy more drinks." So there, that's the reason. Yes, that was it. It seemed convincing enough.

When we were punished, it was immediate. There was no time-out chair, no lengthy discussion, and sending us to our room to think about what we did. My parents did not count to five or other ridiculous attempts to deal with our behavior. We did not have meals or dessert taken as a punishment. But, when we did something, our punishment came quickly, and we would remember it for a long time. If we were promised a spanking but Mom did not have time at that moment, we would get it later. She never forgot. I only received two spankings from her, but rest assured those were enough. She could look at me and I stopped what I was doing immediately. I was scared of my mother, and I minded her because I knew better. It was always a good tongue lashing along with lost privileges or our allowance, or the worst, a spanking. And punishment was given based on severity of the crime.

The worst for me was the talk about disappointing my parents, oh, I hated that. I always felt horrible. You were the lowest of the low when they felt disappointed in your behavior. This time, I sat there waiting for what I was sure was coming next. This was a spanking moment; I just knew it. Mom asked my sisters why they were not supervising us as they were instructed to do. They always had some lame excuse for everything. Mom stood up smiling at us, "Well, you learned something tonight. You saw some incredibly sad people, in a dark and bad place and I hope you will never want to go to those places in your lives." What had just happened? *Was Mom not going to give me a whipping?* There was no relief like that. I had escaped what could have been a very severe punishment. My brother and I were elated but confused at Mom's reaction.

The summer was my favorite because we were out of school. We could stay up a little longer and sleep in a little later. But one thing I hated that was associated with summer was a four-letter word, camp. It was the worst. I hated everything about camp. Usually, long before they started talking about it at church, I was already priming my parents with reasons why I could not go to camp that year. Oh, I loved being outdoors at home, but I did not like being in the woods, and around masses of water. It was all concrete where I lived, and a small patch of yard that suited me just fine. I never wanted to sleep outside or eat outside or do anything that required being outside at camp.

One night, we were at the table finishing dinner and my mother brought it up. Oh, the pit of my stomach hurt when I thought about it. I rambled on about not wanting to go and looked at my dad for help. Even he thought it was not a big deal to attend camp. He would give me reassuring looks like I am trying kid, but my mother was not having it. To her, it was a magnificent opportunity to get in touch with nature outside of the city and somehow draw closer to God, having forged in the wilderness for a week.

No, thank you. I would beg and promise anything, just to not have to attend camp. It was church camp and since I was five years younger than my brother, I would be away from him for an entire week.

He would leave after I came home, so it would be two weeks until we were together. After that, my sisters would go and that was fine. Often, I wished they would stay at camp. But they usually did come home a little different, a little less argumentative and especially for my middle sister that was a miracle for sure. It was the same every year. We would arrive at church on a Sunday afternoon for the dreaded meal of sloppy Joe's. Oh, to this day, I detest anything that resembles oil-soaked bread with some type of mystery meat. I would usually eat before we got to church because I could not manage the food and then a long bus ride afterward.

We stashed our stuff in the bottoms of the rickety old school buses and filed on board with one or both of our parents off to camp FA HO LA. It was only a couple of hours away, but between the bouncing up and down as the bus hit every bump in the road, and ninety-nine songs, I would be over it once we arrived at our destination. My ears would be ringing and my stomach churning at what was ahead. It was pandemonium once we arrived. All the busloads of girls from churches across the state arrived at the same time. You would have thought they would stagger the arrival times, but, no, that never happened. We would be checked into the cabins, meet our counselor for the week and our parent (usually my mom) would help me settle into my cabin. She would be asking me if I was sure of what I brought the entire time I was continuing to give her reasons why I should go back home with her. The worst time, was when the bus left with my mom on board headed back to the city and I was left in camp FA HO LA.

Cabins were just small units with a roof, concrete floors and screen doors and walls. Everything was screen, and I would think about bears or other critters with large nails scraping down the screens to make entry in the night and kill us all. All, meaning the three other girls in my cabin and me. Right off the bat, they got into a click laughing and whispering. I was usually in a cabin where the girls knew each other. I never got to be with people I knew from church. Girls were the worst, which is why I liked playing with boys. Boys were not complicated. They did not get mad and run off pouting or talk about you. But girls, oh they could be cruel. My mother sent me with a bathing suit and the only pants I had to wear over them for when I went swimming.

She bought me pants to wear so my legs did not show around the pool because we had to be decent. God forbid, if anyone in that blessed camp out in the wilderness saw my sad scraped up knees.

I don't think she even knew her own daughter, or anything that went on at camp. First, there was never a pool there, it was only mucky lake water that I would have never gotten into for love nor money. Second, I would have never put on the bathing suit she sent with me because it looked like a tablecloth and had little thin straps that you had to tie up at the shoulders. I could never get it on right. One shoulder was higher than the other because I would tie a bigger bow on one side, and I looked like a hunchback. No, I would never wear it and never even took the tags off it or those dumb pants. A lot of the girls were running around in little colorful bathing suits with nothing covering their legs. And third, it was summer, pants in summertime at camp, in the heat! really, Mom?

The counselor assigned to our cabin would start yelling for us to get up so that we could get showered and dressed, make our beds, tidy our rooms and be at the meal hall by 7:00 a.m. I never understood why, because we had to wait forever in line once we got to the food hall. And I always tried to get up quickly and shower because we would run out of hot water if we waited too long. Oh, how I hated mornings there. I would lie awake listening to girls' giggle, noises from outside and strange shadows the moon made on our ceiling, and I would only doze off in the early morning after I could not protect our cabin any further and gave into sleep. It was usually then that we heard someone yell, "Get up!" We walked through the woods to the food hall; I never did know what the proper term was for it. We stood outside in line until it was time for us to go in. The exhaust from the cooking would push out through large vents in the kitchen. And I would get so sick smelling all the breakfast fixings.

Usually, right after breakfast, it was off to chapel and then free time. I longed for free time. You could do many things. But my favorite was going to the store for a cold pop. That was what we called cokes or other carbonated drinks in the North. It would settle my stomach from all the morning activities. Then I would go to the office and beg them to call my parents to come and get me. It got to be a daily routine. Most mornings, the ladies in the office would start shaking their heads as soon as they saw me. And, even with my most sincere pleas, they refused to call home. On a few occasions I would wander down and watch other campers swimming carefree in the lake. Since I was terrified of the water, I could only watch for a few moments and then find something else to do. I did enjoy arts and crafts and evening worship in the big tabernacle.

My age group was the first to attend camp for the summer. So, all the new improvements would be made. Just entering the tabernacle, it smelled like fresh-cut wood and new paint. I loved the way it smelled. And it was such a special place.

Of course, there was no air conditioning in any part of the camp we were allowed in except the offices and the infirmary. But there were fans that circulated cool air around the large tabernacle. After the music would be playing for a while, it was like the fans kept perfect time with the beat. The summer was warm but not unusually humid, so it was tolerable. I loved the services at night. The evangelist geared the meetings to our age group. I loved going to the altar and praying or watching other girls pour their hearts out to the Lord. That part had a way of freeing a person. Your worship was your own. No parents, pastors or older siblings were there to watch over your shoulder, it was freedom to worship independent of everyone in a no judgement zone.

My imagination would be on high alert at night. The woods were so dense and dark when we went back to our cabins. Most of the camp was mowed, but there were places in the woods where high weeds covered the ground and I just knew something bad was lurking in those weeds. We did have a few minutes to get something at the store if the service did not run too late and I would always try and do that. I learned that smuggling cokes to my cabin was not allowed. I started at the beginning of the week to stash as many snacks and drinks as I could. I was desperate enough because of sick stomachs in the mornings that I would have drunk a warm coke. I didn't get them at home a lot, but we did have it in our house, and it did settle my very temperamental stomach. Thinking I was all set, I failed to realize that counselors could rummage through belongings. So, once I went for my stash and it was gone. There was a note that said it had all been taken to the store with my name on it and I could get it there as needed. As needed? Well, of course! I needed my snacks. Just another thing I did not like about camp.

I would usually run as fast as I could through the woods screaming from the top of my lungs at night until I reached my cabin safely, and then locked the screen door behind me. I never watched a single scary movie. Well, except for the Wizard of Oz and those awful scary flying monkeys. But my mind would be filled with all kinds of horrible scenarios. The other girls would drag in laughing like they did not have a care in the world. Sometimes I wanted to make them stay outside, but I always gave in and let them in. I must have been the only one that was terrified of snakes and bugs and whatever else lurked in those woods and water after dark.

When camp was over on Saturday, our parents came up to ride back with us. Dad usually came then with my mom and brother, and I would be so overjoyed to see them. They would have programs and sporting events that everyone could participate in, and you could compete against your parents, but I wanted one thing, to get out of there as soon as possible.

I had trouble sleeping and would wake in the mornings so tired from wrestling around with my thoughts and I didn't want to tell my mother. I would relive my brother trying to leave our home and would wonder what he was doing, or if he ever thought about us.

I would think about my friend that drowned and imagine what he could have felt or thought right before he sunk into the water for the last time. And, that awful night my family had gone through not long before was still fresh in my thoughts. Those memories danced around like devilish acrobats in my head. I would draw my cat closer into me and begin to sing quietly to myself with hopes that it would stop me from hearing the noises and clatter inside my head.

My mother would tell us that God had not forgotten about us and that He would take care of everything, we just had to believe in Him. I was mixed up. If God knew about us and saw what happened, why didn't He stop it? I would hear my mother praying and I wanted to believe like her, I tried to have faith, but I saw the situation, in cruel black and white and nothing seemed right. There is a unique way a child perceives faith differently than an adult. A child trusts that if you tell them something, it is a given most of the time. They have not yet learned to approach something with variables, reasoning, or doubt.

I think when God refers in the Bible to have faith as a child, or childlike faith, He means take it as it is; do not add all your interpretations, attitude, or cynical reasoning into it. Believe it because He said it to be true. And not one time in the Bible did He not come through for believers. A child believes without everything making sense. When I was told I was loved by someone when I was little, I had no doubt that they loved me. I did not have to question it. They loved me and that was enough. Even though I had issues I knew I was loved. But once we become adults, or when our world is rocked, we put too many restrictions on our faith. We question God why? And we muddy the waters. God must remind us that we need to become as a child again, with a child's faith to believe not only in the work that He can do in our lives, but to get into Heaven.

Life can be full of obstacles and there are more reasons as an adult to question not only your faith, but your relationship with God. It is like going full circle. You believe so simply as a child, then you become and adult and hit the speed bumps and barriers that life throws at you.

Your faith wanes and your trust in God fails. You lose the passion and wonder that you knew as a child that believed God was loving and faithful. Then after all your questioning and denials, you return to the Lord and become like a child again starting over to fully trust Him.

As a child I believed in the wonder of God, that He was my savior, but trusting Him in the tough times was exceedingly difficult still. I had seen a lot as a child, but Mom was always there to give me direction and to listen and she was never deterred in her faith no matter what came along.

There were no sacred cows in our family; we could discuss everything freely, especially with my mom. It doesn't mean that we always did. Dad was a little more reserved and we did not rely on him for our spiritual guidance. But he taught us so many things to watch for in life. Mom, on the other hand, was trying to teach us to trust God for ourselves. I knew that if she believed that it was going to be OK, then it was. I trusted her when she spoke of God's faithfulness to us even with our circumstances difficult and things looked bleak. She didn't have all the answers, but she knew God did. She would say, "Do not trust me about this, trust God."

God had given my mother unmovable, unshaking, and unwavering faith. I did not understand it fully, but I trusted her, and I loved God so that would have to carry me during this dark season in our lives. We did not understand as a family why our faith was tested in such a way, but we would need to rely on God. We were all still dealing with the aftermath of this the following summer.

It was exceptionally hot that year. Even the news people would say how incredibly and uncharacteristically hot it had been. Dad watched the news every night and read the paper every day. Sometimes, we watched the news with him. He would say, "I wish they would stop talking about the heat, and people being bored, they are going to stir something up, you watch and see." He had friends and family all over town so he would glean from different ones about newsworthy events.

It was the morning of July 23, 1967—a normal sweltering day in Detroit. I was nine years old. We were all up getting ready to set out for church since it was Sunday. Dad was up and told us that we would not be going to church that morning.

There was some trouble brewing downtown. He had been watching the little black and white TV we had. It was on a cart that rolled, so we could turn it around or move it to other places. He reminded us of what he had said earlier about the restlessness in the city this sizzling summer. When the picture on that ole television was hard to see or fuzzy, Dad would give it a couple thumps with his hand. Sometimes that corrected the problem, other times it did not, and he would get aluminum foil from the kitchen and put it on the ends of the big rabbit ear antenna. It was two long metal rods that looked like ears. Not attractive at all, but the foil on the ends did help and you could move the rods around for a better picture.

The Detroit riot had begun in the wee hours that morning. We watched as the news captured the rumblings across town and showed violent scenes that were scary to watch. Mom had worked a night shift and was detained at work because of the rioting. They needed extra staff for potential victims and injuries, and they were also afraid to let anyone venture out because of the danger downtown. We were glued to the TV watching every minute and awaiting any updates. On this day, Dad was particularly agitated.

We were watching stores being looted and burned right before our eyes. Places we often shopped at were being destroyed. What started with only a couple people had now swelled into many people in the streets, with a mob like heightened anger at everything. They hated white police and white people, in general, and it was getting worse as the day progressed. The news reporters were edgy, and it looked to us like some were way to close to the situation. Since the city had never experienced anything like this and since it was racially charged, no one knew where it would end. We were not allowed to go outside, so we found things to do inside to keep ourselves occupied. And we were all starting to get worried about my mother who had still not left for home yet.

Dad had tried to call but by now the lines at the hospital were busy so he could not speak to my mother or find out if she was all right. We had no way of knowing if she had headed home in all this or not. I tried to pray for her, and we all were thinking the same thing, would she be OK in this madness that had overtaken the city?

Places around the city were up in flames, and no one was sure at what point it was going to escalate. We just knew it was not ending anytime soon. I tried to get alone for a bit in my room to think about Mom and to pray for her safety. She was the binding agent for our family, she kept us together, kept things moving. She and Dad ran a tight ship, but we had a stable home because of them and Mom's faith in God taught us to believe and hold on in challenging times. We used to say she had a direct line to God's throne. If you had ever heard her praying, you would understand the reason we felt that way.

I tried to have faith that she would be OK, and that God would bring her home, but the TV showed a vastly different city than our quiet little street. It was full of people that were railing out at anything and everything and I did not want my mother to be in harm's way or in their path. I do not remember the exact time, but late in the day we went outside for a minute to look down the street and see what may be happening in our area and we saw her walking towards our house. She was in her stark white uniform and white shoes, but she had taken off her nursing cap. We were all overjoyed to see her coming home safely. She was a target in all that white, and we all knew it.

Later in the evening, she told us that it had been horrible where she was, and that she had started walking, not knowing what else to do. She usually took the bus both ways, but they were not operating. Everything in the city had been paralyzed by the violence. She prayed as she walked, and, after a time, a bus pulled up, the door opened, and a black man was behind the wheel. He told my mother to get in quickly and that he would take her as far as he could. And he did just that. He was my mother's angel that day. God had used this wonderful man to help her get home safely. He told her she would not have made it much further being white and in that white uniform. the area she was starting to walk through before he pulled up was like a war zone.

For several days, until July 28, 1967, the riot continued. It was the worst story of violence and destruction in history at the time. There were military guards surrounding our neighborhood, and military snipers were on the rooftop of Chadsey High School where my sisters attended. Military jeeps and men in uniform paraded down our street that week. I would wave at them from the porch since we were not allowed on the sidewalk or the street, per our parents' instructions. There was also a curfew for the entire city.

At the end of that week, forty-three people had been killed, 342 were injured, and 1400 buildings were torched or burned to the ground. Over 7,000 National Guard and Army personnel were called into action to combat the violence. Detroit was never the same.

After the riot, my parents decided that we needed to leave Detroit. The decision was made to move to Saginaw. It was a couple of hours from Detroit. Dad would take a civil service position to finish out his work time and then retire. I was beyond unhappy. Mom got rid of Candy around this time. She had begun to not let anyone near me. Once she had even attacked me while I played with my brother. Now, I know that everyone does not see how a pet can be so important to a person. But I felt that I did not have a lot that was truly my own. I felt different. And I often felt alone; even when everyone was around. I could not explain it then, but now when I look back, I see myself as an island. Separated, but still with everyone. So, this cat meant the world to me. She was truly my comfort, especially at night when those terrible memories came knocking. And they cluttered my mind till I fell asleep. She was a one-person cat. But they had to send her away because of her behavior and I cried every night for her. I grieved for Candy. She and I had been together for so long and we did everything together. I had begged my parents not to get rid of her, that there had to be another way. I was lost without her. Now, the thought of leaving her behind was unbearable. Along with that, I had to leave Mr. Stacey and the band I loved and worked so hard to get into. And then there was Carol. I told her through tears one day that we were leaving Detroit. We both cried.

My parents tried to talk Carol's mother into letting them have custody of her, with the assurance that she would get the best they could give her and that she could always stay connected. Her drunken mother refused and said she would do better by Carol, but we would need to leave her behind. And Maude. We left Maude, too. My oldest sister was still dealing with some things, and she remained in Detroit to continue healing.

Even while I am writing this, I am in tears. It brings back so many emotions and sadness to my heart. I was rebellious, and I was on Mom's bad list. I was refusing to leave because I wanted things to stay the same. I wanted Christmases in that same house with all my siblings like it was in the past. I wanted to run home, jump on the counter in the utility room and sing with Maude, and tell her how much I loved her. I wanted my cat back. I needed my best friend, and I would miss my sister.

Everyone tried to tell me that it would be OK. That I would meet new friends, and this would be an adventure. But I did not want adventure; I hated change and I could not stand the thought of leaving there. It was home. It had always been home, and I did not see how I would ever be able to leave.

No matter how often they would console me and try and make it better, it did not make things better. Each day was a reminder that we were leaving soon. They said I would love it in our new place. It was hard on all of us. I have a photo of Carol and me on that last day together. She had become family to all of us. She gave me a little ring to keep, and I cherished it for many years. But I never saw her again. I have wondered so many times about her and what her life was like after we left.

I had groveled with insecurities about my place in this family. I always had. I had kept it inside. Too afraid I would hurt my parents or my siblings if I explained my feelings. I wish now all these years later that I had shared all of this with my parents. Maybe I would have gotten the answers I needed. I knew beyond a doubt I was loved and what I experienced was an internal struggle. Maybe, there was nothing to it, and I was just that kid with the big imagination. I was slowly starting to come to grips with some of my memories. And especially since I was getting a little older. It was becoming easier to sort things out in my mind.

But I had the cover of this home where things were familiar and there were people and animals around me that made me feel safe. And they gave me the ability to explore my thoughts in a nonthreatening environment. These walls and this home were my haven, filled with my hopes and dreams. It was familiar and safe. I was and still am a person who is contented with a status quo. I do not need adventure, or change. I am perfectly fine with things staying the same. But we would leave all the people, and everything I loved behind. I had felt so alone so many times in this family. I could not explain it, but I felt like an island and now the only things or people that gave me comfort we would leave behind. My heart was broken. What a horribly sad day that was, to say goodbye. I knew my brother felt the same way.

We lived about five miles from Frankenmuth near Saginaw Michigan. I hated it. We all had trouble adjusting. But Mom got us into church quickly. We attended First Assembly of God and Pastor Thomas Trask was the pastor. He is a great man of God and years later became the eleventh General Superintendent of the Assemblies of God.

He was instrumental in getting us kids back on track again. We all loved him. We were supposed to be baptized in water one Sunday. I was still terrified of water. He had counseled me about it and promised that he would be right there. That Sunday came and we were all in the back room preparing and I was getting ready to change my mind. He came over with his big smile and said, "Now, Gaye, it's going to be fine, I promise."

It was my middle sister, brother, and me. Other people were baptized that morning as well. I remember all of us dressed in thin white robes. The plan was, when you got inside the big tank you would give a little testimony and then he would baptize you. I had my hair braided that day and I remember freezing up in front of the microphone. I was not scared to talk, but I feared being in that water. I mumbled some words and Pastor Trask dunked me quickly. He knew I was a runner. When he brought me out of the water, my arms were flailing. A while later, we moved to another Assemblies of God church closer to where we lived where my sister and my brother had met friends, and Pastor Kapaz became our pastor. They had many more young people and we liked it. I was in the church band playing my clarinet. It is also where I had met my first boyfriend, the sweet pastor's son. I received the Holy Ghost in that church. What a wonderful day that was!

We had not been in Saginaw long when Dad had a terrible car accident and nearly died. He was hit head on by another driver. It was a few days before Christmas. We spent days at the hospital so we could be near him. Even Christmas Day. Mom brought some of our presents to the hospital with us so that we could open a couple while we sat in the waiting room. He was in ICU, and it was touch and go for a long time. He survived but experienced some heart trouble shortly after that. He made the decision to finish what work he could do quickly and retire.

Mom had a friend in upper Michigan, in Petoskey, and she had also found a job at the nursing home there as a nurse. My parents decided we would move there because it was a small town and Dad could retire, and it would be safer than Saginaw for us kids. We were used to moving by now, and I for one did not have attachments to people anymore. It was too difficult to say goodbye.

Everyone else left for Petoskey with the big moving truck and I stayed behind so that when Dad got finished working that last day, I would ride up with him. I did not want him to ride alone. I had been sick all day after my family left and was staying with the neighbor.

Dad came to get me, and he was driving an old pickup truck I had never seen before. It had seen better days, and I wondered how we would be able to make the trip in it. I asked him where he got it and he said he needed to bring a few things up with us. So, we got in that dilapidated truck and headed to Petoskey. There was no heat, and I was miserable. It was freezing cold and made for an extremely uncomfortable trip.

I was never happier to be in our new warm home when we arrived in the wee hours that next morning. I was so happy to see my mother even more. She had gotten up when she heard us come in. I had not noticed the cold outside because we were in that old truck and I was frozen to the bone, but the next day I thought about what kind of place we had come to. This place was freezing! I thought Detroit was cold, and Saginaw was colder. But Petoskey was like being at the North

Pole. We had moved there towards the end of winter, but it was still bitter cold into the spring. We had not been up that far. Eighteen miles from the coldest point of Pellston MI I believe. We had no idea how much colder it could be.

Petoskey is a quaint tourist town in the upper peninsula. Our house stood at the top of a big hill. It was white and looked a little Victorian. It seemed so large until I saw it many years later for sale and it looked smaller than I had remembered. At night, we could look out over the city. The new neighbors beside us were the Kigamaugh family. They were Native American and great people. There two younger kids were around my age. You entered our house into a sitting room with a large window seat. The open area flowed into the living room and dining room. As you went to the back of the house there was a large kitchen with a breakfast nook and short windows across the wall that let the sunshine in early mornings. And there was a thickly wooded area with a creek that framed the house in the back. Narrow steps off the dining room led to bedrooms upstairs. My sister, brother and I had rooms on that floor. My room was wallpapered in pink and white stripes. It was smaller than the others but fine for me. My parent's room was off the sitting room downstairs, and there was a basement with a large cellar.

For several months, Dad worked in Saginaw and would drive up to see us and then go back. We would talk to him on the phone when he was not able to make the trip home.

We had started church at the little Assemblies of God church down in town. I do not really recall much about it because it did not leave much of an impression on me. The pastor's last name was Padgett, and he had a daughter my age named Michelle. She was very heavy and abrasive, and we did not get along from the onset. She was spoiled (and I was a little too), but she would try and tell me what to do and that did not work for me. She would say, "If you don't do what I say, I will tell my dad on you, and he's the pastor." I do not know why, but her parents were adamant that we were going to be best friends, but that was not happening. One day, her dad came to visit specifically to talk with my mom about how Michelle and I could be better friends and that Jesus wanted us to get along.

My sweet mom tried to make him understand that some people did not hit it off, and that she and I were incompatible. He tried for a while to get us together, but then gave up thank goodness. Since we had arrived in Petoskey near the end of winter, it was now becoming spring. Everything bloomed, and the city looked beautiful. The waters that framed this quaint community were blue and clear. Events were scheduled for every season. Ice fishing on the lake in winter, and festivals and water activities in spring and summer. And the air seemed much cleaner than Detroit. It was a busy place though and congested with tourists. Many came for skiing or other snow related sports, so it was critical that we had snow in the winter months. I loved when Mom finally drove and we would go downtown, less than five minutes from our house. We would wander through shops, and I would buy Petoskey stones. I also found some separate times, and I still have them today.

There was a tree swing on this huge tree that overlooked the valley next to the Kigamaughs' house. I wore pants now because the winters would be much colder, and I was more comfortable than in my dresses and tights. Mom had given in and had become a little more relaxed in the way I dressed. We would all take turns grabbing hold of the rope and swinging way out and then back and catch our feet on the bank to pull back up.

Once, everyone had taken a few turns on the swing, I decided I would take one more before we went in for dinner. I swung out far and the rope broke plunging me down hard into the grass mixed with rock on the steep hillside.

My body stung from the fall, and I had scratches all over my arms and legs. I could see my brother at the top of our hill looking down at me.

He yelled down to see if I was OK, and I was not sure I was. Finally, I made the walk back up. I could not talk at first, I think the jolt from the fall took my breath. The side of the hill was jagged from overgrowth and tree branches that weaved their way around rocks and dirt. I never played on that rope swing again after it was repaired.

My middle sister had gotten a job at a local restaurant and would bring home food at the end of her shifts for my brother and me. She was eighteen now and had decided to rent a room from one of the restaurant's regulars. The woman had property around the city and made her income from teaching and renters. She was so strange though. My parents were less than pleased about my sister's decision. They wanted her to attend college and stay at home.

My sister rebelled as usual and told my parents it was her decision and moved out. My brother and I had mixed feelings about it. She and Mom had words quite often and she felt everyone was against her. She was confrontational and had a chip on her shoulder as tall as she was. Even with us kids, she would agitate and belittle us. When she left, I thought that we would see her often, it was a small town, but she was influenced by this woman and started coming home less and less. Mom would call her, and I knew my folks were worried about her, but she was strong willed and if she got something in her head, she would do it or die. By now, I was used to being left. I could not forget what we left behind in Detroit, and I still resented my parents for the move. But it was not easy watching our family become so broken. It was just my brother and I now and we stuck together like glue. I felt that he was all I had left.

One day, we were outside, and this long sleek black car pulled up in front of our house. We watched as a little man got out dressed in a black suit and hat from the driver's side and hurried around to open the back door of the car. An older gentleman stepped out in what looked like an expensive suit, even a kid like me noticed. Mom had been baking and cooking all morning, but that was a normal thing for her when she was off work. It was her way of relaxing, so we did not think anything about it. He acknowledged us and then headed to the front door. Mom answered the door and offered for him to come in and we were right behind him. He sat at the kitchen table and visited with my mom for a few minutes, laughing at every word she said with sheer enjoyment. Mom laughed and packed up the food and desserts she had made that morning. When he started to place a substantial amount of money on the table, she refused it. She let him know that his money was not necessary. Mom explained that her baking was for us and others to enjoy. We knew that anyone who got to sample her food or baked goods was fortunate.

My brother and I would have gladly taken it, that was a lot of money. But after much insisting from Mom, the man promised not to offer to pay again. He told us that we were fortunate to have a mother that was such an exceptional baker. We were aware of what our mother could do. She was the best cook and baker around. Everything was made from scratch and all of it was delicious. The little man that had guarded the car had come in to assist the man in carrying out the food to the long car. The man came a few more times, and each time we would visit with the chauffeur who always stayed by the car. He was a kind little man and very attentive to the older gentleman. I had asked my mom on one occasion if this man was wealthy, and she had laughed and said he was extremely wealthy. But she was never fazed by it.

My mind was always clicking like a bomb, and I was old enough to know that my mother had no earthly idea this man may have feelings for her. One day, I said "Mom, he is so wealthy; he could have food flown in from anywhere, why do you think he comes here? Why do you think he sits and drinks coffee with you and does not want to leave?" "What do you mean, Gaye Elizabeth?" she asked, looking surprised. "Well, I think he likes you, Mom." "Oh! That is ridiculous," she said, jumping up from the table. I could tell when mom received a compliment, she would get fidgety and nervous. Nothing about her was pretentious, or fake. She was genuine to the bone. Mom felt that she was not pretty and would laugh uncomfortably if you told her she was. But she was intelligent, funny, and gifted in so many ways. I did not blame this man for thinking she was special, she was.

Dad was still in Saginaw for a little longer, but, in no way, would my mother have ever led someone on or done anything to lose my dad's trust. And this older man was a gentleman and I think just genuinely liked my mom as a friend, and her food of course. She could do so many things, he was fascinated by her talents.

We went with her a few times to drop off a pie or some type of baked goods to the nursing home the man owned, but the big black car never came to our house again.

The fall in upper Michigan is one of the most beautiful times of the year. The colors are vibrant, and the crisp air lends itself to big fires and cozy settings. By the time fall came around, we had been there almost a year. We were settled into a routine of school, and work and Dad had finally come home for good. We were walking to school both ways each day, up and down the big hill. It did not take long to get there or anywhere for that matter. Most every child walked to school. Just the way of life in a small town. I think we all still missed the big city. I missed the noise, traffic, and the stores that towered over the city of downtown Detroit. Here it was quiet. Too quiet. Little quaint and expensive shops replaced big chain stores, and the town was always full of tourists. Especially in fall when the leaves changed colors so beautifully. People crowded in from all over the country to this small town.

I would go up the creaky steps at night to my room. It was my space, I could think about home, and what and who we left behind. Not really thinking about the time in Saginaw, except for the wonderful people we had met there. We knew it would be temporary though, but Detroit, our real home. I missed everything about it. I did not care about riots or crime, I just prayed to somehow go back home. I would lie on my bed and sing songs Maude and I had sung together. They comforted me like a warm blanket. Singing always did. Since we had the cellar in the basement, I would take books down there and close the big door and read. I pretended it was my girls club, or my library. I did not really care about having friends around. I had my brother, and I did not care about anyone else. He was up in his teens by now, and often doing other things, but he still took time to spend with me.

I noticed a small cut on my arm one day. It was not deep, but, after a week, it was still there. My mother had looked at it and tried treating it, but it would not go away. I also developed a low-grade fever around the same time, so she took me to the doctor. He assured her that I had a viral infection, and it would be gone in a few days.

But after a few days, neither the cut nor the fever had left. I had become a little stiff when I got up in the morning and some days it took a little longer to get ready for school. My hands did not want to work, or I would have to stop and rest.

I noticed that the walk there and back was becoming a little taxing for me, and I would have to stop and take breaks to get up the hill in the afternoon. My brother and I would walk down together in the mornings but in the afternoon, we would catch up with each other. My school got out a little before his did.

One day, in class, I was having difficulty concentrating on an assignment. It had become something to deal with. I was feeling stiff that day and ached like I had the flu. When the teacher wrote something on the board, I just copied it down not even thinking about what I was doing. To be honest, I had not been paying much attention. I just wanted to get home and lay down and I dreading the long walk back up the hill. She called my name and asked me why I had cheated by looking at the board. I did not know what to say, I certainly had not meant to do that. I was above average in all my studies except math. So, I had no reason to cheat. Besides, she was doing this in front of the entire class, and I could not process it all, I felt so bad physically.

I explained that I had not cheated, and that I did not feel well. But she laughed at me in front of the class and said it was a shame that I would pretend to be sick to get out of trouble. I can still see her little elf like face that came to a point under her chin. She wore tiny eyeglasses that made her squint and skirts that looked like carpet pulled up high on her waist. Her hair was always one big clump of curls, and she would talk and laugh at the same time as if it were a nervous tic or something. She had humiliated me that day. But I was terrified at how I was feeling more than anything and dreading the long walk home. I was spent. Exhausted and in pain from head to toe.

My mother took me back to the doctor who now diagnosed me with growing pains. I could tell mom was agitated when she began quizzing the doctor. "How can she have a low-grade fever, a lesion that will not heal, and flu-like symptoms all the time?" She would ask in rapid fire. He offered medication and referred me to an orthopedic in Detroit for a second opinion.

Nothing was taking the low-grade fever away, and I was starting to miss more school because of it.

A few weeks later, Mom and I hopped on a Greyhound bus well before dawn and headed on the four-hour trip to Detroit. Of course, it took much longer on a bus. They stopped at every small town between Petoskey and Detroit. By now, it was getting colder on these mornings. I could not get warm no matter how much I layered my clothes. It was difficult for me to get my body moving. I would get up so stiff and it was painful to move around. Since we took the bus, we had no way of getting around downtown Detroit, unless we walked, took a city bus, or taxi. We would opt for a city bus, and finally got to our destination and the office of the orthopedic doctor. At that time, there were not any specialists for me in Petoskey, just general practitioners. So, you had to travel to get in-depth care. Supposedly, some of the greatest orthopedic doctors were in Detroit. Ironically, I wanted to go home, but not to see a doctor.

The doctor was unremarkable. He talked about growing pains and took me off the medication the other doctor in Petoskey had put me on. He advised my mother that this new medication he would prescribe was powerful and could cause side effects in a child, but, with my symptoms, we would need to try it.

All we wanted to know was what was going on, was there something they could pinpoint about my symptoms or diagnose me with something treatable. But no that seemed unreasonable. We would be back on the Greyhound bus headed home with medications that could or could not help me. Medications that could destroy my teeth and potentially cause harmful side effects. And that was it.

When the snow started that winter, it was fast and heavy. Accumulations were higher than anticipated that year, and you could almost watch it climb higher and higher outside. It was like fluffy frosting heaped in piles on the ground and weighing down branches of trees and bushes. Nothing was moving except snowplows. Even for a city that was accustomed to harsh weather, the weather people were dumbfounded at the amount of snow. It figured. We moved there and the snow showed up in all its greatness for us. Even the ski resorts close by, and down toward other cities were paralyzed from too much snow. We opened our back door only to find snow had drifted high up onto our door, with no way out unless you shoveled heaps of it away. And, it was level with our mailbox.

It was scary to see it come so quickly and mount so high. My brother would let our dog Nikki out and would watch for fear he would get caught in a drift. I was feeling rough this one day, but my brother and I decided to go out for a bit and see the snow. This kind of snow made the best snowmen. It would last for days in the cold. Even the Sun must have been pumped in because nothing warm could last in this place. We promised to only be out for a few minutes and bundled in layers for the trek. There was a beautiful park across the street from our house, and we had played there when we had first moved to the neighborhood.

This day, it was covered in the white stuff, and we were trying to measure the level to see how high it was at the deepest point. We could hear our boots crunching down on the snow and ice as we made a little trail through the snowy park. We walked and measured for a few minutes, and we were both beginning to freeze. Our boots and socks were no match for this cold. Suddenly, as I was walking behind my brother, I fell into a deep snowdrift. It was cold and became tight the more I thrashed around, and I could not move. Tangled in too many clothes and snow that would not budge, I began to scream for help! And for him to get me out.

Thank goodness he was close by and shoveled me out with his hands because I was panicked. I no longer cared about the snow after that day. I grew to hate it and everything about that place. My poor brother would try and help Dad shovel the snow and just when he got the walkway or driveway partially cleared the snowplows would come and push all the snow right back where they had shoveled. It was never-ending. Our driveway looked like a big kitty litter box. Dad used litter to try and keep the ice at bay.

I was beyond the beauty of it, and I could not believe we had come to this place where the temperature got so low so quickly, and you wore sweaters in spring at times. Life went on there no matter what on lesser snowy days. Schools were open, people worked and drove, and they went about their day like it was a godsend. The shops and ski resorts thrived because of this. Ice fishing and other winter events relied on this to survive. The economy was based on tourism and the snow brought people in. I remember being downtown with my mom after a doctor's visit and watching people drive out onto the icy lake. It was the strangest thing I had ever seen. They would park their cars on the ice, dig out a hole and place a tent over the top to keep the frigid air out and then fish.

There was no internet back then; you relied on telephone books or dialed the telephone for information and talked to a live operator. Somehow, my mother had researched and found another orthopedic doctor in Detroit and decided we would go to him. The days leading up to our trip my knees looked like large apples. They were hot to the touch, and I could not move my legs easily, or bend my knees. Swollen and stiff it was difficult for me to walk or step up into the bus. And the trip was terrible. I was achy and cold, and my legs throbbed the whole way there.

We had waited a long time for this doctor to come into the room and when he did, he threw open the door and startled us. He was tall and completely bald but young and very arrogant. He would talk to my mother and totally ignore me, and I was old enough to converse with him. He blew off my symptoms and, my mother gave it right back to him saying, "We won't be leaving with another growing pains diagnosis today. We need answers!" And she meant it.

He was neither gentle nor empathetic to me and twisted me like a pretzel, pulling my arms and jerking my hands and fingers. I was in so much pain that I began to tear up. When he examined my knees, he told my mother that he would need to remove inflammation from my left knee. It was worse than the right knee. That was obvious, it was bulging and hot to the touch. I was terrified of needles and began to cry.

There was no comfort or understanding from this man. He had no bedside manner whatsoever. As he went about setting up for the aspiration my mother comforted me. Not only was I scared of needles, but I was in horrible pain, and could not imagine him puncturing my tender knee with a needle that size. He flashed the biggest needle contraption around and told me to stop being a baby. I asked him if there was anything else he could do besides the aspiration.

"Did I want the injection or not?" Was his smart remark, and I just sat on the table while tears streamed down my face. He aspirated a large amount of green gold-colored goo from my knee and then injected cortisone into the spot. He told my mother that he was not sure what was wrong with me; I was too young for it to be anything major, and to keep me on the anti-inflammatory drug the last doctor had given me.

I sat there thinking how strange, to keep me on a drug for inflammation that was not working. Had he not seen what was aspirated from my knee? What was that? We were both let down after that visit. My mother was furious when we checked out. The woman had asked when my next appointment was, and my mother told her plainly that we would not be returning to this man and that he needed to learn a few things about treating people and manners. She left the woman sitting there with her mouth open.

The trip home was awful. Of course, it was cold, it was always so cold. And then, the pain had really kicked into my knee once the anesthetic had worn off. There was no place to stretch out my legs and I would twist and turn to try to get comfortable. Mom was sleeping after our long day. I knew she was overtired from working and taking me for doctor visits in the early hours of the morning. But at one point, I hit the button on the side of her seat and propelled her straight up, making her jump and come alive. She was like a windsock with her arms flailing. "Mom! What is going to happen to me? Am I going to die?" She cradled me to her like she did when I was small and said, "No dear, this is just a speed bump in life for you, and for us. God will take care of you; you do know that don't you? We've got to have faith and trust him even when things are at the worst, we think they could ever be."

I wanted so badly to believe her, and to trust God. I knew her faith was strong, and I wanted to be like her, but I could not. At times, I would be in so much pain that she would put the tea kettle on for us to have tea, which was a cure for everything. Hot tea soothed our souls. And she would hold me and pray that God would give me relief. My brother began taking me to school on a sled, down the slippery hill. He would drop me off and stand the sled at the entrance. No one bothered it, everyone used sleds or even snow machines to drop off kids. We lived in an igloo surrounded by ice, snow, and temperatures that were unbearable to healthy folks, let alone a sick kid like me.

I was sick and tired of being sick and tired. Forced to try and participate in gym class or play outside, where the teachers would say, "Go get some of this glorious cold fresh air in your system; it will help you think better this afternoon." I hated it, I hated that school and those teachers with their freezing air cure-all for everything. What I wanted more than anything in the world was to get out of that horrible cold! The cold made my bones ache to the point I could not stand it at times.

The medicine I took was strong. It hurt my stomach and had started making my white teeth a gold color. I would grab a blanket and a book and curl up in the window seat. Everything felt drafty and cold. Mostly, I tried to pray. I was struggling with what faith looked like. Mom had stayed the course. She was doing something right, but was I?

Whenever things went wrong, and they did all the time it seemed. She was never rattled or scared. She put her trust in the Lord. It was just that simple with her. But not for me. I was finding my way. Still young and questioning everything. My prayers and faith had not resulted in much success up till now. My brother gone, my oldest sister trying to find her way, my middle sister never around. We were five minutes from everywhere there, but it seemed like she was a million miles away. Mom and I stopped by one day with things Mom had bought for her little place. It was a nice visit until that lady, the property owner, showed up from downstairs and stood around like she was a guard protecting some valuable.

It made me mad to be interrupted by her, we did not get to see my sister that often. My mother was gracious, but my sister had become distant and completely changed when the woman showed up. "That woman has a real hold on your sister, and I can't understand it," Mom said as we drove home. After that, our visits were rare. My sister would come for a birthday celebration but not much else. I was not getting any better and the fever was continuous.

One day, the teacher in my homeroom showed up with my assignments. I was curled up on the couch and did not recognize her car until she got out. I could not believe she had come to my house. My mother answered the door and ushered her into the living room where I was. There was one thing that I understood, if someone came to visit, you were to be kind and welcoming no matter how you felt about them. So, wanting to bite my tongue, I said hello to her.

She immediately looked surprised at me as if taking in a site she had not been expecting. I knew I looked terrible. My eyes were sunken in from lack of sleep, I had lost weight and I was too weak to stand. She initiated a conversation with my mother after laying my assignments on the coffee table. She said she owed her an apology. Of course, my mother looked curious. I was too. She went on to say that she and I had an encounter at school on a day when I was attending full time, and she had accused me of cheating. That was not a word used in our home.

We did not cheat, lie, or steal. We did not even eat candy (Jolly Ranchers), that would cause us to lose our testimony. Well, my brother did not lie. I had lied a few times when I was younger, but I had felt terrible afterward and I always had a good talk with the Lord at night before bed. I would explain in detail why I had gone astray for those few moments. My mother seemed troubled and asked me if I had cheated in class. I told her no, I had not cheated. And the teacher in her usual animated way, said there had been a misunderstanding. She had also thought I was pretending to be sick to get out of school, until that day. I guess when she saw me, it proved I was not. Mom let her know that accusing a child or anyone of cheating was a serious accusation, but more importantly, to presume a child was pretending to be ill was downright disgusting. Oh snap! Mom had a way about her, she could cut you with words so sharply but still leave you with some dignity. She advised the teacher that her apologies should be directed to me. She had hurt an impressionable child that was enduring things beyond her years, and with no relief from this illness in site.

I remember this so well. I was lying there, and the teacher gave me this look of both embarrassment and regret. She was not expecting such a lashing from my mother, so I knew she was a little deflated. And to be honest, I was surprised that my mother had been so abrupt to her. There were two things I could do at this point when she finally apologized to me, I could accept her apology or decline. The little devil on my left shoulder wanted me to tell her what I thought about her humiliating me in front of class and laughing at me. The little angel on the other shoulder was quick to advise me that Jesus would want me to be kind and look beyond what had happened. It was hard for me. I never liked to be made fun of. But in the end, I accepted her apology. There was some satisfaction that came with vindication.

She came often after that and would bring little gifts from my class or books along with my assignments. I was home for the rest of the year because of the fever and the increasing difficulties of functioning outside of my bed or the couch. I mostly stayed downstairs now since it was difficult to climb the stairs to my room.

CHAPTER ELEVEN

My brother and Dad had really bonded over the years. They had always had a great relationship. But now it was the two of them since Dad was retired. They would tinker with the cars, or parts or do projects. They would stay out in the garage trying to get Mom's car started due to the weather. The battery never stayed charged even though it was new. It was funny, there would always be cars on the roadsides where the battery went out or something due to the cold. One-night late, Dad came in mad, stomping the snow off his boots. He said, "Why on earth did we move to this place? colder than…" well, I cannot say what he said. But suffice it to say he was not happy in the cold of upper Michigan.

It was apparent that there was nothing that could be done for me. Doctor visits included me telling them how I felt and them draining which ever part of my body that was full of inflammation. I would get refills for medicine that made me feel worse, and sometimes they would give me pain medication for a few days. The standard verbiage was, "This will take the edge off for a few days." But what about all the other days? I could not sleep, I could not stand a sheet to touch my body most of the time, let alone a blanket. And I cried alone. I was at home, could not play, and could not go to school because of the fever I kept. It was then that things got worse. When it was dark and quiet, it bothered me so much more. It was like the pain knew when to have a party and would dance all over my body.

I watched TV until it would go off at night. Around midnight, the TV signed off after the national anthem played. A test pattern showed up on the screen. And that was it. Television with its three channels was no longer my company for the night. I would just lie there mostly. Sometimes I sang to myself. I spent many long nights alone. Mom worked the midnight shift at the nursing home, so my dad and my brother would be asleep.

On occasion, I got scared in the living room. It was nothing but the thoughts in my head playing tricks on me. I would be on the couch and would see the wind sway the trees back and forth as if they were monsters raising their arms. Do monsters have arms? Well, they did in my mind. Shadows on the walls and creaking boards all participated in making my imagination worse. And the old furnace would rumble on at the worst possible times sounding like it was saying boo, as the air kicked on. I would get up and turn all the lights on and just lie there, miserable and pray for sleep.

When we moved to Petoskey, Dad got my mother a new Plymouth Fury, in a gold color. She would drive it around town but was never happy about it. She said driving made her nervous. One day, she, my brother and I were downtown. One of the worst things about living there besides the winters was the crowding when it was tourist season. However, we did not get many breaks from it as people traveled there all the time through the year for festivals, or events. But the town could get congested, making it difficult to maneuver around the narrow streets. People could park on both sides of the streets.

We could walk from our house easily to town in less than ten minutes, but in my condition, Mom had to drive me. One day, I was in the front seat and my brother was in the back. Mom was driving, and suddenly someone crowded her off the road and into parked cars. Three parked cars to be exact. She hit one and it started a domino effect down one side of the street. One hit the other and the other until we finally stopped. Four cars total were involved. All parked cars but ours. Mom was crying. We did not use seat belts then, so I hit the floorboard hard with my body and contorted my neck and shoulders. My brother was pulled towards the front of the car from his back seat and then jerked back.

People gathered when they heard the commotion and reassured Mom that it was OK and that their cars could be repaired. They were kind and wanted to get us all to the hospital. My mother was pitiful and so apologetic; I know they felt sorry for us. But Dad was not happy when he saw her car. I do not think he believed that she was crowded off the road. He thought she panicked in the close traffic. I was in excruciating pain for days afterward from trying to brace myself. My neck and my arms throbbed horribly, and my body was stiff. Thank goodness she and my brother were fine, just sore from the impact. She wanted us to go to the hospital to be evaluated but we said we were fine. Neither of us wanted our mother to feel any worse.

When I caught a cold, or something happened like this accident, it took a lot out of me, I was having difficulty getting around. It took so much time in the morning to get my arms to move, and then I would try moving my legs. My neck would be stiff, and my knees always felt tight and feverish. One of the doctors had told me to try and do range of motion slowly when I got up. I would try and move my fingers which felt like stiff sausages first. They would itch from being swollen. It was a lengthy process to just get moving each day trying to get all my extremities moving. And Lord help me, I could tell when it was going to rain.

I was having a rougher week than normal, and my pain was off the charts. I had read and watched TV all I could. I was so tired of it by now. So, I had an idea, I thought we could make cookies. I always enjoyed that when I was small, getting in the kitchen with my mom, baking and singing. It had been a long time since we had done that. The rain had visited for a few days and was well past its welcome. So, I thought baking may take my mind off it and the pain.

Mom helped get everything out of the cabinets that I would need, and we began. It felt good doing something different for a change. But shortly after we started, I had to lie down. In that brief time, it had taken a toll on me just putting ingredients into a bowl. I was so depressed that day. I got pep talks, but we all knew something was horribly wrong. But not one person on this earth seemed to have any answers. I am sure there were other sick kids out there, but at the time I did not think much about it. There were no advertisements for children's hospitals on TV. No fundraisers that I recall except the Jerry Lewis telethon and that was related to muscular dystrophy. So, I did not know if there were more like me out there in the world. None of my doctors gave us any feedback about other kids with similar conditions. Knowing would have helped me not to feel so alone.

The medications were not working. And the last orthopedic in Detroit referred me to a child psychiatrist. My mother was stunned, and I cannot say what my dad thought about it; he was so angry. But sure enough, we were back to Detroit to see a child psychiatrist. The wise minds thought I had mental problems. No matter my symptoms, my fever, or how my body looked, I had a mental problem. I was ushered into this exceptionally large room with long windows across one whole side of the room leading outside to a wooded area. On another long wall were different toys and games on shelves, and along two walls were books, floor to ceiling. I loved the thought of all those books. I could have gotten lost for hours, just reading. My parents were asked to sit in the waiting room, which adjoined the room where I was. It was a combination of play area on one side, and then multiple seats with tables.

I sat down in a big chair alone in the room for a brief time, before the doctor walked into the room. He was thin and not much taller than my dad. He wore dark glasses and had gel in his hair that made it look shiny. I was not sure how old he was, but I thought younger than my parents. He introduced himself and placed a long notebook on the table. Then he asked me to go and select an item that I found interesting from the long toy and game wall. After I found my item of choice, I sat back down across from him at the table. He asked if I would show him how it worked. And so, I completed it quickly.

"Now Gaye," he started, "What made you select this item?" I thought for a minute and said, "Well it had pretty colors and looked interesting." "That is great! And what else do you like to do?" "I like to read." "And why is that?" or something to that effect. "It makes me forget my pain, when I read." "OK, what else do you like to do?" "Well, I like to sing." I replied.

"Wonderful! What do you sing?" "Hymns. I sing hymns." "Interesting," He shook his head at me. "And why is that?" And he leaned in like I was going to tell him a secret. "They make me comfortable, and I forget." I will always remember how his expression was changing as we talked. He was writing at this point. "So, Gaye what do you try and forget?" "Well, I forget about dying." He leaned in further with his arms on the table looking intently at me. He was surprised at my comment. After a minute of studying me, he asked if I was afraid to die. "Yes, I am," was my reply.

He asked me about my doctors and if they had told me that or what they had told me about my condition, and I said, "Nothing, they haven't told me anything." He asked if I liked school and I remember telling him that I liked some of it. We talked about my best subjects and my worst. Of course, I told him math was my worst. At times, he would write things down on the large pad. And he showed me pictures of things that looked like spilled ink. He seemed very curious about what I said I saw in those spatters. My imagination was wild, so I am sure I saw things he had never heard before.

After time that seemed like forever, he told me we were finished for the afternoon and that I could go out and sit in the lobby, and my parents would be joining him. I would be returning the next day as well. When I went to the waiting room, my parents went with him. I stayed behind near the lady behind the long desk. She would smile at me periodically, as if reassuring me that it would not take that much longer, he was just telling my parents how mental I was.

The next day, we did similar things and just talked about how I was feeling.

When we were in the car that day heading home, Mom told me that he had told them I was a very thoughtful girl, advanced beyond my years and that there was not one thing psychologically wrong with me. I was desperately trying to adjust to constant physical pain. I was suffering from a physical problem and that someone somewhere would need to get to the root of the problem sooner than later. He advised my parents that the medications I was on were well beyond what a child could manage and that they would need to be adjusted. He promised to send reports to all the doctors listed on my records and my parents would receive a copy in the mail.

We were all a little relieved. I did not think my parents thought I was faking or had mental issues, but it was nice to hear it from a professional. It was like vindication in a way. I would have loved to have been on hand when those "specialists" received the report about me.

We had made trips to Tennessee while living in Detroit. We would go for a week in the summer, or to attend a family member's funeral. Dad was homesick for his family, and there was not a lot he was interested in, in Petoskey. Yes, some of the weather was good, but for the most part unless you were a tourist or liked sporting activities, you were out of luck with things to do. Dad was not an outdoorsman to say the least. He became more agitated the longer we lived there. My care was at a standstill, and there were no great colleges around the area that my brother wanted to attend. He had wanted to attend Lee College (now Lee University), to get his ministry credentials. Dad had talked with his family in Tennessee, and he wanted to be closer to them now that he was retired. Mom, as a nurse, could work anywhere really, so the plan was made to move to Tennessee. Chattanooga more specific.

Having only been in Chattanooga for a week at a time, we were never really bothered much by the heat. However, now coming to live, it was a dramatic change. I remember telling my mother that we came from the Arctic to an inferno.

It was that different than the north. But Dad was happy to be closer to his family and content. Mom began working at a hospital in Georgia. My brother was excited to be thinking about college, and I was miserable.

We rented a small house by Lake Winnepesaukah, a local and well-treasured amusement park. Not knowing where we wanted to settle in the area, this was a steppingstone. I was enrolled in middle school. It was a struggle every day. Getting ready in the early mornings to catch the school bus was difficult. But the culture change was much worse. My middle sister had decided to stay in Petoskey and that was painful for all of us. We wanted her to come with us and start fresh, but she refused. My oldest sister had her life together now and had come ahead to stay with my aunt until we arrived. She began attending a Church of God of Prophecy church close to my aunt's house and had told us all about it before we arrived. It was the happiest I had seen her in an awfully long time.

The school I attended was run down and had little portable buildings with heaters and fans depending on the weather. Everyone talked like they had all the time in the world. I could not get accustomed to the language difference, and they certainly could not get accustomed to the way I talked. Several had a southern drawl that added additional syllables to their words, and I was a fast-talking northerner. My classes were behind what I had already studied in the north. And my body was not adjusting to the humidity and dampness. Physically, I was worse. I could not keep up no matter how hard I tried. Petoskey had been a beautiful place to leave, because of the severe cold, but this place held a host of vastly different problems, and I had no doctors.

Poor Mom would try to dress in her nursing uniform and would hover over the small window air conditioner to get ready for work. It was that miserable. It was that hot. My hair was frizzy from the humidity and my body ached from head to toe. And it rained constantly for days at a time. We were all trying to adjust for Dad, but it was so extremely difficult for all of us. I was bullied at school for my clothes and because I was new. Mostly because I was from the north. Not only being new but having a northern accent did not help the situation. People would ask me to talk just so they could laugh at me and after a few weeks of this I was no longer willing to put up with their remarks or their rudeness.

Because I could not participate in physical education I would study during that time. Mom was trying to find a doctor for me, but it took time and she had to threaten the school into accepting a note from her about my condition, so I could skip gym. One day, this girl came up to me. I had seen her before, she would be with a group of girls, and they would stand off from where I was and would laugh or pretend, they were talking about me. And maybe they were, who knew. I realized that to get this to stop, I would need to confront her, the ringleader, since she set the tone for the group. But I would not make the first move.

I was sitting on a short rock wall one day and she came over and pushed my book bag on the ground and commented on my New York uppity clothes, and my fancy talking. She would look over at her friends for support. I adjusted my bag and looked at her standing there with her cropped shirt, tight jeans and flip flops, the style I had guessed but I was not impressed. She looked cheap and well beyond her years just by the clothes she had on. My parents would have never stood for me wearing anything like that. She mumbled something else to me, and not backing down, I replied, "Oh! Did Kmart have a sale? Or is that from the thrift store?" I asked, pointing to her clothes. I never took my eyes off her or her friends, but I was determined to make this all stop one way or another. I was not strong enough to fight anyone and never wanted that to begin with, and this was all I had, lame talk. I had to survive here, but I had no fight in me. I would need to show my strength, or what little I had.

My heart was pounding. I could tell I hurt her feelings, and I wanted to say I am so sorry I did not mean to say that, but I could not back down. And from then on, they left me alone. I felt like a mean girl and no different than they were. I was not physically able to protect myself, but words can hurt so much more. And I certainly was not proud of myself. We had come from the cold and dryness to heat, rain, and humidity. All extreme in their own way, but, to someone sick, it was even worse. The rain would last for a few days, and the humidity would set in. My bones and joints would be penetrated from the dampness, and I would ache until I could not stand it any longer. Nothing I would take at the time would relieve it; nothing would give me a minute's peace from it. I would come home from school and crawl into my bed and cry out to God for help. "Have you forgotten me, Lord? Did you not move here with us? I can't manage this pain." I went without sleep because I could not even turn over in bed without excruciating pain. That, along with no appetite, and a healthy person's schedule, I was trying to keep up with school and church. I was beyond miserable.

Mom had come home from work one day and said she had talked with a fellow nurse about a doctor in the area that she had recommended for me. I was relieved, but also skeptical. How could there be a doctor in this place that could measure up to the ones I had in Detroit? Even though they were not willing to invest time in my case to really figure out my problems, they were some of the best. But we had nothing to lose.

I wanted to just give up. It had been a long struggle. I was growing into a young woman; I experienced all the normal girlie things earlier than most my age. So, compounded by this illness it held me down like a heavy weight. I was a bundle of emotions, frustration, and hormones. We arrived at the doctor's office one afternoon. It sat behind the duck pond in Rossville Georgia, I will never forget it. When we went inside, it was smaller than it looked from outside. An old waiting room, filled with big heavy chairs, outdated magazines and fake greenery left for no great first impression. There was a small window that an older lady sat behind and directly behind her were tall cabinets with what looked like paper folders. They were people's charts I assumed. Very outdated and mundane compared to the shiny modern offices to which I was accustomed. But then again, those doctors had not helped me in the slightest. The sweet lady had a welcoming smile when she greeted us.

When she called us back, Mom and I went into a large examination room, and she asked that I sit on the exam table. She did not ask me many questions, which I thought strange since before I was asked everything imaginable by the nurses in the other doctor's offices. Dr. Stanley G. Legner, a general practitioner, was a tall man with salt and pepper hair and a beautiful smile. He wore the usual white coat with his name emblazed on it, and when he entered the room, he had such a presence about him. He was so distinguished. I liked him immediately. It was as if I could trust him, and I did not even know this man. He made me feel like I had hope for the first time. I could always read people and usually I was correct in my thoughts about them. He went over my information and examined me and then he took the stool he had been sitting on and moved it right up beside the examination table where I was. I will never forget what he said. "Young lady, I don't know what is wrong with you, but I will not stop until we know. And that is a promise." And we shook on it.

He went over a plan of action that would change my life. He began by removing me from school entirely and placing me in a program for sick children who were home bound. Teachers who were trained to work with sick kids would come to your home and teach you instead of putting you in the general population where you were susceptible to everything imaginable. My resistance was so low at the time. I was a candidate for every cold or flu. The second thing he did was wean me off those powerful medications. And he began to research my symptoms.

There were times he would call and say, "Bring Gaye in, I need to draw blood," or "Come in; I need an x ray." He would not share anything or updates but would assure us he was on the case. I had never been happier to know that he was so interested in helping me. My parents were relieved as well. By then, I just wanted to know what was wrong with me regardless of what it was. One glorious day, he called and said, "Come in immediately!!" We hurried to his office, and he had that larger-than-life smile on his face. "Gaye, you have rheumatoid arthritis," he announced. I remember saying, "Isn't that what old people get?" "Not anymore," he would explain. "There have not been many cases, it's the juvenile kind that children get. And you have it!"

Of course, you would never be happy to know you have a diagnosis of anything, you want to be well. But knowing that we could put a diagnosis to everything I had experienced now four or, so years was more than a relief.

He explained that he had been in touch with doctors around the country, some who had patients with this very thing, and he had read about it in his research. I could not believe it when he told us that blood work was the key to finding it. There were a series of special blood studies, and a process the blood went through, that would give either a negative or positive reading. Once tests were completed, they would have to be repeated and studied all over again for the same results. He had taken a substantial amount of blood from me over time, and he advised that it was all part of making the diagnosis accurate. There was much more to it than that, but the jest of it was that a few blood tests could have diagnosed my problem much earlier had the doctors cared enough to do some research.

It was music to my ears. I was placed on medications that would not only reduce the inflammation in my body but would also help control the pain and they were in doses that were suitable for a child. Now, we knew. Dr. Legner, was my hero, he was an angel from God and our prayers were answered. I could finally begin to tolerate the disease. I would learn to thrive and, better yet, I was not dying from it. The edginess left my mother as well, she was so relieved to finally get answers.

I began therapy at Siskin Rehabilitation almost immediately. Back then, it was a much smaller organization. I would go a few times a week for hydrotherapy and physical therapy. Therapists would place me on a large hammock, and it would slowly ease me into a huge vat of warm water. The water would swirl and flow around my body and help loosen all the tightness and pain. I also had therapy for my throbbing hands. A concoction of oils and paraffin wax was stored in a large metal container that remained warm. A little warmer than you could manage but I adjusted to it quickly. It would coat my hands as I dipped them into the liquid wax. Just holding it on my hands would generate warmth down to my joints and it felt amazing. I would peel it off and then re-dip my hands several times until they were pink and soft from the paraffin but warm and not so achy.

We started keeping a pot of the wax on the back of the stove and would melt it down on days my hands were throbbing. I was starting to be able to deal much better with my condition. The fact that someone other than my parents was in my corner fighting for me gave me such relief. My grades climbed back up, except for math. That would always be a thorn in my side.

CHAPTER TWELVE

We started visiting the church my sister had been attending. It was odd. People were nice and welcoming, but again the culture was different. The first Sunday we were there, they were having a building fund dinner after church and the entire place smelled heavenly. We were invited as honored guests since everyone loved my sister. The ladies had lined up the food on the large counter in the church kitchen and you served yourself. My brother was in front of me, and we had never seen some of the food choices. The ladies fell in love with my brother's accent and personality. They would say in that good ole southern drawl, "We are going to fatten you up," and he would laugh. But not knowing what he was eating, he passed on a couple of things and the ladies pointed out all the different greens. "Try um," they said proudly, and my brother, looking closer, quizzed, "Are they grass clippings?" The ladies laughed at my brother's joke, but I knew he was serious. They took the time to explain collard greens and mustard greens and whatever else green they had, and we sampled some of everything. The food and the fellowship were wonderful.

They would say, just talk to us. We sounded so different from them. Some had more of a southern accent than others and it was fun to hear everyone. And they would laugh when we started to talk and tell us to slow down. It was a new day and a new place, but we felt at home.

I was trying to stay limber. My joints were so stiff that my legs and arms throbbed when I tried to move. I still took therapy at Siskin, but I decided to take karate which sounds strange I know. I wanted to do it for the stretching exercises.

Of course, I was not able to do the more difficult aspects like spar with a partner, but I needed stretching and Dr. Legner thought it would be an excellent way to stay limber. Mom took my brother and me to sign up. He came for quite a while but went on to do other things with college and then left home. But I tried to go when I felt I could. I usually had school classes around 10:00 a.m. in the morning until noon and then I tried to go in the early afternoon before classes filled up.

A Korean master owned the karate school. A midsized tornado that was not to be messed with. He was dangerous and taught the classes like a drill sergeant. He understood why I had come there, and never forced me to do anything I could not do. I moved through the belts until I was a blue belt, and that was from knowing the forms, and not from sparing. That would come later in the next belt, but not for me. I was only there for stretching and light minimal impact exercise. One day, I was off school for teacher in-service, and decided to go to the karate school around 10:30 a.m. that day.

Mom dropped me off, I was fourteen at the time, so safer there than anywhere based on the owner's ability to fight to protect me, I thought. Mom had not been worried to leave me. I had thought more people would be there since school was canceled that day. The master saw me come in and I just went to the girls dressing room to change. In a couple minutes, I heard the door to the dressing rooms open and shut. He wore soft soled shoes, little black slippers, so you could not hear him walk up on you. But I had heard the door. I thought one of the girls had arrived for the class early as I had.

I saw the door handle to my room turn and I was scared that we were alone in that building. Women would usually just barge right into the area talking and laughing.

He came in and just stared at me. I told him that I was dressing and started to tie up my uniform. He came towards me, and I thought to myself, *what is he doing in here?*

He never said a word, just eased his arms around me and started touching my hair. I was trapped, and I did not have a clue what to do. I was stunned that he was in there and even more scared that he and I were alone. I knew he was extremely strong and forceful, and I was no match for his strength in my condition. And even a well, strong person could be overpowered by him easily. Not only was I a kid, but, I was a sick kid, and did not have the strength to defend myself from anyone. I tried to talk to him to diffuse the situation and I continued to try to remain calm, but he began to nuzzle my ear and rub my neck. I was pinned against the wall by now, and I was terrified. I continued to talk to him to try and convince him that this was not right, I needed to get to work. Trying to play it off well my body shook from fear.

I remember laughing, like I do when I get nervous while trying to combat his arms and hands from my body, like I was swatting flies. It was difficult. He was used to making quick moves, and man handling people in class. And, there was a lengthy line of experts in his family. He had been so kind to me, I could not understand why he had changed so drastically. I would see his family from time to time in the studio and think to myself what a beautiful family they were.

I began to pray for God's protection in my mind, and, suddenly, I got boldness from somewhere. I know it was the Lord; it had to have been. I yelled out, "Stop it now! I mean it!" At first, he smiled, but then he realized I was not kidding, and that smile turned to an evil look which made him more determined. And I could tell he was getting angry.

He pressed in a little harder against me and now had my hands behind me against that wall. I had no idea what would happen at that point. But I remember saying, *"God, please protect me"* in my mind as my heart was pounding into overdrive. *"Cover me with your blood and stop this, Lord, I am at his mercy."* I had an assertiveness that came over me again and I was not about to back down. Whatever was going to happen, it would not be without the best fight in me. I told him to "Get out!" as loud as I could, and I began to fight back. He stopped like he had heard something on the other side of the door, and turned around, he looked back once at me and then left the little dressing room. I fell into the chair that was there. My legs were like jelly and my heart was racing. All I could think of was that I needed to get out of there in case he returned.

I fumbled with my clothes trying to hurry and hoping he did not come back. I was shaking all over and nauseated at the same time. I had been in so much pain that morning, I had not even wanted to come, but I thought it would help me. I was so wrong that day. I got my things and left the room looking in all directions. I did not see him when I came out, but my mission was to get to the front door. I ran with every joint throbbing, as I pushed ahead as quickly as I could. The entire front of the building was glass with one glass door to enter and exit. It was a miracle that I was running. I could not walk at times, let alone run. There was a small restaurant across the parking lot in the little strip mall, and I ran there as fast as my body would take me and took a seat to get my breath. I had been in there before for snacks, so they knew my face.

I asked if I could use their phone and I called Mom to come and get me. In the meantime, I huddled in a booth waiting and watching to see if he came after me. I was that scared.

But by then, a couple other people were coming into the school so I knew he would never try anything with other school attendees present. I did not have to tell my mom; she could tell by my face that something had happened. I begged her not to tell Dad or anyone else. Mom wanted to call the police, but I begged her not to. I had no idea what triggered him. But I felt so bad afterward. I felt guilty, like I may have done something to warrant this advance. As usual, I internalized the situation. I struggled for a long time afterward with feelings of violation. I just could not trust anyone it seemed. I never went back.

One Sunday, several weeks after this occurred, a friend from church asked me to go home with her and come back for the Sunday night service. I went with her, and her brother went home with my brother after church. She drove a sporty car, which meant nothing to me, and I remember that she had reddish hair and was five to seven years older than I was. She was not the prettiest girl, but the youth group liked her because she was funny and sweet. We had not been at her parents' home for more than a few minutes when she asked me if I wanted to go to a local place and get a coke. I said sure, although I thought it was a little strange, we always kept cokes and things at home, and I thought it was a long way to go back into town for just that, but we did anyway.

When we got to the restaurant, she began circling the place where you called in your order, you could drive up and order from a little machine on a stand and eat in your car, or if you liked, you could go in and sit down in the restaurant. I noticed a lot of guys in cars beeping horns and calling out to other cars where girls were laughing and talking to them. For some reason, this did not appeal to me in the least. But my friend seemed to be enjoying herself. She enjoyed how they admired her car, and the attention we were getting.

I had thought we were there for a coke and finally, she stopped in one of the places and we ordered our drinks. I had not planned to go anywhere that day, so I only had enough money for a coke with me. Some older guys pulled in beside her on the driver's side and she began to talk to them. They would lean out and try and get me to talk. A lot of girls would have loved that attention, but not me. I had never done anything like this before. And I was uncomfortable.

She had said something to them and then we pulled out, and I was thinking, *good, phew, we are leaving*. But she only pulled over to an isolated space near the restaurant. The guys she had been talking with zoomed in beside us and jumped into her car. They started making small talk and then turned their attention to me and were saying suggestive things. I looked at my friend and said, "We need to leave now!" She laughed and explained to them how old I was, hoping they would ease off. But that did not happen; it only got worse. I tried not to look at them in the back seat but soon one of them began to try and put his hands on me around the seat. I panicked and said I needed to use the restroom, and I jumped out of the car and ran to the restaurant.

Once inside, I went into the restroom to try and get my composure. I was shaking at the words coming out of their filthy mouths, and I was shocked at my friend's behavior. I had just been in that terrible situation at the karate studio weeks before this. There was a young pregnant mother with her small child in the restroom and she asked me if I was OK. I know I must have looked terrified. I told her what had happened, and she had warned me not to go back outside, just to stay in the restaurant. I had no money to call my mother and I did not know what to do. I stood in the restaurant watching the two cars side by side and I had no idea what was going on with my friend. I was scared for her, but I was not going outside regardless of what happened. I watched from the interior window of the entry doors of the restaurant for a good thirty minutes. And, then I saw what looked like my mom's car driving into the parking lot, with a police car right behind her. I finally got a good look as she was scanning the parking lot for me.

I ran outside and flagged them down. I was never so happy to see my mom than that moment. She had my brother and my friend's brother with her. My brother was driving and parked near my friend's car, and the police got out quickly and went over to remove the two guys from the car. I had no idea how Mom had known I was there. I had not asked anyone to call because I was embarrassed to ask. So, there was absolutely no way she would have known. Mom walked over to my friend's car and told her how disappointed she was in her for subjecting us to the dangers of dealing with strange men. And, I was thinking, *Mom, you do not know the half of it*. The police had taken the guys off somewhere, I am guessing to have them explain the threats to a noticeably young girl. But I never knew the outcome to that.

On our way home, I said, "Mom, how in the world did you know where I was? And, who called the police?" She looked over at me as calmly as she could be and said, "I was making lunch and God told me Gaye was in trouble! He showed me where you were and told me to bring the police." My brother and my friend's brother confirmed what had happened and I was overwhelmed. I always knew she had a direct line to the Lord, and I knew he showed her things, but this was amazing to me. I was even more cautious than before on who I became friends with, and who I went anywhere with after that. God had spared me from an extremely dangerous situation that day and I was beyond grateful to him and to my mom's faith and trust in him to follow his lead.

I became more active in singing. I sang in services when I was feeling up to it, and they had a great band to accompany me. The music was full and uplifting. I enjoyed the worship service. I was comfortable with a little more formality, but I was adjusting. At first, when people just walked up to the choir to sing, I thought it was strange. But after time, I realized that they were not playing what I call puppet church. Meaning, two songs, a couple of claps, a quick sermon and then dismissal. And God forbid if that changed, or the Holy Spirit wanted to move in the service. There was no time, and the lights went out at noon. No, it was not like that, we worshipped in the services without watching the clock.

Once when I was older, I was already on the platform to sing. It was the beginning of the service and people just started coming up to the choir. It was so relaxed at that church, and I was not used to that. The song began and the worst and loudest voice I had ever heard stood right beside me. I did not know her. I must have had a funny expression on my face. I was not judging her; I had just never heard that noise come out of another human being before.

My mom said later, there was laughter around her pew, apparently, people had seen my reaction. My face always gave me away. But God did not say only the best voices need apply; He said, "Make a joyful noise unto the Lord." He knew there would be singers like that, and it was wonderful no matter how it sounded to me or anyone else. It is all about just praising the Lord and using your best gift.

I genuinely enjoyed attending there for a time. I was never comfortable when someone would grab the church flag and begin to parade it through the service though. I felt at times too much emphasis was placed on that flag. I know it was displayed in the churches but for some reason it made me uncomfortable. There were other things that troubled me about the Church of God of Prophecy. One thing was how judgmental some of the people were. When we began to attend regularly, we could not find an Assemblies of God. My sister liked attending there and we wanted to all be together.

They pushed us to become members. It was as if you were not a member then you were not part of the church. People often reminded us that you had to be a member of that church because it was God's only church. I became really troubled because my mother was not allowed to become a member, and the emphasis was more on membership than a relationship with God.

When they found out that Mom had been divorced through no fault of her own, and remarried, she was shunned by many. Oh, she attended, she paid her tithes, but they would always make the distinction that she was a friend and not a member of the church. No one wanted to admit it, but they looked down on divorced people. It did not matter the reason for the divorce or whether the person had been abandoned. It was sin to them, and they acted superior and judgmental. And I could not handle that.

There were occasions I spoke my mind to ones talking about my mother not being able to become a member because of her past. It did not matter if they wrapped that church flag around themselves until the cows came home, their judgmental attitudes were questionable and sinful. And, if Heaven was going to be this church alone, with this behavior, I did not want to go. I have been in services where the preacher preached on being divorced and remarried and I wanted to jump up and shout, "Your judgment towards others is no less a sin."

It was strange that they preached often on divorce and what they called costly array, meaning the wearing of jewelry. But I do not remember many messages about love or forgiveness. So many other things were displeasing to the Lord. I certainly did not want to become a member, but Mom insisted that my siblings and I join so that we would feel a part of the church more. That was a real stumbling block for me. Their words cut deep, and they were painful. My mother was the godliest person I knew. She was faithful to the Lord. Whenever they needed help for the building fund, they were quick to call her. When someone needed a wedding or a party, they contacted her. She was kind and helped every time free of charge, and it infuriated me. There was great jealousy over the singing at times. Once, I sang a song and a group got up right after me and sang the exact same song!

I prayed about it often, asking God for wisdom and to calm my temper. I attended because I had too. In my deepest thoughts, I felt they teetered on being a cult, to be honest. My opinion. When you preach that you are the only ones going to Heaven, and you critique who can and cannot be part of the body of Christ it's dangerous. When more emphasis is placed on a flag and a man than God, it borders on cultish behavior. We had heard the story of A.J. Tomlinson so many times. And that was wonderful, but he was just a man; he was not God.

My brother was going to Lee College and working. I hardly saw him with his busy schedule. I was having school at home and going to therapy at Siskin and church and that was the extent of my activities.

Dad had heard about a place in Ft. Oglethorpe, Georgia that had the best ice cream around, and, one day, he, mom and I went to check it out. Next door on the little strip mall was a large music store. I left my parents and went in to check out Dan Williams Pianos. It was filled with beautiful pianos and sheet music stacked neatly in shelving to the ceilings. Back then, you purchased sheet music in the key you wanted to sing in, or if you were fortunate, the pianist accompanying you could transpose a song to the appropriate key for you. I loved the covers on sheet music, and it had the lyrics, so it was a great tool for a singer. I ran my fingers over the pianos and thought how beautiful they were. There were large grand pianos in a deep black color and small pianos in rich wood tones. I was in love with this place.

The owner, Dan Williams, came over to talk with me that day. I had selected some sheet music and had placed it on the counter to pay for, but I was roaming around when he introduced himself to me. He was a tall man with a large bald spot. His thick hair grew around it so that it looked as if the bald spot was on a pedestal. He was a little chubby and wore dark glasses with dress pants and white shirt. He had an inviting smile and I liked him immediately. He was one of those people that smiled with their eyes. He had asked me my name, and if I was interested in a piano.

"Oh no, I am just enjoying looking at them, they are beautiful." I left that day but was back in the store in a few weeks and he had remembered me. We talked about music this time, and he even remembered how I had admired his pianos. This time, he told me to pick out my favorite piano, which I did. I had fallen in love with one previously while looking around the store. He told me I had made a brilliant selection. This was an upright piano made by the Grand Company, it had ivory keys, and nickel-plated strings in a beautiful wood tone. When he began to play it, I was off on a journey. Before long, I began to sing the song and we had a wonderful time. The piano stood proud sharing it's melodious sound and he assured me that only the best materials had been used on this instrument.

Mr. Williams told me that day that my voice was a great gift, and he assured me that I would be playing the piano one day. The piano had a price of a little more than five hundred dollars and the piano bench was a separate cost. I knew that was out of our budget. I would never even ask for something that I could not use, let alone an expensive piano. But each time I would go in for sheet music, I would pray that piano was still there and had not been purchased. Mom had seen how much I loved it and, one day, she asked Mr. Williams if he had a layaway plan where she could pay a little at a time, but the piano would not be sold to someone else. And, once we paid for it, it would be mine. I was shocked. My mother was one that encouraged us kids to go for it, reach for our dreams and she knew music was one of my dreams. They had talked while I browsed around the store, and then we left.

I had come in many days to walk around, purchase sheet music and look at the pianos. He knew I was sick and that I was taught from home. I had never said anything until one day he asked why I was out of school. It was a great comfort for me to be in that store.

It was getting close to the holidays. Mr. Williams and I had struck up a great friendship. He called my mother one afternoon and said he would like to bring the piano to me as a surprise; I heard Mom on the phone talking with him. She refused and told him she appreciated it, but the agreement was that I would get it once it was paid in full. I understood completely where she was coming from. It was a huge investment for my folks and waiting would not be a problem for me. Especially, knowing that I would eventually get this magnificent instrument.

It was late afternoon on Christmas Eve, and I was not feeling good that day, so I was resting. Late afternoons and evenings were difficult for me for some reason. I had a lot of pain that day and nothing would ease it. There was a knock on our front door and my brother looked out the curtains and said that a truck was in the driveway. Mom came from the kitchen, and I was curious as well. My brother opened the door and there stood two men with a clip board and an invoice to sign. My mother told them there had to be a mistake, we had not ordered anything, and they said that Mr. Williams had sent something for Gaye. I yelled, "That's me!" They told my mom that they would need to put this item on an inside wall because it could be damp against an outside wall, and, again, we were wondering what was happening. Then they brought in the piano bench, and my mouth dropped.

Mom told the guys that there was a mistake, and that the piano was not paid in full, but they smiled at her and kept working. After a few minutes, they were inside with my beautiful piano. It was now against the inner wall of our living room looking like a celebrity and I was in love. My mom cried. The man said, "Well, he wanted your daughter to have the best Christmas and he thought this would do it!" They wished us all a Merry Christmas and were gone, leaving this wonderful gift. I could not play anything, but just sat looking at it in all it's glory. I could not wait to see him and thank him personally. It truly was one of my best Christmases ever.

A few weeks later, I was playing the piano. I would pick out songs and play by ear. I began to sing and play, and then I began to write music lyrics with a melody I could remember. Later, some of these songs were put to music by a dear friend, published and copyrighted. This piano has always been such a blessing. I have cried playing it and I have laughed playing it. I have prayed playing it. All these years later, it still sits in a place of honor in our home. I would not take anything for it.

CHAPTER THIRTEEN

I wanted to work with the candy stripers at a local hospital. Dr. Legner thought I needed an outlet since I no longer took karate. And walking would be good exercise for me when I was able to tolerate going. So, I began to work in their physical therapy department. I thought that was what I wanted to do, until I had to bring my first burn victim to therapy. The stench of burned flesh made me so sick, I knew I did not have the stomach for anything in the medical field. One day, a man with some notoriety came in for therapy. He and others in his community had been on the local news several days for being part of a snake-handling church. I remembered his name, and while he took therapy, I could not help but ask him some questions. He was a kind man, small in stature with dark curly hair. There was an exceptionally long scar on one of his arms they were treating from a recent snake bite.

We began to talk, and I asked him how he had gotten the scar. He said something like, "Well, we were on the news because people are not too keen on the way we worship." I knew, I had seen the news, but I wanted him to tell me more about it. I was fascinated with him. He said, "On that day, I guess I did not have as much faith as I should have had, and I got bit right along there." And he pointed out his long fresh scar. I knew from the therapist that they had to cut away and drain his arm from the snake venom. I asked if he would do it again, and he said yes without hesitation. We talked about other things, but faith was really the focus of our discussion.

"One thing for sure, I would want you to pray for me if I needed it. You sure have strong faith," I laughed. He had thought that was funny. I told him I was terrified of snakes, so I would not be visiting his church any time soon. There were many days I had to miss going to the hospital because I was not able to walk, or the weather made me feel worse than normal. But when I could, I would go and loved meeting and talking with people. I had a heart for those that were sick, I knew so well how they felt. The staff knew I was sick, but they treated me like anyone else, and I met some wonderful people. I went on to become president of the club with over seventy-five girls. I achieved honors, and I was awarded the highest award given. The Florence Nightingale award was for outstanding service. That doesn't sound like a great deal, but, to a sick kid that could scarcely move at times, it was a tremendous accomplishment.

Several articles were written about me for the local papers. Since I was sick and still gave of my time, apparently it warranted a lot of attention. One article had placed in bold print, "Even in great pain, she gives of herself," I was mortified that people would read that. I was not comfortable in the least, but the hospital thought it gave worthy attention to the strides they had taken to acquire great volunteers. The volunteers were vital to hospital operations. One Sunday, the pastor and I were talking about the man who handled snakes. He had come to visit one afternoon when I was too sick to attend morning service. He had not been at our church exceptionally long, but I loved he and his wife. They were godly people and he and I would laugh at everything. His personality was the best and he dressed like a celebrity. I told him that we needed some snakes at church, it would sure separate the believers from the fake ones. Usually, the man had told me, those who had been bitten and died had their photos on the walls of the church as a reminder. I did not think that was true; he always made me laugh though and the pastor and I had laughed about it the day of his visit.

I could read people well from an early age. Sometimes I did not care for this gift or curse as it sometimes felt. It was difficult seeing someone for the way they really were and not the façade they hid behind. And, I was young, so a little confused that I had this ability in the first place. Discernment is a spiritual gift, of seeing things as they really are instead of as they appear. I was in tuned with the Lord as we began a revival at the church one night. I remember taking the stage and walking by the evangelist and looking him in the eyes. He looked at me in the strangest way and I knew that we were in for trouble. My spirit did not jive with his at all, and I was uncomfortable around him. I was not scared because I had the Lord's protection, but I knew in my bones he was a total fake.

I was sitting by my brother after I sung my song. When he came to the pulpit, I could not bear looking at him. He was a disgusting man. Heavy and brash and he talked about things that were not appropriate from the pulpit. But if you looked around, the people were lapping it up. He was a friend of the pastor who was oblivious to his actions. It had surprised me that he could not see his shortcomings or read this guy better.

The first night of the revival was strange. During the preaching, he would look at someone and tell them some bizarre prediction or jump from the stage, run up to a person, get in their personal space and shout in their face. He would spit on the carpet, of all things. And he would call young married couples to the front and ask inappropriate questions during the message. At the altar call, people went down, but I did not feel a thing. On the way home, I told my brother what I knew about this man, and he and I prayed for God's covering. It was going to be a long week of services. If you can discern someone's spirit, it is not an easy position to be in. It causes an uneasiness, and you almost feel like a traitor or spy, knowing things you should not know about them or their intentions.

It is like being alone in a large crowd at a sporting event and everyone is cheering for the player to score, but you. And you sit there among them knowing something they do not know. It is hard to describe, but it has happened to me so many times and started when I was about twelve. A night or two had taken place in the revival. This con artist had young married couples do ridiculous things under the guise of being led by the Holy Spirit and told more pitiful outlandish stories than I had ever heard. He lined people up and told them things that they would do in the future, as if he were a fortune teller and, each night, more people fell in line with this behavior—hungry to see what he did next.

People were bringing gifts for his family, taking up huge offerings for him and he was playing them like a fiddle. All under the pretense of the sacrifices he was making being on the road. He sat and cried at the altar, saying how he missed his family, and the congregation was completely caught up in this charade. I was tormented by the entire thing. I was shocked that the pastor and congregation could not see that his actions were out of line and a mockery to the Lord. He had grieved the Holy Spirit many times, and I just wanted the week to be over so he would leave.

I never let on to him or anyone how I felt, but, on that Thursday evening, I had been feeling sick all day and thought about not attending that evening. But the pastor had planned on me to sing as I had done every night that week. So, at the end of the service, during the altar call, I just made my way down to one of the front pews and spent some time with the Lord. It always made me feel a little better to go down and sit in the Lord's presence as I totally relied on Him for my life and especially in dealing with my illness. There was a chorus, and then this evangelist went to the pulpit. He began to smirk at me. I had just sat down in the front pew when I finished praying. He said, "Well, well, well, look at her? She got up here and sang like she was an angel falling into Heaven." I never took my eyes off him. "Yeah, she was down here asking for forgiveness for what she did last week out there," he continued. By now, the pastor was looking around stunned and adjusting his collar nervously, and others in the congregation were puzzled and I felt their eyes on me for a reaction. It had started to dawn on some that this guy was attacking a fourteen year old from the pulpit and spewing lies.

He started to hurl more outlandish accusations towards me, but the pastor jumped up and went in front of him to the pulpit, where he quickly dismissed the service. I got my things and left quickly. I did not stop to talk to anyone, and I wanted to get away from the pure evil I had witnessed. My mom and brother were shocked when we all got in the car to go home. I reminded them of what I had said early in the week when he had arrived. I made up my mind I would not be returning the next and final evening of the revival, Friday. All during the night I replayed his words and actions. And I could not believe people had been so gullible. It was still early in the morning on Friday when there was a knock at the front door of our home. Mom answered and I could hear her talking and a man's voice. It was the pastor, and he had brought the evangelist with him.

After small talk, the pastor said, "Gaye, what happened last night was awful and I am terribly sorry. Obviously, you are owed a huge apology for the words that were spoken." He looked at the evangelist as if to remind him of why they were there. Up to that point, he had just sat with his head down. My mother remained present during the visit. But she was quiet. I just looked at him waiting to see what he did next. He could hardly look at me, but, after a period of silence, he mumbled that he was sorry. I wasn't taking this; I knew he was not sincere, and it was my time to speak. I said, "I have known from the beginning of this week that you are a fraud, sir. There is nothing genuine about you and the Lord showed me that you are a total fake. You have grieved the Holy Spirit and said and done ridiculous things this week and the people fell for your lies, but I have not. God showed me the first night what you are."

The room got completely quiet now, and my mother was moving nervously in her chair. I would not take my eyes off him; he was pure evil. The pastor sat there dumbfounded. I had not let on to anyone that week what I had been shown about this man, so no one knew. The only thing this guy was aware of was that a kid had his number, and our spirits could not dwell together. He looked at me with such hate, I will never forget it. But I felt empowered, and I went on, "You go from place to place telling lies of the devil about your family and pull in tons of money under false pretenses. But you will be found out soon, mark my word." The pastor was pale now, and they both jumped up, excused themselves and left.

I had promised to attend the last service, which I did, and I sang. The evangelist spoke a very lowkey sermon and quickly turned it over to the pastor for dismissal. No bells and whistles or group participation that night. He wanted out of there as quickly as possible. A few months later pastor went to the pulpit and said he needed to make something right. He began to tell the congregation how the evangelist's lies had caught up with him. They found he was an alcoholic and that his family had left him long ago for his behavior. And that everything about his ministry for many years had been a lie. He said, "I don't understand how I did not know, but Gaye, you did." I felt bad for the pastor because the man had been his longtime friend. It became clearer to me as I grew up that I could tell a lot about people by talking to them. Or, in some cases just passing them or shaking their hand.

Discernment sees beyond the smoke and mirrors. I have dealt with people from all walks of life, and I can read them so well most of the time. Even church people, unfortunately. I have learned to keep things to myself. But I have told my husband things in confidence over the years. I believe God will always uncover someone's true motives and intentions when the time is right. There have been two instances where I had nothing, and in both I got really hurt. So, possibly God just let me go through those things so that I could learn something, or I was not in the proper place to hear from Him, I do not know. But most times I know from the beginning when I first meet someone. I have felt their spirit of jealousy in an initial conversation which always saddened me and eventually surfaced. My gift was highly active during the years of my early teens.

Sammy Hall was a great singer in the gospel world, and he traveled with family that made up the Sammy Hall Singers. There was a Church of God youth camp in Chattanooga one year. I decided to attend as a daily camper. That meant I only stayed through the evening service and then came back the next day. I was not sure if I could manage the entire week, but I wanted to go and hear them. They were one of my favorite groups at the time. During one of the daytime events, there was a plea from the camp staff for soloists, or groups to sing during the services. I did not approach anyone, but for some reason, I said yes when I was approached and was to sing in the evening service on Friday. The services were regular worship services, and then they would turn it over to Sammy Hall for their singing and ministry. He was my favorite and I envisioned singing with his group. I admit I was a groupie in the best way. There ministry was powerful. And his testimony touched many hearts, including mine.

I remember coming into the exceptionally large building and doing a sound check early in the day, and the night I was to sing the place was packed. A lot of locals and fans were able to attend along with campers, so it was a huge crowd, and open to everyone. Someone had said in the high thousands. I was always a little nervous when I stepped onto the platform. But as soon as the music started, and I took the microphone I was fine. I became caught up in the song. And this night was no different. Before I knew it the song was over, and I was leaving the platform. I could hear clapping and I saw people standing, but it did not dawn on me that I had been given a standing ovation that night, until after the service. My parents were there, and Mom had said it was amazing how my voice carried in that place and the anointing was upon me.

I was grateful people had been touched by the song and that was all I ever wanted. Later, I attended a Church of God of Prophecy music camp with a friend who was on staff, and I was able to roam around and partake of classes I wanted to attend. I selected a voice class. When I arrived at the studio, the instructor was a tall woman that reminded me of a librarian with her bohemian look. Her hair was pulled in a large bun tightly planted on top of her head and she was profoundly serious about teaching voice. She started by asking me to sing a little something for her. I started, and, partway through the verse, she stopped me and asked why I was there. I misunderstood because I said, "Well, I've never been to music camp before." "No, why are you taking my class?" she asked. I told her that I had never had formal lessons and wanted to be sure that I was giving my best to the Lord when I sang, and I was there for pointers.

She advised me that I did not need her class, and that I would need to find something else to fill my time at camp. I thought she wasn't serious at first and I laughed. But she went on to say that what I had was God given and that she could do nothing to enhance my gift. Later during the camp, a well known instructor was preparing all of the young ladies for a choral group to do some backup vocals for an upcoming album one of the church leaders would be making. He lined all the girls in the choral group up and there were many of us. He instructed us that we would be singing unison at the beginning and that we would all need to sound alike. So, to do this, he was going to go down the line and each of us would sing a line from the song and he would select the singer that everyone would need to sound like. Easy enough.

There were many voices that blended well, and everyone sounded great to me. When he got to me, he asked me to repeat the verse twice. Then he went on down the lengthy line of girls and came back to me. He asked me to sing it again, and then said, "Now, sing like her." Girls I knew and even strangers began to laugh and say, "We can't do that, we can't sing like her." But he was adamant that they try. I was so embarrassed. But we did sing, and they even did some backup vocals when I sang one of my original songs in the Sunday morning service. We had all been invited to sing there that weekend.

I was singing everywhere by now if I was able physically. I sang on television and even at a grocery store. Yes, the owner loved gospel music and had promised a good offering for the building fund if I would come and sing. So, after much convincing by the pastor, I sang there. You could see me on aisle three next to the bread, not really, I was planted at the front of the store with a microphone and sound system. It was a unique experience, but the shoppers enjoyed it. I only agreed to do it once, and once was enough. The customers would walk by while collecting their groceries and smile or wave at me while I sang. I could not believe I was doing this, but it was for the building fund. However, I do not recall anything ever built with the building fund money. But we sure contributed a lot to it over the years.

There was a great man that became interested in my music. He was a terrific talent in his own right, both in playing the piano and singing. His voice was effortless and like smooth butter. He played for me and arranged my original songs for copyright. I wrote many songs over time, and I would play them for him, and he would cord the songs and then add the music to them before we submitted them for copyright. He became my mentor, my cheerleader, and a manager.

His plan was for me to sing any and everywhere. He introduced me to people in the church in other states that I did not know but that could be of assistance to me, and he was a great friend. His wife and children were also precious, and I loved them so much. Mom got the idea that we needed to move to Nashville so that my singing career could get underway. I was reluctant and had no desire to move again for any reason. My doctor was in Chattanooga, the people I cared about were there and I did not see my career taking off in great strides just because we would move to Nashville, two hours away.

My oldest sister had left Tennessee now for the Air Force, and we had not heard from my middle sister that had stayed behind in Michigan. Mom had tried to contact her, but she would not respond. Unfortunately, when we left for Nashville, I lost touch with my mentor in Chattanooga, not because of anything that he had done; it was my own insecurities over my singing and my hurt over things that had been said to me from people in the church. It was jealousy, and, at the time, I was too young to really deal with that from anyone, so my way of handling things was to run from them, and the move came along at the right time. I have regretted that I did not let him know more often that I appreciated him for all he did for me. And, that I didn't share the things that troubled me with him. He had been so good to me, and I know I hurt him. I have tried over the years to locate him, and I still hope I can one day.

Before we moved, one Sunday morning, my brother was to preach at our church. I was so nervous for him, but I did not dare tell him. Mom and I sat in the front so that he could see us. I knew he was nervous, but he began to preach. There were a few places where there was silence as he collected his thoughts or moved along in the Bible. But I could hear laughing behind me. I turned around in the pew and saw some of the ones laughing. And, then others on the far side of the sanctuary started laughing as well. The sad thing was that these were adults mostly.

My brother never let it get to him; he kept right on. It was his first time speaking in front of the church. The pastor, who had not been there long, was not really my favorite He wanted competition between others and me in singing. In my mind, there was room for everyone to use their gifts. But at one point, during my brother's sermon, he got down and held my brother's legs pretending to pray for him, which made me furious. It was as if he was mocking my brother and it generated laughter.

After the service, I went to everyone that had laughed at my brother and I confronted them and the pastor for his ridiculous move and let all of them know how I felt about it. While I was at it, I talked about how they looked down on people that were not part of the church and that there wagging tongues held the church back from what God wanted to do. My mother knew that I was too angry to try and stop, and she let me do what I needed to do that day. When I got mad enough to cry it was best to leave me alone. I would protect my brother no matter what. He was kind and caring and never said one ugly thing about anyone in his entire life. He wanted to be a preacher from the time he was a little boy, and none of them were going to stop him if I had anything to say about it.

The next time he preached, it was at his ordination. He had become an ordained minister in the Church of God of Prophecy. I was so proud of him. I had very mixed feelings about him being ordained in that denomination, but he had to obey God. We moved to Nashville not long after that. I met great people that I had hoped would make a record with me at some point soon. Dad was at a satisfactory level, and my brother had just finished receiving his ministry credentials and was waiting to know where the church would be sending him. As usual, Mom found a nursing position right away, and I had my music. I was still having school at home and having good and bad days. I never lost touch with my doctor.

One lady that we met was the wife of a singer who was in a musical group and well known in the church. She and I became quick friends. She had two little precious boys and stayed home with them while her husband was on the road. She was so gifted in piano and singing, and she also wrote beautiful music. We would play and sing, and she began to play for me at events. I was getting a feel for gospel music and thought that it was God's plan for my life. I was very self-conscious at the time. I got a lot of attention, and to be honest, I was not sure how to process it. I was a singer, but I was still a girl, a young girl. My hair was long, and people would complement me, and I had my share of boys coming around. But I always remembered what Maude had told me; never sing when your heart is not right. So, I tried to protect myself. I wanted to protect my gift. There were a few awkward times meeting new people, especially men and I did not manage those times very well. I had become much shyer than I realized.

And, of all things, I did not want anything to jeopardize my testimony. One night, my sweet friend and I had dresses made alike and I was to sing at an event that was going to give me great exposure. There were popular gospel artists in the lineup and of course, scouts and record labels would possibly be in attendance as well. They would often show up at events, I had heard from other singers. We arrived early to familiarize ourselves with the stage and the surroundings. A little distant from the large stage, we waited to find our seats, and a very well-known group was up doing a sound check. If I said the name, you would know immediately who I am talking about. One of the members, an extremely popular member, began to stare at me. Other people had started filtering into the large auditorium, but he kept his eyes on me.

I would look away, and look back, like you do sometimes when you cannot help yourself if someone is staring at you. And he just kept on looking me up and down with his eyes. I felt so uncomfortable that I finally said, "Do you know what? I am too nervous to sing tonight; let's leave." She tried to get me to stay, and I never told her the reason I wanted to get out of there. I was so embarrassed that a popular man, a married man, singing gospel music, would look at a young girl that way. She thought I just had stage fright, but it was much more than that. I could have never sung in front of him, and to this day, if I see him on television, it makes me sick to look at him. He is old now and would never admit to doing such a thing when he was young, I am sure, but he did it, and sadly, I do not think it was the first time.

I missed a fantastic opportunity that night to sing in front of powerful and influential people. I missed others as well. Sometimes, I was a victim of my own self-sabotage. I had been raised in an extremely strict home and thought that everyone who professed to be a Christian was one, because how dangerous it was to profess to be something you were not. The thought of lives tainted with the lust of the world, especially while singing gospel music to large crowds every night, was unthinkable to me. I learned that not everyone that sang gospel music was a true believer. It was a business just like any other, for many.

There was a death that surrounded my sweet friend's family, and we had all attended the memorial service. I had no idea that The Sammy Hall Singers would be in attendance that night. I sat in front with the family, and I was shocked when Sammy Hall came out. They had been asked to minister at the service at this exceptionally large church. The place was packed. He stared at me during the service, and immediately afterward came off the stage and headed my way. I never thought for a moment he would remember me, but he had it appeared, and I froze when he stopped in front of me.

"I know you," he said to me. Those sitting around me were looking on like what is happening? "You're the girl. You sang in Chattanooga that night at camp?" he said, smiling. "Well yes, it was me." I could not believe he had even seen me that night at camp, let alone would remember me a year or so later. He took my hand and said, "You brought the house down with that song, your voice…You got a standing ovation. Tell me, are you still singing?" I told him that I was not singing. Which was a bold-faced lie, because yes, I was singing. *Why did I tell him I was not? Why did I do this to myself?*

He talked to me a few minutes and was so sorry I was not singing any longer.

He had said people needed to hear my voice, and then someone came and swept him away. I would never get that chance again. I learned a while back that he had gone to be with the Lord.

I was so taken back that he knew me in that crowd at a memorial service two hours from Chattanooga and over a year later. And I admit I was a little star-struck that he had even talked to me.

Could he have offered me a place to sing with his group? Would he have offered to help me or let me do backup vocals for the group I so loved, who knows, but it was a great meeting. He had no way of knowing how much their music meant to me because I was too silly to tell him that night when I had the chance. He had done most of the talking. And I did what I did best, sabotage myself. I was nervous, and tongue-tied. Just like I always was. I was my biggest problem.

We moved back to Chattanooga. Dad was more content, and happy and I figured I could sing anywhere. Chattanooga could be a good home base for me. My brother moved to Wisconsin, to work in a church. We did go up for his wedding. And, then he would go on to do church plants in desolate areas, so we hardly saw him. Now it was just Mom, Dad, and me.

I was seventeen now and had settled back into a routine. I had never really adjusted to life in Nashville. None of us cared for it. I loved being back in Chattanooga and close to my doctor and friends. It had been raining for several days this one week. I thought it would never end. I remember how very sore and uncomfortable I was. I could hardly move and was to fatigued to even think about it. But we were having services at church, and they had asked me to sing this night. The evangelist was older and seasoned in his preaching, I had not heard him before. I had enjoyed the service and was glad I had come out even with the terrible rain.

After the service, and during the altar call, he said, "There is someone here that needs a special touch from the Lord. I want you to come now. You know who you are." Several people went to the front, but I stayed behind. I knew a lot of these people and knew what some of them were dealing with physically, so I was praying for them, standing at my pew. Again, he extended the offer for someone to come who needed a special touch from the Lord. I was so caught up in praying, and not even thinking about my illness. I had carried it like a worn handbag for so long that I had adjusted to it somehow. It was always with me.

A few minutes later, he said, "I am going to pray because there is a person here that is sick in body. You have struggled for many years, but God is saying tonight is your night!" I began to wonder if God meant me. Was I who he had been talking about? Could this be my time?

I just began to pray that if it were me that God would have free rein in my life to heal me or continue to give me grace to go through it. I remember starting to feel heat at the top of my head, and it slowly moved down through my body like someone was pouring warm liquid over me. I began to cry, and the warmth turned into heat to the point that sweat beads were forming above my top lip. I became so hot by this point, but it was not unbearable or uncomfortable; it was stopping the pain in my shoulders as the heat touched them. Then it moved down into my arms and hands and the aching went away. It traveled down my legs to my knees that were swollen and throbbing and immediately the throbbing stopped. It continued down to my feet and my ankles and into my toes and by now there was no pain whatsoever in my body.

I remember turning my neck and feeling the heat again covering me as if to do a second coat of warmth. I was standing tall, not bent over like I had been, always favoring one sore leg or the other as I balanced myself to stand. I was standing on both of my feet, straight as a board and there was no pain. I had no pain anywhere, and I could hear the rain pounding the outside of the church. I was warm, comfortable, and feeling good for the first time in many years. The tears would not stop, and I looked up to see the evangelist smiling at me, knowing that God had touched me. I have wondered many times, what if I had moved that night, when he made the call the first time. Would God have touched me in a more unique way? Or, what if since I had been disobedient, had He not touched me at all? I did not know initially that I was the person, but I was one that needed a touch from God desperately, so I should have moved regardless. I had not been obedient. But even though I had not, God still healed me. He still had mercy on me.

The heat turned into an internal warmth that lasted well into the night. It was as if I had an electric blanket on the highest setting, covering me. Most mornings, before rain even came, after rain or during a downpour, I could not move. It would take me forever to just move enough to get out of bed, my body would be so stiff and sore. The next day, I jumped out of bed! And ran to the kitchen where my mother was. I said, "Mom! It's still raining and I'm up and I feel wonderful." She was shouting praises to the Lord. It was the greatest thing. I went to the doctor, and he took tests and confirmed that yes, the disease was gone! He would shake his head and tell me that there were no signs in my blood, and my hot inflamed joints were no longer affecting me. He could not believe it, but he was as happy as we were. No more would I suffer from pain and stiffness. No more would I lose sleep and feel tired and fatigued. No more would I have to take medications or therapy or lose weight or anything else because of juvenile rheumatoid arthritis, God had healed me finally!

I would no longer suffer with bruises that would develop for no reason or scrapes that took forever to heal. Even my teeth were whitening again from the effects of the initial strong medications that nearly ruined them. I had that disease for over eight long years, but it all changed when Jesus touched me.

CHAPTER FOURTEEN

Now everything was happening fast. I wanted to make up for lost time. I was graduating one year early from high school, and I could not wait to start college that summer. My life was really starting it seemed. Gone was the sickness that had kept me like a prisoner for so many years. I was free! Free to explore, to get out and live my life.

My oldest sister was in the Air Force. So, she was off living her best life and we were happy she had found some peace. My middle sister had joined the Navy after leaving Petoskey and I had gone to visit her once in Memphis after she and her "friend" had come to Chattanooga after a trip to Disney World. I was in my early teens then. We had gone to a dinner theater right across the street from Graceland called the Gaslight Theater, and Elvis was still alive at the time. I wanted to see him so badly, but only got to see his Cadillac parked in front of his stately home.

I also visited her shortly after in Pensacola Florida when the Navy transferred her there. It turned out to be a horrible trip for me. We knew that my sister was a lesbian, but we did not talk about it. She had become a Navy photographer. My sister was also very artistic in paints and drawing which began when she was a young girl at home. Her paintings were unique and when you looked at them, it was as if you could walk right into the scene. Her job, now in Florida, was with advertising, designing, and taking photographs on base.

When they had come to visit at home that one time, they stayed during the day and left in the early evening. My parents and I knew that her life had taken quite a different turn, but they were cordial and welcoming to them even though we did not agree with her lifestyle. I was always just waiting for Dad to come out with something, but he kept quiet, I think for my mom's sake more than anything. On the Florida visit, she had taken me to the Naval base to pick up some things, and I was not at all used to being around men like that. Sailors were everywhere, and they would hoot and holler at me. My sister would holler back, "She's a kid" And, immediately, they would yell, "Sorry. You're a beauty, honey" or "Wish you were older." I did not like it and was so happy to get back to her house. Her friend, a proud atheist, had mannerisms like a man, brash and abrupt. And her hair was cropped off short. She was supposed to be brilliant, and I know that she had a high-level position in the science field, but she could not have been that smart if she did not believe in God.

When I had visited in Memphis in my early teens, she had been super quiet and inviting. But I could tell from the onset of this visit to Florida that the mood had changed. At lunch, on my second day there, she began to talk about church and asked me questions about why I believed what I did. She even asked if I was a so-called "Christian" because my mother forced her beliefs on me.

My sister kept silent during this conversation, but I knew what was happening. I would glance at my sister, and she would move uncomfortably in her seat or lower her eyes so she would not have to look at me. And it all made me angry. The more the friend questioned things about God, and laughed off my beliefs, the more upset I got. This kept on later at dinner, and by then I had enough. I told them both that I would be leaving in the morning and flying home. I was not putting up with this ridicule of my life and my relationship with God, and I questioned my sister about why she had fallen away from what she knew was right and led into this lifestyle.

They wanted to persuade me to leave my life, denounce God and the home I had grown up in and I was not having it. The friend had left for work in the morning when I was getting ready to catch my plane home and I had a little time alone with my sister. I said, "This woman is an atheist; she is also a sick individual and lives a lifestyle you should not be a part of. No amount of money or status will ever replace God in your life." I explained that I knew Mom was strict, and there were rules, but that we had lived a great life sheltered by church and what was right. I told her I would pray for her and that I loved her. I made it clear that I would be there if she needed me. I caught my plane. I never saw her again.

I found out many years later, after my brother and I reconnected for my mother's funeral, that she had left the military, became an art instructor at a university, and that her friend had died. My sister had a debilitating back problem that caused great suffering, and after dealing with it for as long as she could, she committed suicide, not able to deal with the pain. I had no way of knowing my three siblings had stayed in touch; I was not included. Except the letters from my oldest sister with her stories about life in the Air Force she sent to my folks, I hadn't heard from anyone. I regret that I never tried to reach out to her, tried to help her. I did not know all of this at the time; did not know she struggled with pain. The last I had seen her she had told me that she was happy and did not want to stay in touch with me because I did not approve of her lifestyle. I could have helped though, because I knew all too well what dealing with constant pain was like. It still breaks my heart when I think about her. My brother had tried to help her but to no avail.

I received a call one day from a company in Nashville after we had moved back to Chattanooga because things were not really happening like I thought they would there, and I missed the people and Chattanooga more than I thought I would. I was asked to bring a demo tape to this place. So, Mom and I made the trip. Dad was not physically able to travel; his health had declined in Nashville. Mom and I arrived with demo in hand and met the guy. He looked like a used car salesperson to me. Tall with his dark hair slicked back, and a suit that had a shimmer to it. He wore long toed boots that looked like they could round a corner before the rest of his body could. And he talked with a southern drawl.

I thought how ironic it was to be back in Nashville after living there and nothing happened, now this. He talked in generalities with us for a few minutes, how was the trip up, traffic and mundane things. And then asked for my tape. It was large and round like a Frisbee. Thin tape circled round and round on the plastic holder and it was tucked in a cardboard box. It was a reel-to-reel tape and back then, if you had a demo tape you were something. Everyone that was anyone had a demo tape to shuffle around to record labels. I still have that tape. I only had one song on the tape, and I had recorded it just for this day. I had to admit I was excited. This could be my chance I thought. He put the tape on this large recorder that faced us, and the tape started to turn. When the song started and I heard myself, the man shifted from sitting with his hands planted on his desk to lying back in the big chair and closing his eyes.

I felt strange and a little awkward sitting there while he listened to me. You always feel when you hear yourself that you could or should have sounded better or at least that is how I felt. I never felt good enough. I was glad my mom was there with me for support. At the end of the song, he jumped up and turned it off, rewound it and sat and faced me. He said, "Young lady, you are not a singer; you, are an artist." I did not know what to say or if I should say anything. I just stared at him, and then glanced at my mom who was smiling. I did not even know how he had gotten my name or knew I sang. He grabbed paperwork and began to talk while moving things around the desk. "You are the whole package. You have the looks, the body, and the voice, that voice," he said.

Something was not right. And I was thinking, why would I need a body or looks to sing gospel music? Thoughts were running through my head, and he began his pitch to me. "You're going to make us both rich! I have not heard a voice like yours in a long time. "Country music is about to get a star!" What? country music? I knew something was wrong with this. I said, "Sir there must be a mistake. I don't sing country music; I sing gospel music." "Well," he waved me off, "You can sing that on your own time. Country music is where it is at. We will want to sign you." "I am sorry, there must be a mistake. I came here thinking this was about gospel music," I said firmly.

I think back now and how naive I was. I tried to explain that I was a Christian and that God had just recently healed me from a serious condition and my goal was to sing gospel music and share my testimony. I did not even sing secular music, never really listened to rock n roll until I got to be older, and then only rarely, maybe a ballad. He just laughed, like he had no clue what I was talking about. I asked, "Well, if I decided to sing, would I be able to sing gospel music along with country music?" And he shook his head no. He talked about a brand and other things, but I had drifted off in thought. In my heart, I heard do not be a sellout. Maude had always told me not to take the stage unless my heart was right. "Your singing is a ministry, honey," she would say. "Don't you ever forget it." How could I sing worldly songs like this with the gift God had given me? Writing this makes the tears flow all over again. I felt so let down at that moment. I had thought I would know God's direction for my life, and this would confirm it.

I asked if I could think about it, and he looked at my mother and shook his head. "Do you know what people would do for a chance like this? Talk to her, Mom." My mother had been quiet and then she said, "Well, it's her life. I trust her to make the right decision. I want her to be happy." We left there that day with the idea of thinking about it, but, on the trip home, I knew without a doubt that it was the wrong choice for me to make. Not only would I be singing country music, and it is not bad, but back then the songs were different than what's available to artists now. I could never sing about people cheating on each other, that was so foreign to me, regardless of the money or success it could bring.

But he had instructed me that I would not be able to make choices about song selection, dress, or where I sang. I would become a commodity, a product that they would paint and dress and send out to perform. It did not take me long to decline, but the hardest thing was telling my dad. First of all, he was a believer in my singing voice. So, I had to convince him that it was not in my best interest. Secondly, he liked country music very much and felt it was a terrific opportunity for me. And thirdly, he knew I had the potential to make a lot of money. It was the one time I felt I truly let him down. He was so disappointed that I had turned down what he thought was the opportunity of my life.

I went on to record my gospel album that year in South Carolina. It was a fun time and I met so many great people. Many were in the Church of God of Prophecy, and I knew some from music camp the year I attended. My dream of starting my singing career had finally happened. All the years, I had suffered and thought it would never happen, and now here I was at the beginning step of making my first album. It had been a lengthy process for me.

My brother and his family had come back to live in Chattanooga for a few years and long enough for all of us to fall in love with their little boy. From the time he was born, Dad referred to him as his little buddy. There are so many photos of Dad and that baby. They had another little baby boy shortly before they decided to move back to Wisconsin, and we were all crushed, especially Dad. He missed those babies more than any of us anticipated. But it was now just the three of us Mom, Dad, and me, again.

If something needed to be done, I did it. If the house needed painting inside or outside, I painted it. I got on a ladder and did what I needed to do. A guy drove by once and saw me on the ladder outside trying to reach a high spot with paint and he may have thought I would fall, or he felt sorry for me. He stopped his car, jumped out and asked if he could do it for me. I was not used to help, so that was a pleasant change. I kept all the balls in the air. I never wanted my parents to feel guilty that I was the only one at home, but it took its toll on me. There was no one else. I did not have anyone to really talk to about it. I was responsible, or so I thought.

The friends I had at church were all getting married around the same time. There were a few young people but mostly a group of older people that talked loudly during service and made change out of the offering plate on Sunday morning. Mom was a great wedding planner and event coordinator. She could put a party or wedding together in no time. My friends took advantage of her gift of hospitality, and she did everyone's weddings. It was her hobby and she loved doing it as a release from her work as a nurse, so it made her happy. We were a package deal. She planned and coordinated the weddings, and I was the token wedding singer. And I was none too happy about it.

I would sit on the platform waiting to sing those sappy songs, and watch them walk down the aisle thinking, what are you doing with your life? Dad had always told us kids to get married when we did not have anything better to do. "Get a job, travel, make money," he would say. "Don't tie yourself down too early." But here they were. Sadly, I do not think many of them stayed all that happy.

Along with weddings, church, and school. I even got involved with several campaigns against the cruelty of animals. If I found an organization that needed help, I volunteered my time. I collected signatures for petitions regarding animal care. And I protested against animal cruelty and the wearing of animal fur long before it was trendy to do so. I had heard about a shelter down in Georgia where I could get a dog. I had been thinking about getting a companion and a dog was much better than people, you knew where you stood with a dog. They either liked you or not, no running behind your back or deserting you when they felt like it. They were trusting and loyal. So, I jumped in my little red Gremlin and headed down there one day. It was cold, and I drove my little car through the back roads of Georgia thinking I would never find the place.

No cell phones, no GPS, just an idea where it was from directions on the phone from a guy who sounded like he could have cared less about being there. When I arrived, dogs and puppies were on the cold pavement with no shelter, water, or food. There were metal bowls that had once held water, but they were now dirty and empty. Puppies were shivering and there were so many of them. There were a couple of cats too, but they had a place to go inside out of the cold. The guy with attitude showed up and I asked him how much the puppies were. He shrugged his shoulders and said they were free. So, I said, "Well, I will take every puppy you have." He looked at me like I was insane, and I may have been, but I was not leaving one puppy behind. I grabbed them like they were the hottest items on the shelf and put them in my little car. Every single puppy was in my vehicle when I left that place.

They were cute little bundles of fur that settled right down when they felt the warmth of the car heater. I could have cried leaving the few older dogs and cats behind, but I would take care of them as quickly as I got these settled. And I did. I brought all the puppies into the house, bathed them and while I was doing that mom had called her friend that ran the Humane Society downtown, and he was happy to take every one of them to place in good homes. After that, I contacted the city commissioners, took photos of the shelter, and forced them to either remodel it for better conditions or close it. They chose to close it, and all the animals that I promised I would take care of got homes.

I was a bleeding heart for any animal. And I truly felt gratified that my actions had worked. I had wished everything in my life worked like that. To be honest, I resented my siblings. They were living their lives and I was stuck here waiting on mine to start. Dad was not well, and I would go to class and come home and be with him. He could not really be alone at that point, and Mom had to work. I felt like a shaken-up coke bottle about to burst. The day the albums came was strange. A man came to the door and said he had several boxes for me. When he started bringing them in, I could not believe it. There were so many boxes. Each box had twenty-five record albums in it, and he was stacking them up all over the living room. I was excited and disappointed at the same time. Here they were, but what was I going to do with them? I could not go on the road, and to be truthful, I hated the road.

I was a creature of habit. I did not like change. I was not a fan of traveling or eating other people's food. I had done that in Nashville some, and I did not care for it. It is a hard life being on the road. If I could have had my dream situation, I would have just stayed in a recording studio cranking out records, and never traveling to promote them. I loved meeting people and talking with them about their walk with the Lord, but travel was not my preference. However, now here I was with no option to even do that.

One day, I received a call from a university. The man was kind and seemed excited to talk with me. He said that they had heard me sing and wanted to offer me a full scholarship to attend school there. All I had to do was sing in their choral group, and I did not even have to do solo work if I chose not to. He explained that they just needed my voice in their group. I explained to him that I was not able to because I had to stay close to home to help with Dad. But I told him how honored I felt that they had asked me. But for a moment or so, it felt good to know that someone somewhere was interested in my singing. And, I had thanked him for his generous offer.

There was no way I could have left everything for my mother to manage alone. But it was bottled inside me and eating away at my self-esteem. I would go to bed at night and ask God why? Why was this happening? The investment had been made. My parents paid for all of it. I know they sacrificed to do it. But they believed in my gift. I was not as confident in myself as they were. I was afraid of failure. I did not want to let them down. And, I had a beautiful record album, just waiting to get out there and use my instrument. The people at the company were wonderful to me. Several well-known individuals worked on this record including Lari Goss, someone I admired. Lari was a gospel luminary Hall of Famer, a key producer for the great gospel talents, Grammy and Dove award winner. He produced of music for Warner Brothers, Capitol and RCA among other attributes. And he did backup vocals on an album for an unknown girl like me. There was also a great brass band from Atlanta that did tracks on the album as well. I was so touched by their generosity and the time they took to make my record great.

Dad and I did not talk about music or singing. He really was not interested in the details, or the happenings of the recording process. It was a sore topic for him and always came down to what-ifs. What if you had taken the chance and tried country? No, Dad, that was not an option. What if you had made a lot of money? No, Dad, it was not about the money. So often I heard, "You are throwing this away." I do not know, maybe I did throw that chance away. I thought I was doing the right thing.

People only wanted to hear fast up-tempo songs that were entertaining and worked the crowd into a frenzy. That may have been other people's approach to their music, but it was not mine. When I sang, I sang to the Lord. It was my way of expressing my love to him and no one else. I wanted to touch people with the words and the message. I felt a heavy anointing that would make me weep often after I sang when I went to sit down. I could not explain that to anyone. But singing was always a comfort to me. It soothed me growing up. When I was so sick or troubled, I would sing.

Every day, those stacks of records bothered me. They reminded me I was trapped. Reminded me of failure on my part. I got so sick of seeing them I started to put them in the attic just to get them out of my sight one day and my mother stopped me. She said, "They will melt up there." I laughed, "So what, big deal. I don't need them." I wanted to call my siblings and say come home! Do your part! But I knew that was not going to happen. One after another, seeds of dissension and resentment began collecting in my heart. And I was letting them take root. There comes a time when those same seeds are cultivated and begin to bloom and burst out of your mind and heart. I was bursting at the seams with questions to God about why He had even let me do all this. Why had we gone through all the work and expense to get to this point where I sat and looked at boxes of albums. For what? Nothing like feeling sorry for yourself. I had become good at that. My folks had believed in my gift, and they had sacrificed for me to make that album, so there was a lot of guilt associated with it. And every time I looked at those huge, stacked boxes it made me feel more inferior. But I was lonely too. I dated some, but there was not anyone special. I was trying to take care of everyone's needs and I felt like I had holes in me that life was just spilling out of.

I went to church and sang and tried to stay positive and have faith that everything would turn around. One time after I sang, the Lord had moved in the service in a powerful way. I was leaving, and a woman stopped me. I always sat at the piano and prayed about what I would sing beforehand, and I wanted it to be a blessing more than anything. She was one of the church's gossips and had a voice that could grate cheese with its raspiness. "Why don't you ever sing a fast song?" she said in that long gravelly voice. Mom was behind me, and I know she thought I was going to be less than kind to this woman.

I began explaining to her that when you sing you are ministering, and my songs were slow and thought-provoking so that you were convicted and would apply the song to your own life. I do not know what else I said, but I was trying to make her understand. It went right over her head, because she reiterated, "Well, I wish you would sing something fast, for a change."

She walked away clueless. And, I stood there thinking to myself, why I had even bothered explaining anything to her. My mom was smiling and said, "Oh dear, you managed that wonderfully." I had to laugh, "Mom, she doesn't get it and that's sad." Whenever you are on the platform either singing or preaching or whatever, people will critique you. Christians can be some of the worst, but that's part of it. You are dealing with all kinds of people at different walks in their journey with God. I knew her reputation for negativity and for some reason, I felt sorry for her.

In my weak moments, I wanted to say well, you get up there if you think you can do better. The music was too loud, the songs were to slow, this or that. People never failed to amaze me with their quick tongues and criticism. Someone once told me about something they did not like about their Sunday School teacher. Why tell me? I was a kid with no say in anything regarding church business. Nor did I want to be involved. I could only imagine what our poor pastor had to deal with.

I did manage children's church for quite a while, and that had been wonderful fun for me and the children. The children needed their own services where they could learn on their level. The church did not have paid leadership except for the pastor. It was all volunteer, and that was not always popular. As Mom would say on many occasions to me, "Put it under the blood, honey," and believe me I did a lot of that. No one wanted to do it, but everyone had opinions on how it should be done.

I was a mix of emotions. Both happy and sad, I ran the gamut. If I felt bad or trapped, I felt guilty for it. But I had never experienced normal things. I had a home bound teacher until I graduated early at seventeen. I did not get to enjoy drama or music in school or go to prom or graduation. I was fortunate to have a godly and wonderful teacher that I had for several years. Mrs. Varner was one of a kind. She was the epitome of southern grace and class, with her gift of storytelling and ability to make learning fun even for a sick kid.

We would laugh and have little parties. She would show up in beautiful pant suits, with her hair short and curling around her face and her bracelets would clang together when she was animated or telling me something grand. On days when I was too sick to work, we would visit. I would lie in my bed, and she would entertain me with her wild imaginative stories or talk about her childhood. But God had healed me now. Why at that time at seventeen, I do not know? But he had, and I wanted to enjoy my life. I wanted to get out and shake the dust of being home bound off and live my life. I loved when someone came up to me and said, "Your singing is a blessing to me, it touched me to the core." That is all I ever wanted. Not the accolades, but for people to be touched and changed by my singing. We are all just vessels God uses in one way or another. Each of us has our own unique gifts to enhance the kingdom. No one is better or greater than the next. We all have our place serving the master.

One day, I met a Methodist minister. I was at the courthouse in a little town in Georgia for a college project and he was there. I had signed up for a class at the beginning of summer eager to get going with my degree. For some reason, we were in the large court room in the late afternoon with not many people around and he began to talk to me. I told him I was researching something for school, and we got to talking about church, and somehow about my singing. He was so excited. He asked me to bring albums and come and sing at his church. He warned me that this would be a first for his congregation, but he thought it would be good for them to branch out. We agreed on a date right then, and I will never forget going there. It was a good-sized brick building with soft pews and an ornate front with lots of brass and statues. I was not accustomed to that at all, our churches were nice but not elaborate. But he had asked me to come, and I was going to give it my best.

It was not the most inviting crowd, and when I placed my tape player on the front pew people started getting fidgety. I used cassette soundtracks back then, as a lot of singers did. I did not have a piano player so that would have to do. I displayed the albums and began to minister after a generous and heartfelt introduction from the minister. When I began singing the people looked restless as if I did not belong there. Or more like, the music did not belong there.

It was difficult judging by faces as to whether anyone was enjoying it because I sure could not tell. I gave a bit of my testimony and still no reaction. It was the first time I had ever experienced that before. This was the Sunday night service, and I did not know until I got there that he had dedicated the entire service to me to sing. Happy I brought several cassettes, I gave my best. No one clapped, no one raised their hands, no one worshiped. It was Jesus, this sweet minister and me.

People just sat there like they were sitting on hot coals fidgeting and looking into space. When I was finished, I mentioned my album if anyone was interested in purchasing one. I had a bazillion at home, so I had hoped a few would be sold. Only one was purchased, and the offering they took up was not even enough for a fourth of a tank of gas to get back home. But it was fine and had been a wonderful experience. And, I had got to meet this wonderful minister. One woman told me that she had enjoyed having music in the service, so I hoped they would continue because music welcomes the Holy Spirit into the service. It touches hearts and prepares us for the preaching of God's word.

I had received my high school diploma at home with no frills, pomp, or circumstance. Just from my amazing teacher who told me I could do anything I wanted. The school system did arrange for me to have graduation photos taken. I had been attending college now for a month or so and it was finishing. Summer classes were much shorter in duration but more intense.

I was fighting endometriosis even more and it was becoming much worse. I was diagnosed at sixteen with it. I went often to my doctor, an older man about to retire, but seemed to know his stuff. He explained to me at one visit that I had a slim to none chance of having children. I was young and for the first time free to explore the world after a prolonged illness and his words did not cause me any concern at that stage of my life. Getting married and having children seemed too far in the future to even worry about.

One afternoon, after I had seen the doctor, I was a little downhearted. I decided I wanted to seek adventure and do something fun and carefree. I was restless. I had dealt with so much for so long, and this was just the thing to get me out of the city and I would get a different perspective on things. Dad was doing ok, and Mom had encouraged me to have fun for a change. And so, I got a wild idea to travel out west. A friend and I decided to take a trip to California on a Greyhound bus. I was looking for adventure and fun and she was too scared to get out of the bus. All along the way, we stopped at rest areas and restaurants that catered to people that could manage the hottest, spiciest of foods. So, once I had begged the driver to stop at the Dairy Queen so that we could get something gentler on the stomach. He stopped, and several of us got off to get something we could eat. It had taken us three days to travel to Los Angeles and I was not about to stay closed in our room.

My friend had been so different at home, so outgoing and independent. But once we had arrived, she had locked herself away and was terrified to venture out into the city. I finally talked her into going on a tour of celebrity homes and Universal Studios. I admit our hotel was not in the best area, Hollywood and Vine to be exact, but, back then, you did not have YouTube videos or hotel reviews and I wanted to get close to the action. Well, believe me, we were staying where there was action, but not really the kind any good Christian girl needed to be exposed too.

We stood outside waiting for the tour bus the day after we arrived and people were honking and waving at us. I had no clue why they were doing it and she was just as naive thinking they were being hospitable. Finally, the hotel manager walked outside, eased up beside me and whispered to me that these people thought we were looking for work in the worst conceivable way! Oh Lord! Mom and Jesus would surely not be happy about this. From then on, we were careful when we went anywhere out there. And we never stood outside the hotel again waiting for a ride. We waited in the lobby.

When we got back, I signed up for a chemistry class at the University of Tennessee in Chattanooga. It turned out to be an accelerated class and my first morning in the amphitheater I knew I was in deep, when I saw it filled with pre medicine students.

My other classes were fine, but math and chemistry were not my preferences. It was the strangest thing, I did so badly in all math subjects except statistics. Who knew? For some reason, it was understandable, and I did well in it. That summer was filled with those two classes, church and being available at home for my folks. I was still grappling with doubt about what to do about my music.

I was feeling great physically, and that was amazing, and I was so thankful to the Lord. When God heals you, He does a thorough job. I was also off the medications, and my head was clear for the first time in a long time. But since I had been on medications for so long, it took a long time to get everything out of my system.

I had sung at a service one night and a lady came up to my mother afterward and said she would like to meet me. When we met, she said that she had someone she wanted me to meet.

This next part is difficult for me, even after all these years. I have tried to forget it, so I am leaving out quite a bit. I must share it because it played a pivotal role in changing my direction. I thought it a little strange, but there were people that had tried to set me or my friends up with family or friends before. It wasn't that unusual. So, I thanked her and did not think much more about it. However, she was persistent. The plan was put in place that I would meet this young man after church at a local restaurant where we could get acquainted. I had dated and had liked people before, but nothing ever came of it. I did not really have an outlet to pursue anything like that because my life was pretty much planned out for me for the moment.

The night we were to meet, I was nervous, I had never liked being set up. But I thought it would not hurt, and maybe, it could be fun to meet new people. It was after an evening service when he walked into the restaurant. He was the most gorgeous man I had ever seen to that point in my life. He was dark and very handsome. Taller at about five eight or nine and he carried himself like a celebrity. He drew so much attention just by walking in the place that night.

His hair was curly and short, and, when he smiled, his teeth were snow white and sparkled from the shine. And that smile, well I could not believe it. His eyes lit up when he smiled. I loved that he dressed so well, and he was engaging from the beginning. He was more serious than I was, but he was also about ten years older than I was. So that was the reason. I found out that evening. And I was not sure what I was getting into. I had always dated older young men, but he was much older. After we talked for a long time, he said he wanted to hear me sing again and that he had been in that evening's service. I had not noticed anyone, but that was not a surprise. I did not pay attention to who came or went. And I was usually on the platform anyway and my mind was on the service. Somehow, I thought I should have noticed him though. He asked me out and took my number.

I was pretty taken with him from the onset, and I could tell he felt the same way. It was great chemistry. We started dating, and he would come to church with me and smile from ear to ear when I was up singing. He said he had left the Air Force and would be starting college on the GI Bill. I was happy to know he would be staying in Chattanooga. This went on for a month or so maybe longer, and then he left for Texas. I had not really known why he was going there, but we began writing long letters to each other. When I think about this now, I do not understand why we never talked on the telephone. It was always through letters that we communicated. I would be so excited when one would come, and I would read it several times.

I was still wrestling with decisions about my music and trying to figure out what to do with my life. I had all those albums to distribute, and it seemed every door that opened closed just as quickly.

My faith had been waning for a long time. I could not understand anything other than the fact that I was still the only one at home to help my parents and resentment towards my siblings continued to grow. I never resented my parents because it really was not anyone's fault, I guess. Dad could not help being sick, nor the fact that it was just the three of us. That is just how it was. My siblings had a right to live their lives. But I was not managing it well. Faith can come so hard, but bitterness and doubt come so easily. I had thought I had clear direction with what I wanted to do, and what God had wanted. I could not find the answers on how to proceed. But we know that plans are made to change. No matter how you set out, things are bound to change, and life throws in a few speed bumps along the way.

It was quite a while before he returned from Texas, but when he did, he said he would be reenlisting back into the Air Force. I was surprised. We had not talked about it, and it was really his decision. But I never had a clear understanding as to why this had happened. He had started school here, so it seemed so strange that now after being out of the service a brief time that he would do this, and so soon. So, again, he was off to San Diego California for a few weeks, and we wrote letters back and forth. I knew I had feelings for him, and his letters were always filled with affirmations and love. I was trying to do so many things at once, making up for lost time, but I found myself always thinking about him. A year had passed.

He came home and asked me to marry him. I knew it was quick, but for the first time in a long time, I thought this was what I wanted. If God had something for me to do with my singing, I could still do it. Of course, there was no engagement ring, since the church did not condone wearing jewelry, but that was fine with me. He was a Christian, and that is what mattered most or so I thought. I had met him in church, so he was perfect for me, right? Aren't you always safe with people in church?

Every waking hour I was waiting on news from him. He had gone to Texas again, so he stayed gone a lot it seemed.

When I think back on this, and I don't because it was such a horrible time in my life, there were so many unanswered questions, so many red flags. Even writing it now, I wish it had never happened. Why was I just OK with writing letters and never calling? Why had he re-enlisted shortly after getting out of the service? And, why Texas? When we were together, it all seemed to fit. I was happier than I had ever been. He seemed happy and we began to plan our wedding, and even the sting of having to put my music on hold seemed easier somehow. One day, Mom and I were talking, and she said something about my moving to Texas. I was surprised! I do not know what kind of fog I was in, but it never occurred to me that I would be leaving Chattanooga for Texas. She said, "Well, of course, you would go to Texas with your husband." But it had never come up in our conversations. And what was I thinking? I could not leave, could I? All I knew was that I was young and had missed so much, I wanted to grasp all I could from life.

I was so torn from then on thinking about the possibility of moving away and my parents needing me. Maybe I had needed them just as much. And, during that time not one thing was ever packed up to move. No plans were made, and it was just odd, thinking back. It is like we were playing a game. I was trying to figure out what direction I would take with my singing and dealing with him and my parents. It was overwhelming at times. We never talked about it. I did not know if he was planning to leave me in Tennessee and just come back for visits, he never said. He never opened up, we never discussed difficult things or defined our plans. He did tell me that he could not live without me. I was second guessing myself at every juncture. The wedding plans proceeded somehow. I cannot remember one thing about the plans. I have blocked most of this out of my mind. So, it is incomplete at best, and I am just trying to get through this part because it was the beginning of a downward spiral in my life that became serious and dangerous. But if I could leave this all out, I certainly would.

One night, I had not attended a revival service at our church, but my mom had gone. The lady that had set the two of us up was there. She made a remark that she was so happy he had found me because he had not been happy in his first marriage. His first marriage! Mom came home and asked if we had ever talked about anything like previous relationships and I thought that was a peculiar thing to ask. I had not had any previous relationships. Oh, a crush here and there, dates, but nothing else. "Of course not," I remember laughing. I made a joke about it, but I could tell she wasn't laughing. "Honey he's been married!" she hesitated. I could not believe what I was hearing. She did not know answers for any of the questions I was flinging at her. She reminded me that he was older than I was and had a past, and that a lot of men do in the service.

Not only was this something that would break my trust in him, but the church was against divorce and remarriage. And I certainly did not want to get caught up in some situation with an ex-spouse.

They had treated my mother terribly because of something that she was a victim of, and here I was contemplating something similar without even knowing it. And the very first person I had really been interested in was someone who had been married. I had no way of contacting him in Texas, and I do not know why I did not ask his mother for his number, but I did not. I wrote him a letter. I was miserable for days until I received his response. He was sorry, he had not mentioned it. Sorry! That is an important thing to not mention I thought. However, it was she who had not wanted to stay married, he would explain. So, in the eyes of the church, he was free to marry. And, to him, it was that simple. But not to me. Why did she not want to remain married to him? There had to be more. But I could not get answers. I needed answers that would somehow make me feel better about all of this. I thought I loved him, but could that be enough for me? I was not sure.

Oh, I proceeded with the plans not really knowing what to do and anticipated him coming home two weeks before the wedding. When I saw him in person, I was happy but still guarded. But when he was away, I was restless, and I missed him. Down deep I wondered if I could really trust him. It had gotten to the point where letters were not enough.

The first few days he was home were great. We went out and talked about our plans and our future. Nothing was clear about Texas or the big attraction it held for him. It weighed on my mind. What pulled him there? It was a mystery. And the fact that I had no information about his previous marriage caused me great concern. There are always two sides to a story. I was afraid to discuss it. We were two weeks away from a wedding that would change both our lives. It was a tough situation; things had soured on my end, but there was a sugar glaze of a wedding looming over everything. And, then one night my oldest sister was home for some reason, the wedding, I guess? I do not remember, but someone knocked on our door. Well, they pounded on the door and Mom, or my sister, answered as I was in bed asleep.

It was about 3:00 a.m. in the morning. He was standing there in the hallway after my mother had let him in and he was demanding to see me. He had not woken my dad thank goodness, but my sister and my mother were wide awake now.

Invitations had been mailed out a few weeks prior. I did have a wedding dress hanging in my room. The lady that made my clothes for singing engagements and church had made it. I do not remember fittings, or anything about that process. The dress was hanging there, and I did not rush to hide it. I was too shocked that he wanted to come into my room. I had never had a man in my room, and I almost felt violated at his intrusion. He began to tell me that we needed to go ahead and get married as quickly as we could. He did not think there was any reason to wait until the wedding. I was over eighteen barely, and could have easily eloped, but I had no intention of doing that.

That was the least thing I wanted to discuss. There were more important concerns at that moment. I needed to know where this erratic behavior had come from. Why had he changed so drastically, and in a brief time? Nothing made sense to me. He kept saying he loved me more than anything, and there was no reason to wait to get married.

After I calmed him down, and reminded him of the time, I sat watching him sleep it off. I went out and apologized to my mom and sister and we sat there dumbfounded at what had occurred. I was angry and hurt. I knew we would have a long talk about this, and I would get answers one way or another. In the early morning, just after daylight, he woke up and looked at me sitting in the chair. I could tell he was embarrassed, and hung over, but I was past ready to talk. I began to ask him why all of this had happened, and he got up, looked for his keys and started to leave with no explanation. He refused to talk about anything with me. Not even the blood stains on his white shirt or his busted lip. I felt that same rush of rejection I had experienced as a little girl. And, my heart was broken, so much so that I could not breathe. *What had just happened? Was I that horrible of a person that someone would have to be drunk to want to marry me?*

My mom was up early and had watched him leave, and immediately came to me and put her arms around me. I was crying uncontrollably, and I could not talk about what happened. She had become concerned about me, especially with the chance of me moving away with no friends or family. And, now his erratic behavior made her question this relationship even more. After a few days had passed, I knew we had to have answers as to our future together.

Our mothers thought that we should face each other and iron all this out. It felt like I was in a movie or spy show, who does this? Trying to see what my best approach was to confront him. I was barely nineteen now, and I had not been out in the world. This was all foreign to me. And to see someone I cared so deeply for acting in this manner, and especially a week from our wedding now was beyond anything I could handle. I had carried a burden around so long, trying to take care of everyone and now my chance at happiness was drifting away unless things changed drastically. I was beyond doubtful because his actions had scared me. I did not want to live my life like this, and at that time I did not know if he would change or not. Nothing was clear, nothing was right. In my heart I was already planning a funeral for what once was a relationship based on lies. I wasn't sure that I could even go through with it even if he had turned around. It all left a bad taste in my mouth. He was wrestling with something, and I had no answers.

Mom rode with me to see him, and sure enough his little sporty car was where it always was. I knew he was there, so I went inside, and Mom stayed in the car, letting me know she was praying. She was always my right or die person when I needed anything, and I surely needed her this time. I poured out my heart and tried to get him to talk to me. I was desperate. We needed to pray, we needed to figure this out. I realized nothing was going to happen and he was not going to talk to me. It was like a wall had gone up between us. And I knew walls so well. I had often put my own up. So, I got angry. It was the worst kind of rejection I knew all too well. When someone that is supposed to love you watches you pouring your heart out to them in need of answers and they do not care enough to stop your pain. Or, to just give you the answers you need. It is cold and calculating. And after I had said what I came to say while he was silent, I told him the wedding was off, and I never wanted to see him again. I had no closure from it. Just like many things in my life had been. I shut the door on that part of my life that day. I never saw him again.

Big tears were falling down my face when I got into the car, and Mom asked if she needed to drive. I told her what had happened, and she said she would oversee everything and cancel all the plans. I was embarrassed and so hurt. I asked what we would do if people showed up at the church. And she shrugged it off like it was no big deal. My mother had such strength for me at that time, I will never forget it. I would not have made it without her during that time. She was my rock. When I got home, I took scissors and tore that wedding dress apart until it was in shreds, heaped on the floor. There amidst that mound of tattered material was my heart. I had given it to someone I thought would cherish it, but that was not the case. I thought because he said he was a Christian and went to church, I would be safe to give him my love. But it only brought me unbearable pain. I stayed in my room and cried for what seemed like days. I had remembered those times when I had such horrible physical pain when I was sick, but I could not tell which was worse, the pain from sickness or mental anguish when your heart is broken. They blurred together and I was beyond miserable.

What had I done to make this happen? I internalized and analyzed it. It had to be me; thinking the burden of what occurred rested on my shoulders. I must have done something, and I racked my brain. It haunted me so. Had I sabotaged myself?

No one called to check on me, that I recall. No calls to see what the plan was for the wedding, and no one checked on mom. She would see people out and they would be apologetic and hem and haw about not knowing what to say. It was like people had made a mad exodus from my life. Some of it was me. I did not want to see anyone. But I did not need to worry, no one was coming. I could not count on anyone. When I promised someone something or that I would be there for something, I was there. I learned through the course of many things in my life that people were not true to their word.

My poor mom was dealing with it and with me and I was broken. Oh, if Mom could help, people always came around or if they needed a favor or a singer, they were quick to call and ask. But now, it was silent. People were living their lives, and good for them. We had been alone with my dad for some time, so it was not really anything new. I felt worse for my mom because she had to take care of me now. I was worthless. Something stopped in me. It was a combination of things building up with my siblings being gone, my career, this situation, I do not know, but I changed. I was fragmented, in pieces, and nothing mattered.

I stopped attending church. I refused to go because I did not want to see anyone. I was too embarrassed to face anyone. I was crushed and I felt betrayed by what had happened. The day that would have been my wedding day, I spent lying across my bed. I could not understand anything that had happened and now I was just void of feelings. I had cried enough tears to last me. I could not eat or sleep. I just lay there wondering how this turned out as it had. I was not thinking rationally; I was asking God why He had even let me get in this situation in the first place. I had tried to live right, and I tried to do what he wanted from me. I only wanted him to be glorified in my life. But here I was. Every door shut, and now my heart had shut down as well. I was raw, and I rebelled. My poor mom took the blunt of it. She would try and talk to me, and I would tell her I did not want to hear anything about how much God loved me or what His will for my life was. It was lying in rubble at my feet with my dress and my happily ever after.

That was the turning point for me. My life spiraled down deeper and deeper in hate and bitterness, and it covered everyone. Family, friends, this man, church, God, everyone. Before, when I was hurt or scared, I would sing and it would give me peace, but now, I could not stomach singing songs about faith and trust. It was laughable, look where I was? I could not even do the normal things people do, fall in love, and get married. Having a career, being happy, none of it was in the cards for me. I disconnected from everything and everyone. I had tried so hard to keep everything going at home. I was not a martyr, but I had made sacrifices to help my parents.

I did not begrudge them, but someone had to step up and it was left to me to do it. Everyone had left me with it. They went to live their lives and I was stuck because I was the youngest and at home.

But now, I was tired. I did not want to take care of anyone anymore. I did not care anymore. I wanted to stop the world and get off. And, all the memories of tough times, of insecurities would come to my mind like uninvited guests. From the time I was a kid trying to carve out my feelings and where I fit in, to now with rejection once again. Mom would come and sit on my bed and try and comfort me. She had told me that she had gotten all the deposits back, and the vendors had sent their best to me. It was like a funeral around our house. I was waiting for someone to put one of those awful ugly wreaths on our door. Because I felt like I was dying inside. Not just from lost love, but all of it came crashing down around me. It had built up for a long time and then erupted. I had let people and circumstances tarnish my once strong armor of faith. It was now filled with gaping holes. My strength was gone along with my joy. I blamed God, and instead of running to Him, I ran from Him.

I went through the motions, school, work, and home. It was just a cycle of events. Oh, I could smile and be cordial when I had to be, but other times I was mean. Just so very mean. I did not even care what came out of my mouth. I was belligerent and just ugly to be around. One evening, Mom said she wanted to talk to me about something. I knew it had to do with God or church, it always did. So, I really did not want to talk, but she looked upset, as we sat down together. She started by saying she had heard a few things that she felt I needed to know. Of course, I jumped on that with a smart remark and something like it must be our good church friends gossiping. Oh, how my mother hated gossip.

Mom had heard some things. Anything about that situation just got to me even though some time had passed.

She said she did not think his behavior had anything to do with whether he loved me or not and that he had tried hard. "Really, I'm that hard to love?" I just shook my head. "He had to go off the deep end to get away from me?" "No, honey, it's not like that," she went on with a gentleness in her voice. "He tried, but he was fighting an internal battle with a lifestyle he could not just shake off." A lifestyle? What!!! I knew exactly what she meant. I had remembered those awful thoughts that had come to my mind wondering why there were so many things unsaid. I could not believe what she was saying. She went on, "I think he had hoped that in meeting you, he would change, but only God can change someone like that." I was stunned as I reminded her that was a lot to put on me. "So, you see, God protected you from going into a life where you would have been horribly unhappy. God took care of you, honey, can't you see that?"

I stared at her and then I started laughing. I could not stop laughing. I made a joke about it, and I could tell she was not wavering from convincing me that all was well because God had intervened. "Well, why didn't God keep me from meeting him in the first place, Mother? Where was God when all this was happening? Where was God when I was sick, and lost so many years of my life, and where is He now? Where is He while we struggle through all this alone? I was humiliated and betrayed by this man and the people around him, who knew his issues. I don't want to hear any more of this," I told her as I got up to leave the house.

I had come from a long line of hot tempers. And I was becoming more volatile as time went on. I did not know what was happening to me. I could not help myself. I would blow up. I could not control the rage inside of me. We had other talks and Mom tried to get through to me. One night, I was lying on my bed, and she came in to see if I was OK. I mumbled something to her, and she sat down on the edge of my bed. I could tell she wanted to talk, so I just looked at her. Finally, she said, "Honey, I haven't heard you play the piano and sing in so long. I wish you would play some. Daddy and I miss it so much. If you got back into your music, it would help you heal. Music has always been such a part of your life."

"What you really mean is am I going back to church, and the answer is no, I am not," I said. She had tears streaming down her face now, and I knew I had caused this pain. I was selfish and she had so much on her already. "Why would you even want to go to that church mom? They treated you like an outcast. They laughed when my brother got up to preach Mom, and they were jealous and mean-spirited." She just sat looking at me.

"Mom, have you ever given up, just thrown your hands up and said forget it I am done? I know you have had it so hard. You have dealt with so much in your life. Have you ever felt like God left you? Did you ever want to lash out at Him? Your faith ever got shaky, and you wondered if He really could deliver on his promises?" By now, my own tears were falling down my face and on to my pillow.

She smiled at me and said, "Honey, God is all I have really. He has always been there for me. No matter how you feel, I can never lose faith. I will never deny His love for me or you. And I will trust Him until the day I die." I remember saying, "You kill me, Mom." And she laughed a little. "I only pray He can change your heart, and I will never stop praying that He changes your mind." She wiped her face. "You can run fast from Him, but He will be by your side no matter what. You are special, and you are anointed, you have such gifts, Gaye. God will never tire of loving you, never stop wanting you back. He will not stop fighting for you." I just shook my head at her, "Don't worry about me, I'm fine."

I was far from fine, and she knew it. She told me that she wished I could go live my life like the others, but she knew fully well I would not. She left my room and I just lay there, but no song would come for the first time in my life. I had no song to sing. The curtain had come down. I could not rally my thoughts in any positive way. I just felt like I was sinking deeper into darkness.

I worked and finished my associate degree in Business. And I completed all but a couple courses for my four-year degree. I was paying as I went and taking as many courses as I could manage. Dad was doing OK now, and I was happy that at least that part of our world was on an even keel. I had worked at a great company, but they had recently gone out of business. I loved working there and met the greatest people.

When the company closed, I was asked to go to another company, to do the same thing, oversee medical emergencies and process insurance claims for the employees. I was only supposed to stay for six weeks while their other person was on maternity leave. I was young, and this was a teamster union environment, but I needed the experience and a job.

So, I had a lot to get used to and a tremendous amount to learn. I was up to the challenge. The personnel manager, his secretary and I shared a large open office, with a little first aid room at the back. He was usually in a good mood until the union steward came around, and it made him nervous. The corporate people were upstairs, and the plant was on the same level as our office. I got to know everyone fast and loved every minute I was there. However, I was called the kid, and the plant employees struggled with me being in a leadership role.

It was a large plant that made fireplace accessories and other metal pieces for stores like Sears. One of my duties was plant safety director. I had to dress in white, wear huge safety goggles and carry a clipboard. It was my job to make sure plant employees and all departments within the plant were meeting the safety guidelines each morning and each afternoon. The first few days, people looked at me like I was too young to be there, I could hear laughter, and I knew I was not being taken seriously.

I would have to tell ladies on the assembly lines to remove curlers and shower caps from their heads. Most did not take kindly to that, and I would have to advise them that they would be written up and or sent home for noncompliance. One large woman got right in my face one day and told me she would not do anything a little punk said to do. I told her that she would be written up and that I would be meeting with the union steward as soon as I got back to my office. I was scared, at only five two or five three in high heels. And she towered over me. But I had to stand my ground and I did what I had promised. My legs shook all the way back to the office that day. The next day, and for days after that, I had problems with people on the assembly lines and, in the press department and painting. You name it, they really tried to beat me down and usurp my authority.

Once, the union steward came in and said to me and the secretary that people were going out on Friday evening, and asked if we would like to go along. He and I had talked a few times, and he was starting to come around to visit. The personnel manager thought it was great that we were all friendly. I guess he had hoped it would somehow spill over into work and people would not file grievances against him. Anyway, we all met up at a local bar and restaurant on Friday evening and they were all drinking.

I had never had a drink before and had remembered what my dad had told me about his experience. But I was young and wanted to have fun, and I drank a few drinks that night. I wanted to experiment. I had one, and it hit me hard, but it tasted good, so I ordered another, and after a couple more during the evening I had a nice glow about me. I was slightly numb from the drinks and had laughed and enjoyed myself for the first time in a long time. I was relaxed for a change and that felt wonderful.

One day, after my morning rounds in the plant, I heard a commotion in the hall leading to our offices and I saw the union steward, a group of people and a woman holding her arm in the air coming towards us. They were calling for me. I jumped up and had them take her into the small first aid room and because there were so many people that had come with her from the plant, I closed the door for her privacy. I did not need to ask her what happened, I knew. She had tripped the press with her foot while her hand was under it. I could tell her hand had been mangled into the metal glove she wore around the large presses. She was bleeding heavily. I called her by name, and she responded so that I knew she had not gone into shock yet. I said, "Now listen to me, this is bad, it is going to require you to go to the hospital and we have already called an ambulance. But I want you to know that I am going with you, and I will be there every moment with you until I know everything is OK. But I need you to elevate your arm right now, so that you will not bleed as much. And, no matter what happens I will not let them remove your glove, is that OK with you?" She said yes, and began to tell me how dumb she felt having tripped the press with her foot by mistake.

That was the least of my worries at that point. The people from upstairs had made their way down to observe and see what was happening, and managers from inside the plant were checking in, it was a mad house. But I would not let anyone around her, and soon the emt's arrived. The first thing they wanted to do was remove the glove and I refused to let them. I said, "I will be traveling right behind you and if I get to the hospital and you have removed that glove, I will have your jobs, do you understand!" As soon as we arrived, they rushed her back and called a hand surgeon immediately. The personnel manager had come down to the hospital as well, and he was visibly shaken.

His feelings always got in the way of things, and I had wished that he had just stayed at the plant. He was always afraid of the union. Her family had arrived, and we were all waiting for her to be examined. They immediately scheduled her for surgery and were preparing her when the doctor came out and talked with us. He said that he would be able to save her hand, and a couple of fingers due to quick action and the decision to not remove the glove. I was so relieved. Her surgery would last several hours, as they tried to remove the glove that had embedded into her fingers and hand. Her family was grateful. And after I thought I could drive again from my nervousness, I drove back to the plant knowing she was in great hands. I had shed some tears on the way because my heart ached for her. She was never late, never missed work, just a great lady that loved her job and the company. I arrived at lines of people waiting for me. I had called the personnel manager to tell him I was headed back to work, and I guess he had told people.

When I came in, there were cheers and clapping and I was taken back by all of it. I was called a soldier, a trooper, and an angel. I was not the "kid" any longer. And that night when I went to bed I could see her hand, the worst accident in that plant in many years. I had made the decisions that helped instead of hurting someone. Maybe, I had a little value. It took me forever the next few days getting through the plant. I was hugged, given gifts, given food and the main thing it did was create a different environment where people trusted me. I went on to be there over a year and loved everyone so much. I was heartbroken when the woman decided she wanted to come back to her job. I had a great send off, with lots of hugs, tears, and speeches. I would miss them all terribly.

Dad had a heart attack somewhere in this period, I cannot recall exactly when. But I met Mom at the hospital. He was in ICU. Mom had told me to go in the next visiting hours, and I was happy to get to see Dad. When I walked in his room across from the nurses' station, he was smoking. All his oxygen had been removed and there he was puffing away on a cigarette. "Dad what in the world are you doing?" I was so mad.

It had hit me so hard that he had nearly died from a heart attack but was still smoking, and in the ICU of all places. His doctor was at the desk and heard me and called me out of the room. He said he knew this looked very strange, but Dad was more agitated by not smoking and it was causing more stress on his heart than if they let him have one. I was mad, sad, hurt, and angry; I was all emotions. I told Dad we would be in the waiting room, and I left his room. I sat by my mom on a little couch. As I looked around the room, I observed families. Some larger groups and a few smaller ones huddled together. It looked like most of their pastors were there. And there we were, just Mom and me. By now it did not bother me. I could have cared less about people. But I hurt for my mother. Where was her pastor? We were still in the Church of God of Prophecy at that time. Hour after hour we sat there. In all fairness, he could have called the house. But I doubt it. Mom had a lot on her plate. She was working and taking care of my dad and went to church every chance she had. I was doing everything I could to help her. And where were her friends? She was the first person they called when they needed help. She and I had no one. No family that came, no friends that showed up and no church that cared. It is sad and I hate to say it, but it was true at the time. And my heart became harder, seeing her go through these things. She must have known what I was thinking at times because she would smile at me, grab my hand, and tell me that she and I could do anything as long as we had God and each other.

My mother was the kindest and most selfless person I knew. Sometimes she would come home from church, and I would hear pans clanking in the kitchen. I would go check on her and she would be cooking a meal for someone that was sick, or that had lost a loved one. Most of the time, she did not even know the people, but she still took food, gave encouraging words, and was Jesus to people. When our church had church bazaars at the big mall, she brought food, baked goods, and crafts. We usually rode together, I was sick at that point, but I would go with her and sit or try and help. She would carry large cookie sheets of hot homemade bread into the mall and the smell would be wonderful. Her contributions brought in so much money for the church.

People would stop her and want to buy the bread, but she would tell them that it was too hot to wrap, but if they came to our church tables, she would wrap and sell it. Most of her customers were men, and they often took it right off the cookie sheet before she could even get into the mall. Then one year we had to start taking orders for the next day when her bread sold out at the entrance to the mall. She charged two or three dollars for it, which was a lot back then. But because it was for the building fund no one seemed to care. Most times businessmen that worked in offices around or near the mall would give her large donations if they could get extra of her bread and goodies. They would meet us at her car in the mall parking lot. Can you even imagine? It was the craziest thing. Often, they would walk off in their expensive suits with their mouths stuffed with her famous fudge and holding a large bag with bread and other sweet treats. On a few occasions, everything that she had brought for that day was sold right out of the car before we even tried to get inside the mall. And we had to hurry back home to make more.

And for every fundraiser or for the building fund she was first to say count on me when called. She helped people in the church. She took so much of her time to make sure every detail of an event was covered. She carried everything in her purse, like tape, a measuring tape, scissors, you name it. I think years later when glue guns came out it was the happiest, I had seen her in a long time.

I once watched her hem a wedding gown right before the girl walked down the aisle. I was on the platform at one wedding and saw the bride pass out. Everyone froze and no one moved to help her. But Mom came thundering down the middle aisle of the church and took care of the situation. She had been in the back directing the wedding party. She cleaned people's houses when they had surgery, and she never said no to anyone. She gave her last dollar to others. At holidays, she would bake constantly and then I would help her deliver huge trays to everyone she had done business with that year. They would look for it each year and we would start to get calls from attorney offices, and doctors, wanting to know when she was bringing goodies so they could be sure to be there. I had to start keeping lists so that we did not miss anyone.

CHAPTER FIFTEEN

My mother was a Foster Grandparent. I did not know for a long time, but she had become one and would go downtown in the evenings to be with troubled kids in one of the worst parts of town. Kids that needed love got it from her. We knew about it finally because she had to tell me they had done a news story on her, and I always watched that channel. The kids adored her.

But now as I sat in that ICU waiting room thinking about all of this, and her impact on others, it was still just the two of us. I could never change that. I tried to fill the void, but I could not be her husband, or the children she missed so terribly or her pastor, church, or friends. Everyone let her down it seemed. They always did. And that made me feel even worse, more bitter. I saw how she was treated. She knew what I was thinking at one point because she said, "Honey, I am glad it is you and I here together." I wanted to say so much to her, but it was not the time. She was so worried about my dad.

He was finally able to come home, and I was happy. I would wait until he went to bed at night and mom was resting before her third shift at the hospital and I would tell her to have a safe evening and head toward the door, out for the evening. She would say, "You be careful honey. God is not going to let you go, you know that. He will find you because he loves you. He is relentless in his love." I would grab my keys and say, "Love you, Mom," and head out into the night, ignoring her comments.

Dad went to bed super early since he was still recuperating so I was always in the bar around 7:00 p.m. Happy Hour! The bartenders knew me by now, I had become a regular. I usually sat at the bar for a few minutes until my table was ready. It was always two for one during happy hour, and they would bring two instead of one large drink. I would use a straw and suck them down like water as fast as I could and by my third, I would start to feel the tingling around my mouth. And then it came, the glorious numbness after my fourth drink. At this point, I would just sit and sip it. Oh, Dad was right; it did take care of what ails you, even if only for a brief time. I could hear him sometimes in my mind saying, "Don't you ever drink, you understand?" But that little girl was long gone. I do not think he ever knew.

The place I frequented was an eating establishment as well, so early evenings families would still be there having dinner with their children. So, I always felt safe.

I had dated. But after the last experience I was not interested, my heart was fragile. Besides, lost ships gravitate to each other. And I certainly did not want another loser in my life, things were bad enough. If I admitted it, there were so many things about my past that made me unapproachable. My attitude about everything in general was the worst. And there were tall walls around me to keep anyone from hurting me. The bartender and I became friends and he protected me from people. I usually got my special table. First one at the top of the stairs so that I could see the bar and who was coming or going. After the families left, it would start to fill up with two kinds of people. Either you were a serious drinker, or you were there to try and pick someone up.

Men and their shenanigans were fun to watch. But most of the time, I was in my own little world lost in a utopia of liquor and trying to forget why I was there alone, at my little table at the top of the stairs. The New Year's Day prior to my twenty-fifth birthday, I woke up at the bar at around 3:00 a.m., with streamers around my neck and holding a balloon like a teddy bear. So that is what I had become.

I was still working every day, often with a hangover. Mom began to worry because Dad had begun to lose weight after his heart attack. He would cough and choke on his food and even drinking coffee, his life juice, would make him sputter and clear his throat a few times. He had made the decision to go to the Veterans Administration Clinic in Chattanooga, something my mother frowned upon. She was not a fan back then of the care veterans received there. After they had examined him, they explained that he would need testing at the Veterans Hospital in Nashville, and they wanted to have this done rather quickly. So, the three of us drove to Nashville one morning for his evaluation. We had made a few trips to the hospital and each time we would stop at the Cracker Barrel on the way home. My folks liked eating there.

Then one day, we took him, and he was to be admitted. His testing would begin the next morning and it would be a series of extensive tests that were explained to both he and my mom. I had made the decision not to go in to hear the doctor's plan of action. I guess, not hearing would make it all go away, or not seem as real as it was. But down deep, I knew something bad was wrong. Mom did too.

I drove us home and mom got ready for work without much talking between us. After she left, I headed out. I would go to work, get home, wait until Dad called us that evening, and I was gone again. It was hard to stay home. Not that being in a bar made things better, but at least there was laughter, and that is something we had not done much of in a long time. After several days, he was ready to come home, and we went to get him after I got off work. He did not want to talk much and did not offer to give us any details or reasons for his symptoms. The silence made things worse, and no one wanted to stop at Cracker Barrel that night. As I drove us home, I thought the worst, because that is how my mind worked. If I expected the worst, I was not disappointed. There was no good side, or good anything. I knew it was bad news. And I choked to keep from crying and swallowed back the tears as I drove.

My mother was quiet, more so than before. I knew she had a gut feeling too. When we finally got home and got Dad settled, he gave us the news. They had diagnosed him with an advanced stage of throat cancer. That word carries a punch. Cancer, it is heavy and sad and hardly ever means anything positive. We comforted each other. My heart broke for my parents. Was it never going to end, all the troubles? We were always heading up a high mountain or plummeting into a low valley. There was never just a balance, just a time when things were stable for a minute. Of course, I gave them both a pep talk, and we will beat this speech, and then went to my room and covered my head with the pillow so they wouldn't hear my sobs. Nothing was right, and nothing was going to be right again.

I drove us to Nashville the day before Dad's surgery. We had to bring him up the day prior for preoperative testing. He was nervous and edgy that day because he had to stop smoking at least a week or so before the surgery. It had something to do with his treatment afterward not being as effective if he had smoked recently. Dad had not wanted to stop and eat at his favorite Cracker Barrel, and I really do not think he had eaten much once he had received the news. He had lost so much weight. Mom and I were quiet on the ride. I was thinking to myself, after today, I would not hear dad talk again. They were doing an extensive surgery removing his esophagus, his larynx (voice box), and more depending on how the cancer had spread.

I knew he was scared, but he would never say it. We were all scared. I knew he wanted to cry, but he would never show that kind of emotion. And I knew he was afraid to die, but he never felt worthy enough to run to God. He had smoked and it had such a hold on him no matter how he tried he could not quit. Dad became a Christian but when the urges to smoke overtook him, he felt defeated and gave up because he could not let go of his demon. And, no matter what, he was not convinced that God would take the desire away.

And now here we were. The very thing he held on to was killing him. This surgery would slow down the process, but I could not help thinking down the road and what would happen. Or, even how soon we may lose him. We saw him before the surgery, but he was groggy and quiet. I told him I loved him and after Mom visited with him alone, we headed to the waiting room. It was like déjà vu; had we not been in an ICU waiting room not that long ago alone, just the two of us? Mom and I were a pair, we came as a set. She was upbeat and positive, and I was downhearted and negative. She could pray, but I could not. I was so bitter and had been for some time. I thought again, where is everyone? No family, no friends, no church pastor, we were alone in another waiting room hoping for the best but understanding the magnitude of the kind of cancer Dad had and the extensive surgery they were performing.

It was many hours later when the doctor came in and talked with us. He looked exhausted. We were exhausted and anxious. He told us that they had to remove much more tissue, and parts of his stomach. Much more than anticipated along with the original surgery plan and a feeding tube had been inserted. That had hit me hard. A feeding tube from now on. My dad loved food and to think he would be fed through a tube in his stomach from now on along with not being able to talk, hurt my heart. I swallowed back tears to keep from losing it in front of my mom.

Of course, I was not expecting anything less. That dark cloud always hovered over us. He advised us that we could not see dad that evening, they were keeping him sedated until the next evening, so it was best for us to go home and return later. We would be notified if there were problems, but he was stable.

So, from the next day until many days later I would get up and go to work and come home. Mom would be dressed, and we would drive the few hours to Nashville, visit with Dad and then return home in enough time so that Mom could get ready and go to her job on third shift. I would go out for a few hours and drown my sorrows and then return home to sleep before getting up for work. And, then we did it all over again. We were several days into this, and Mom was looking very tired. I came home from work, and she said, "We are not going this evening. We will call the nurses station so daddy will know, but we need a night at home to rest." I knew she was exhausted. She called and explained to the nurse to relay this message to Dad. I answered the phone shortly after to this little noise. It absolutely broke my heart. It was Dad calling. He was trying to use his little machine, (Electrolarynx), to talk. He had not learned to really use it yet, and it was the saddest noise I had ever heard. I was crying so hard but trying to keep it together so he would not know. I explained that Mom was tired, and we would be up the next evening as quickly as we could get there. He made little sounds and

I tried to make it look like I understood by saying yes or OK. I told him we loved him over and over and then we hung up.

Mom slept and I went out. I drank so much that night trying to forget that call that I did not even remember coming home. I woke up in the driveway sometime in the wee hours. What had happened to me? Dad was finally able to come home after a few weeks, and it was a busy place setting up everything he would need. We had to get a powerful blender to puree his food for the feeding tube. One evening, he got depressed about his food selections and made faces at what we were trying to feed him. I jumped in the car and went to McDonald's and got a McRib sandwich, of all things, and pureed it with iced tea while he looked on and smiled big at me. It went down that tube so easily I started thinking of good things he could have. We found out by trial and error what could go down his feeding tube. He needed to regain his weight. Of course, Dad could not taste any of it, but it was a psychological need. And his doctor had laughed when he found out what all I had put down that tube. "Well, if it goes down without stopping up the tube, then that's great; give him what he wants."

Dad remained home for a time, but he began to have complications, so we were back in the Veteran's Hospital in Nashville. One of his long-time military friends came to visit him and that was a wonderful change from seeing us. When he came home this time, we had to agree to place him in a facility where they could give him the care he could not receive at home. I dreaded him going into one of those places, but we really did not have any other choice. I had been out of work due to changes in the company, so I would be able to have more time to stay with him. That was a relief considering the condition he was in and his inability to talk with anyone.

One day, I drove over to the facility later than I had intended. I hated that place, it never smelled fresh or clean and it was so dreary. Mom and I had decorated dad's room, but it was not enough to keep him from being homesick for home. When I got to his room sometime after lunch, he was lying there with a large container half full of what looked like mushroom soup, and it had spilled on his pajamas, where he had tried to feed himself.

His clothes were soaked, and his tube was completely blocked by a large piece of mushroom. He grabbed my hand and was trying to tell me what happened. He was thrashing in the bed and his eyes were wild. I could tell he was scared. I had to do everything I could to keep from crying; he was so pitiful. My heart ached for him. The strong confident man I knew was now reduced to this little scared person looking to me for help. I said, "Dad, calm down, I will take care of this and get you cleaned up and fed. I will be right back." He held onto my hand, and I kissed the top of his little head. He was so upset, and I was furious, but I did not want him to see it.

I left the room with the container of soup in my hand and headed to the nurse's station. The longer I walked, the more upset I got. I asked to speak to the head nurse, and, after a minute or so, she came from around the desk like she had all day. I asked her if she was aware of what my dad had for lunch, and she said "yes" in a condescending way which only sparked my temper more. I said, "Well I would like you to have some." and I threw that carton at her. It splashed on her clothes and shoes and over the desk. It splashed the wall and the floor.

She looked dumbfounded. "Why in the world would you think he could eat this? Why would you think he could feed himself? And why has he laid in this mess without anyone coming to check on him?" I fired questions at her. She gave me lame excuses, and I was in tears by now and said, "Could you let your dad be treated this way, in his helpless condition?" Before she could even answer, I advised her between clinched teeth to get her people in gear and get him bathed. I instructed her to get his tube changed, the bed changed, and to get him something to eat. I gave her five minutes to do it, or I promised to clean the floor with her. I meant every word.

My heart was racing, and I was trying to calm down as I walked back towards dad's room. Before I went in, I put on my phony happy face that I used more frequently than I cared to. I hated fake people and I had become a good pretender myself by now, it seemed. When I got in the room, I told him there had been a great miscommunication and they were handling it now. I even told him they were so sorry that they had upset him. It was all lies, except for the part that they were sorry, because they were sorry individuals and lazy. But I could not let him think people were really like what I had encountered because he would be scared to stay there. He was so fragile and vulnerable, and it was my job to protect him. The room began to buzz with activity and, before much time had passed, he was clean and had something to eat, and I had chosen to feed him. Later, I met with the administrator and let the staff know in no uncertain terms that this would not happen again.

By the night of my twenty fifth birthday, I had been drinking heavily for a while. I went alone most nights. I always saw Dad, and, when I knew he was comfortable and resting, I would head out into the night. I only went to one place, because I felt safe there. It sounds so silly for a girl to feel safe in a bar alone, but I did. I knew people there, workers and bartenders. I never thought about taking drugs because I had been on so many as a child, but liquor was different for me. It was still somewhat of a drug in that it numbed your senses, and made your pain ease a little. I would be sitting there, and old feelings or memories would start to fill my mind and tears would flow only long enough for me to wipe them away and drink a little more until I knew I would not remember anything for at least a little while.

My dad was dying, and my mom and I were struggling financially because of the bills dad had accumulated before he had surgery in Nashville. I helped when I could. Dad had family here, but they did not come around, and my siblings were not here. The only one we heard from it seemed was my oldest sister. I know, you would think I should have initiated contact with everyone with updates and all our wonderful news from home, but I had enough to deal with and so did Mom. I did not need anyone to feel sorry for us, we were OK if we had each other to stay afloat, but it would not have been so lonely had people stayed connected.

Friends and I were going out to celebrate my big birthday. Where had the time gone? One of my friends was at our house getting ready with me, and she was teasing me about picking up a guy on my birthday. I laughed at her, "Well, I have never picked up anyone before and I am perfectly fine not doing that. Meeting guys are the least thing I want to do." Mom said kind of randomly, "Who knows, maybe tonight you will meet your handsome prince." I groaned at her, "Mom, do not hold your breath," and I kissed her goodbye. We were off to a night of bubbly and celebration.

The place was always crowded on Saturday, but this evening March 12, 1983, it was not too bad. We had left around 7:00 p.m. or a little later in the evening. It only took a couple minutes to get my favorite table and my friend had brought a cake. It was about nine o'clock or so, I do not really remember when I saw two people I had not seen in there before. From where my table was up a couple steps and right between the two pillars on either side, I had a clear view of all the bar happenings. I could also see who was coming in and leaving. It was a prime spot for people watching.

I did not notice at first, but then I saw a short man talking to a tall man. And he was taller than anyone in the place. What originally caught my eye was that the shorter man was rattling on and never stopped talking so the other guy could get a word in. I found out much later that this guy was trying to get Bruce to sell drugs for him and Bruce had already told him no, but the guy kept talking. He was surely high on something that night.

My friend watched me watch them, and she could not believe it. I had never looked at anyone in that bar because I was not there for that reason. I was there to forget, or at least try for a little while. But I was fascinated. I then began to look at Bruce. I could not understand what kept drawing my eyes to him. He was good looking. He had longer hair that went down to his shirt collar and it was extremely attractive on him. He wore glasses and a flannel shirt. I did not see until later in the evening, but he had on corduroys, and boots. I got the feeling that he was not there to impress anyone like a lot of the others that came in and tried to do. We caught each other's eye a few times and I would quickly look away. My poor friend was losing her mind at this. I finally told her that I could not help it, and that if she would get up and go to the restroom or the bar, he would come up to our table. He told me much later, that he was waiting for her to leave the table so that he could come up. She said, she couldn't believe how I was acting, but she got up and headed down the steps. He passed her coming up.

I was on the verge of a mental breakdown, I really was. I was tired, frustrated, and I felt so hopeless and lost inside. You get to the point when you keep fighting yourself and trying to make everything better that it starts to wear on you. I could not be everything to everyone, but I tried my hardest. I was depleted. Tired of being a cheerleader, tired of the facade I wore. I was lonely, and I felt lost. Thoughts about the Lord would come into my mind on occasion. Oh, I remembered the faith I had as a little girl when I was all in one hundred percent. But I felt God had let me down. I felt He had left me and moved on. The empty house that was my life was boarded up. As quickly as thoughts of me running to him for refuge would come, they would leave me just as quickly. There was no room left for any of that. Something deep inside me ached for all this madness to stop. And I was not about to trust anyone again.

I was not falling for all of that. I would remember something my mom would say about nurturing her faith in God. "Gaye, when you exercise your faith, God will show up!" I knew that my faith over the years was like building blocks. When I was little, I had faith, it was a simple faith, but things would happen, and I would be encouraged to trust again for something else. I would pray, and God would answer, and my faith would be strong for a time. But isn't that what faith really is? It is little things that keep you encouraged, spots in time where you pray and God does a miraculous thing, and that keeps you encouraged until the next time. Or it gives you boldness to share with someone else who is also needing their faith encouraged.

The more I was determined to believe God was going to do something in my life, He would show up when I was young. He had healed me gloriously. But that seemed long ago now. So, how had I become this person? How had I got so lost and so bitter? I had looked at people and how they had let me down every time and that became bigger than life. Now I was sitting in a bar and a man was coming toward my table and I felt a mix of unusual feelings. I thought, *I am not giving up my heart again, so do not even try.* But there he was, and he knelt by the table and said, "Hi, I'm Bruce." And I blurted out, "I'm Gaye, well not really that's just my name." Oh, the horrors! Had I just said that? He looked a little surprised but just smiled at me. But at that moment, the strongest feelings came over me. I cannot explain it to anyone, never have been able to and never will. We have talked and cried about our meeting many times through the years, but he had no idea of what kind of pain I was in that night.

I felt as if everything was fine for once. I was good. I get so emotional remembering because it was so special. It was as if I could lay my head on his shoulder, and rest. The pain, the rejection, burden of being a caretaker and sheer bitterness had left me for the moment and I was caught up in this man's aura. He was unpretentious, unassuming, and comfortable. The first gentleness I had felt in so long. And he had only just knelt at my table. He did not know what I was experiencing. But he asked if he could sit down. My friend came back to the table, and we all talked for hours. A friend of his joined us and we laughed so much getting acquainted. We realized that we were transplants. Bruce was from Indiana, my friend from Ohio and I was from Michigan, and we were all here because of our dad's work, or in my case his retirement.

I kept wanting to pinch myself. What was in my drinks? What kind of spell had this guy cast over me? I have never felt like that. He was like therapy of some kind. Just sitting by him cast the sun over my darkness. He lit up the place. And to this day, when I see him coming in the door, I get that same feeling. All is well, and the air is back in the room. Whatever it was that night was wonderful, but when we had closed the place down, and headed to the parking lot, my walls started forming again. The chilly wind woke me up fast from this little fairytale. *Guard your heart, do not do something dumb,* kept running through my mind. *It was just a nice evening, but it is over now.* I still felt that feeling of contentment if he was standing there. But I got in the car, quickly trying to get away, and he motioned for me to roll down the window and he asked for my number pulling out a rumpled drink napkin. That is what you did back then.

A guy would ask for a number with a cocktail napkin, and he would not know if he got the girl's correct number or a bogus one until he got somewhere where there was a telephone to check it out. And, sometimes the ink would fade on a few of the numbers from the guy holding that napkin as if his life depended on it. I gave him my number, my correct number, not sure I even wanted him to call. I did not think I had it in me to start anything and I was troubled because of how he made me feel. He leaned in quickly and kissed me fast, just a peck, and said Happy Birthday again. We all left, going in separate directions, and would probably never see each other again.

On the way home, my friend was laughing and talking excitedly about meeting them and how much fun it had been. All the time, I was trying to figure out that feeling I had felt around him. Where had that come from? I had never experienced anything like that before being near someone and being so drawn to them. But it wasn't a romantic feeling entirely, it was sheer contentment when he was nearby. Being around him, that night had given me such peace. I felt everything that clattered and raged in my head quieted with him there. I had almost forgotten what my mom had said before I had left for the evening, about this night, maybe meeting my prince. But when my friend flung open the door to our house at four in the morning, Mom was sitting in the den wide awake waiting for all the details. How strange this all was.

She had wanted to hear all about our evening which I felt was very odd, she had never asked me one thing about being out. In the past she was afraid to ask what I had been up to. But this night was odd in many ways. She had been off from work, and it was strange to see her up and so anxious to talk. I did not say a word, I left the two of them talking about the guy I had met, and I went to my room and shut the door. My head was spinning, partly because I was intoxicated and not totally from the drinks.

This was not a normal meeting between people. I did not really know how to understand the evening, and certainly did not want to talk the next day, as I was still mulling it over in my head. I was hoping he would not call because I was a little afraid of what had transpired with him the night before. I was always in control of my feelings and emotions when I was around other people and always very guarded. But something had happened inside me that night. I could not explain it and I sure was not going to share it with anyone or him for fear they would think I was weird. He did call the next afternoon and asked me to his parents' house to watch television and get better acquainted that evening.

Yeah right, I was thinking. *Come to see your etchings? No thanks.* "I am sorry, I do not know you and I am not coming to your house!" I said. He told me he worked second shift until Sundays when he would work first shift.

He was polite and seemed to understand my concern and we hung up the phone. And that would be that. Had I self-sabotaged myself as usual? I was good at doing that. I had missed so many opportunities by just shutting down. Giving in to the doubt instead of grabbing the moment regardless of the outcome. I was too scared to take risks; I had tried before and got hurt so badly, and nothing was worth that kind of pain again. So, this was all right. But better not start something then be hurt later. What a sad way to live your life. But that was me… that was my truth.

That next Thursday was Saint Patrick's Day, and, of course, I was in my favorite bar early. It was already crowded to the point that people were against the walls two or three people deep. I had not thought much else about everything it had all been too peculiar. There was laughter, and like always people were floating food to me over the crowd. I do not know why, but every time I was there, people sent food over to me. The bartender would say, "Girl, you have it made. You do not have to pay for anything." I paid for drinks, but not all of them. But these people were kind to me. No expectations, just hey she looks hungry send her over some food. This night I had to wait a few minutes for my favorite table, but finally I was able to sit down, and I was in my happy space. The friend of Bruce's that had been with him that first night we met, came to my table. This was not the guy that had talked so much and so fast. This was his friend, and he was funny and made us all laugh. He loved to mingle, and he had a pickup line or two. But he was alone. So, when he spotted me, he came over and asked me where Bruce was. I told him I did not know and that I had not seen him.

He scanned the room and then said, "Here, watch my jacket, I need to mingle, and oh, I know where he is, I'm going to call him and tell him you are here." "I do not need you to call anyone for me, and I do not babysit people's clothes." I said as he was walking down the steps, but he was not listening, and had already found a group to join.

I do not know how much time went by, I was just watching people, when Bruce walked up the stairs headed for my table. I was flooded with that feeling again. It is going to be OK. Everything will be fine. He just sat down and started talking to me. I could not get my words out for my big smile. I was so happy to see him, and I did not even know why. He had no idea the effect he had on me. And I surely would not be able to explain it if he had asked.

From then on, Bruce and I were together. We would talk for hours on end. We would laugh, and he held my hand. I would hold his so tightly, and he would smile at me probably thinking oh, she likes me. He had no idea; I was holding on for dear life. I had mulled this over in my mind so many times, but whatever he brought; however, he made me feel the way he did, I needed that in my life. Every time I saw him, I got that way that it was is all better, he is here. Relief would come over me.

I did not have any idea why this person had such an effect on me. I have said this over and over to myself, but I was beginning to count on him and that was not a good place for me. One way or another, the things, or people I loved the most slipped through my fingers like sand. It was inevitable, that history would repeat itself. I would be rejected again. The more I told myself to keep my distance, the more I was drawn to the way he made me feel. I liked him for sure, but it was more than that. It was something I could not control. I look back now, and we both know that God was in it all along. Bruce had even told his friends way before meeting me that year, that he would be married in 1983.

I usually brought my dad home from the nursing home on Saturday when he was able and felt he could make the trip. If not, Mom or I would go visit with him at the home. He was so frail. But I knew how to manage his tubes, and care for him so it was a time we shared together. And it got him away from that awful place. I had told Bruce, that I would not be available one Saturday in late April. Dad was feeling like he could come home for a day. I had explained about my dad's condition, and that this was alone time for us so he could not come over until later in the evening, after I had taken Dad back. Bruce had not understood why he could not come over, and he did not know that I was very protective of my dad. It had been just the three of us for so long. I was not about to let someone invade dad's privacy, especially now when he was a shell of the person he had been. The cancer had taken a toll on him in so many ways and my heart ached for him. It had robbed him of everything, had done horrible things to his body, and he was wasting away from us.

That Saturday, I got Dad and had settled him on the couch to rest, and there was a knock at the door. We had only been home a short time. When I opened the door, Bruce was standing there. "Why are you here?" I asked him, quizzingly. "Why did you come? You cannot come in." "I want to meet your dad. I have met your mom, and I want to meet him."

"Please let me come in, Gaye; I want to meet him, and I won't stay long if he gets tired." I knew Dad could hear me, so I let him come in grudgingly. I watched Bruce to see his reaction seeing Dad in that condition. I just knew he was going to act awkward and make my dad uncomfortable. I introduced the two and my dad seemed excited.

He sat up and grabbed the little kids board he used to write with. It was one of those boards that had a little plastic pencil, and you would write on the board and then pull up the plastic and the words would disappear. They had given him these at the hospital and they were perfect and compact. Bruce sat close to him. But I hovered like a helicopter pretending to do things in the kitchen, while watching them.

Bruce had surprised me that afternoon. He was kind and funny and they talked for just a little while before Dad lay back down to rest. I did not see Bruce after a time and found him by the bathroom door in the hallway. He was emotional.

"I wish I had known him when he was healthy. This is so sad," Bruce said.

I hugged him and thanked him for being so kind, and I told him I was sorry for being hard on him for wanting to meet my dad. I saw a sincerity in him that day that I had not often seen in an individual. And he was comfortable enough to show his vulnerability, and what a great heart he had.

We were out one evening with friends later and the time was right, the stars aligned and all that corny stuff, and we said I love you. It was fast. I was in love for the very first time. So, this is what true love felt like. This man was the kindest, and most caring individual I had ever met in my life. We liked each other, really liked each other. He made me feel whole. Even if we had not liked each other romantically, I would have wanted to be his best friend.

There were so many moments that people would say were chance, in our meeting, but we both knew it was not chance at all. As much as I fought the realization, I knew deep in my heart that God had brought us together. How else could we explain all of this? And our feelings had grown so quickly. We had only been dating a brief time, but it all fit so well. Our hearts meshed, and it was divine intervention, and even I had to admit it. He was the first person I had met that was without an agenda. He did not need me to change a flaw in himself or to use me to enhance his own self esteem. It took me a long time to understand that. He expected nothing more than I could give.

True love looks beyond your clothes, hair, or weight. It scrapes away at your persona and looks beyond your eyes to your heart. True love is not superficial or fleeting. I learned early with him that love is not deceitful or hides secrets, it is honest. When I looked into his eyes, I saw myself differently than before. There were no games, tests of my feelings, just pure trust I had not experienced before in many areas of my life. I will never be enough for some people. I will not look right, and they will find fault with me, but this man was different. He was and still is the best part of my life and I will protect and guard his heart for as long as I live. In another time, we may not have been attracted to each other. That is why God gave us time to be ready from previous chance meetings or God Wink moments I will explain later. The definition of a God Wink is an event or personal experience, often identified as coincidence, so astonishing that it is seen as a sign of divine intervention, especially when perceived as the answer to a prayer. Squire Rushnell has authored several books relating to this topic. We were not ready. It is almost simple when it is right.

He was different from me, casual to my formalities, open, to my being closed for repairs. My attitude was horrible. I was cynical and brittle. He was thoughtful and honest. We were starting a hand in glove relationship, depending on each other and it was wonderful to finally have someone else in my corner for just me. He had not known the rejections I had faced; he was not aware of anything about me but what he saw before him and that was enough for him. I was enough, for what seemed like the first time in my life.

CHAPTER SIXTEEN

Dad took a turn for the worse in early May, only a couple of weeks after he met Bruce. We rushed him back to the Veterans Hospital in Nashville to be under the care of his cancer doctors. While he was there, the doctors found cancer in his lungs and could not give us a prognosis or how much time he had left. Mom and I were making plans to go up the next day, but we got a call from the hospital that Dad's condition had worsened, and we needed to come quickly.

My parents had a young friend. They had met him a year or so previously. He and his wife were great people. Mom had called him to tell him about Dad and he had insisted on driving us up to Nashville. Bruce was at our house. He, Mom, and I had been watching television.

When she got the call, she hurried around and I said, "Mom, I am going. Bruce and I will take you; I want to be there." Mom told me that this friend was taking her and that I needed to stay home and wait for her call about Dad's condition. It made me angry. There was no reason for her to keep me from going. I was tough; I had to be. So, she did not need to protect me; it was just the opposite. We had done this entire journey alone and now she did not think I needed to be there at the worst possible time.

But Bruce and I stayed behind, and we were quiet waiting for Mom's call. We both finally fell asleep in the den, and around four in the morning, on May 13, 1983, Mom came through the door. I jumped up and ran to her wanting to know how Dad was. She said, "Honey, I am sorry, Daddy is gone. He lost consciousness before we got there, and when we arrived, he was gone."

"You did not get to say goodbye?" I asked.

"No," she said with a crack in her voice, "I did not." I had not seen my mother often in my life be so unguarded and exposed as she was then. What do you say to someone who has lost their spouse after so long together? Oh, my folks did not have a perfect marriage all the time, but they had perfect times, and no matter what, they knew they could count on each other.

Bruce left to go home; he had to work later that day. Mom and I went to bed after she hugged me again and reminded me that the next several days would be tiring and difficult. We both went to bed, but I did not sleep. Dad was gone. What would Mom do without him? What would I do? I lay there and began to cry. I was so mad at God. I had watched my dad lose every ounce of dignity he had, and he was an immensely proud man. He suffered constantly and wasted away more each day. He had been the one my mom had turned to and he rescued us and gave us a good life.

He was there for all of us kids, a sturdy figure in our lives and now he was this mere image of a man. I remember railing out at God, "It must be nice to have such power that you can dangle things in front of people and then take them away. You have done that to me my entire life. And now this! You do not care about me, you do not care about us, and I do not have a clue why my mom cannot see this for what it is, why she continues to trust You." I never slept, but I did lay there thinking the rest of the night about what would come next.

The day we dreaded came early. I had hoped that when I got up with the sun shining like it was, it would have all been just a bad dream. All the grief and sadness we had experienced just hours before would just be our imagination, but it was not. I heard my mom on the telephone. She was making plans to run errands and would meet at the funeral home later in the afternoon when my dad's body arrived back in Chattanooga. She had a list the funeral home had given her over the telephone to bring for Dad's burial. I told her I would take care of that while she ran her errands. She needed a minute alone, and I sure could not think of her preparing Dad's clothes for his funeral. When Mom left, I eased into their room and it is funny, but I could have sworn I smelled Dad's cologne. He always smelled so good. His slippers were by the bed, and I glanced at the few things on his nightstand. I could not remember the last time I had been in this room. Mom had left everything the way it was before Dad's surgery.

I opened the closet and saw his clothes, mostly things he could not wear any longer because he had lost so much weight, but I touched them, smelled them and since I knew I could no longer hug my dad, I held his suit for a long time wishing this day had not happened. The tears flowed as I hugged it close for the last time. I felt they had left off things on the list, so I sent his favorite cologne, and a pair of his favorite socks and underwear. Realizing he needed a new suit, my oldest sister who was in Chattanooga at the moment went with me to the mall to find just the right one for him to wear. If he could not stay with us, he was going to look sharp where he was going. I gathered all his things and closed the door to their room behind me. My parents' friend took her to the funeral home, and again I was upset that she had not let me go with her.

He and his wife were not family and I resented them being included over me. But Mom had said I would be there soon enough, and she wanted to protect me if possible. That was just like her. She always wanted to protect us from everything. I guess that is where I got it. I was a lot like her in that respect. When he had dropped her off after planning the funeral, she told me that she was going to go through Dad's paperwork. The funeral home needed his military paperwork for the military funeral he would be having. I told her I would help, and we began to look through their papers. I was rummaging through an envelope and found old newspaper clippings and I had no idea why he had kept them. And, there was a black and white photo of Dad and me.

The photo was one of those little square ones you would get developed at the pharmacy back in the day. The date said 1958, and dad was cuddling me with a big smile on his face. I studied it for a minute and then said, "Mom, what's this? It says 1958?" And there was one that looked similar that spilled out from behind the clippings and was dated 1959. "Was Dad around when I was born?" She closed her eyes like she was wishing I had not seen anything and said, "Honey it was Dad's decision." "What are you talking about?!" I could feel my head start to throb, so much so that I could hear it in my ears. She went on, "Daddy did not want you to feel different from the other children, so he did not want you to ever know." "Know what!" I screamed at her. "Honey, he was your real dad. He was the other children's stepdad, but he was your real dad. You must know, he did it for you, he was determined that you would always be part of the other children with no differences made. Dad battled with that too, not always feeling that he fit in, and he did not want that for you."

I felt like I had been hit in the stomach with a brick. I wanted to cry, thinking it would calm me, but I could only feel rage begin inside me and hot fluid filled my throat. "Mom, did Dad not want me? Was he ashamed of me?" "No dear, oh Daddy loved you more than anything." "You cannot love someone and not be honest with them. You knew this too and you never said a word to me. I do not care if he had this dumb idea, he was helping me somehow, It did not help! When I was a kid, I never felt like I belonged with the other kids. The four of them were a packaged deal, a set. I felt it whether anything was said or not. I did not have anyone. And, when we were with Dad's family, I did not feel like I belonged with them either. But I could not understand why. I was happy, but there was something that did not seem right and now you tell me this?! How could you do this to me, Mom?! I trusted you more than anyone." "So, they are my half-brothers and sisters?" I shot at her sharply.

She tried to hug me, but I pulled away from her. The tears were coming now, and I asked if my siblings knew, and if Dad's family had known and she replied yes. "So, everyone knew about this but ME! You kept ME from knowing that I had a dad, my dad, right there all along. I felt that since I had the same name as the other children our dad was some loser out there. I did not know anything. It was all a big mystery. But I was little and confused thinking if I got too close to this dad and my real dad came back how hard that would be to choose between them. I did not want to hurt anyone. There were times I wanted to tell Dad secrets and I wanted a strong bond with him. And then I would remember that since he was not our dad, he may leave us too. There was always a barrier. I did not know how to tell you what I was feeling. I was a kid. How does a kid even comprehend something like that?" I said as I slumped over, my stomach beginning to ache in sync with my now throbbing head.

"It was a different time honey; people did not talk about things like they do now. Daddy never opened up about anything. We had been married five years when we had you." "But you knew, Mom, and you should have told me; I would have understood. I always kept Dad a little distant, not knowing he was my real dad. I should have known. Why did I have their name?" Mom was realizing the error of all of this by now.

She began, "Daddy thought that this would never come out, that you would never find out. He wanted you to always feel that you had your four siblings, and you would never feel alone or different from them, he wanted you to belong, so he gave you their last name. It meant that much to him." "All of you betrayed me. And now he is gone, and I cannot ask him questions about this, I cannot get closure or say goodbye the right way between a dad and a daughter. I need to know why?! You all robbed me, and I just do not know what I want now, I am so tired of people knowing secrets that impact my life. You all, that loser I almost married, everyone had secrets. I am getting out of here," I concluded, and got my keys to leave. "You kept this lie my entire life." Mom tried to stop me because I was so upset but I would not listen.

As I drove, I thought I would never get a chance to talk to Dad again. I would never get to say I love you Dad and mean it with no reservations or guilt. Or wondering who my allegiance was with. Some man out there or him. I was an only child technically, and a first-born child, unless my folks had more secrets. That would answer questions about my strong will and drive.

I just could not come to grips with learning this. I felt so sad for things that could have been, talks we could have had on a more intimate level. Things you only talk to your mom and dad about. I had always gravitated more to my mom for everything. But now I would never really know if Dad would have ever wanted a deeper relationship with me if he had known I knew his secret. He was fine to have things as they were but that was selfish and wrong in my eyes. He did not have the right. I was his flesh and blood and I deserved to know his reasoning for what happened. If not for him then for me. I missed having a real dad. I had remembered what my middle sister would say when he corrected her, "You are not my dad! You cannot tell me what to do." I guess when you are a little kid, you just take things as you see them, and you do not look beyond or know enough to ask questions. It did not hold water that it was only about my fitting with my siblings, there had to be more to him doing this, but Mom did not seem to know, and I would never find out from him now. Not only were we burying him, but he was also taking a lot of answers I needed with him. And, I was angry at my mother, angry for the first time. Of all the people in the world, how could she have known something like this and never once wanted to tell me. Or maybe she had wanted to tell me but could not. I could not do that to a child. Who does something like this? Even if Dad did not want me to know, at some point she should have said to him, either you tell her the truth, or I will. This was not a bond that should have been kept between the two of them. And it led me deeper down that dark hole of bitterness, now with a side of anger and resentment for the one person I thought I could trust.

A little girl has her first relationship with a man that is her daddy. What she sees him do, and how he interacts with her, helps her later to become comfortable seeking a partner in life. Their relationship can affect her ability to trust someone. It can affect her self-esteem. She may strive to seek out someone like her daddy, who provided comfort and love to her. Who protected her and was good to her mommy. Or, she could have a very different relationship with her dad. It is a vital bond and critical to her overall adjustment as a child and into adulthood. I did not have a deep bond with my dad. It should have been more, should have been better. I loved him and I knew he loved me in some way. And that would have to be enough.

I dreaded the time when the family was alone with their deceased loved one. I had experienced it before as a family member, part of a large group. The funeral director would come in and present the body to the family before everyone came to pay their respects and would ask the family strange questions, and this time was no exception. The funeral director asked us if Dad looked OK and that struck me as the dumbest thing you could ask a family. Yes, he looks great, he is dead, but he looks great, sure. My oldest sister and my brother were there. I found out that they had all stayed in contact, the three of them, my half-siblings. But I was never included in the loop. There was a difference, I had been right.

I know they felt the division as much as I did although I do not think they would have admitted it if asked. I loved all of them, but there was a gaping hole somewhere that I could not fill. I always wanted to know what they were doing but at this point in my life I was not going to beg anyone for attention or support. I had done my best by everyone, and I certainly did not feel guilt.

I knew my brother was preaching and the Church of God of Prophecy would send him to these broken-down excuses for a church no one else would take. If he did not turn things around, they would chastise him for it. I know there were times his family suffered greatly. His two little boys who I adored, and his wife sacrificed so much during his ministry. The church leadership seemed more concerned about money than souls. It is my opinion, and I know what I experienced, and what he experienced. It is sad but true. He is the most genuine and kind person you would ever meet. He loves the Lord and worked tirelessly in those church plants or struggling out in rural areas that had small congregations with small wallets. They barely survived. But he and I had drifted apart after he married. I knew he was super busy, but I missed him and his family.

So, here we were at the funeral home. At one point, I went up to the casket before visitation started and bent down to tell Dad I loved him. He did look peaceful. And he was not in pain any longer. For that I was grateful. He always wore a burr haircut, flat on the top. When I stood there and looked at him remembering how long he had suffered, I wondered how his hair was still so dark with only a small hint of gray at his temples. His casket was draped in the American Flag, but we had also purchased a blanket of flowers for later. I wanted to be close to him, just alone the two of us. We had such a brief time now to be together. I wanted to say stop! We need more time. You cannot leave me now; you have to tell me my story. Tell me about me. I wanted to shout, tell me what you were thinking the day you put another man's name on my birth certificate. Like that was best for me? Tell me how you would not acknowledge me all these years as your own flesh and blood? I will never know if you ever really wanted children of your own, or if you ever dreamed of having a little girl. I will never know about your past or really what you wanted in your life. I don't know my lineage or what makes me the way I am. I cannot recall a day when you really played with me. Had a tea party or read me a book. I know that was not your nature with any of us kids, but I missed so much. Did you ever question this decision? Or think about what it would do to me? In a quiet moment before I went to bed at night and ran to you for a hug, did you ever want to tell me the truth? I know you loved us in the ways you showed us. You took great care of all of us. But I do not recall many times when you said I love you to me. You hid behind a façade of strength and roughness, but there had to be some tenderness in your heart for your own child. So many more questions that would never be answered.

I was still angry at everyone for keeping this secret, but now that had begun to turn to my being resolved in knowing. Still maybe not yet understanding my dad's reasoning or my mother not telling me. It was a different time back then, and private or secret matters were not discussed. I knew that, but it was difficult still. We talked about everything at home usually, or at least Mom did with us. Dad was always quiet and never felt comfortable discussing anything about life or romance. He would get embarrassed. Although he had opinions when it came to dating or what we wore. So, I was really conflicted understanding why I had not been told, at least when I was older and certainly before Dad had died. We were raised to have an opinion or a say in matters that involved the family. And how had someone not slipped up over the years and told me. How could everyone have known this but me all these years?

Family and friends began to trickle in and soon the place overflowed with people, and Bruce was there as much as he could be. His sweet parents came as well. The dynamic at a funeral visitation is one for a comedian to take on. You have the friends that you have not heard from, who show up. They are skittish and feel guilty having been a horrible friend. But they make an appearance. There may be one or two max that are faithful friends who have really been there for you. They always say, I will be here if you need me, you know that. And they always are. Then you have the relatives. Those can be the worst.

They march in like little ants and head to the grieving wife. She must take them to the casket so that they can remark about how good the body looks in a macabre way. They tell her that if there is anything she needs to be sure and let them know (a lie). They talk about getting together (a lie), and that it's been so long. And, then there are the relatives and one or two that feel the need to show a display of grief. They drape themselves across the casket and cry loudly so everyone can hear them like they and the deceased had been the closest in the family, (Another lie.) So much of it was fake to me. At least I thought it was. My aunt did this and I remember how badly I wanted to call her out in front of everyone. But I just made my way to her side and whispered in her ear instead. And she drifted off to a seat and was quiet the rest of her time there.

Fake emotionalism makes me furious. If you did not care about someone when they were alive, they cannot hear you crying for them now, so take a seat. I watched at how my poor mom was comforting everyone else when it should have been the other way around. It was inconsiderate, and I had enough of it at one point, so I slipped out and went and sat in the chapel. I could not pray. I was in no condition to pray and ask God for anything. I was so mad at Him for not helping us, not healing my dad and for all the turmoil I had experienced up to now. I was in such a bad and cynical place. I had been sitting there a few minutes when Mom came in and quietly sat down beside me.

"Mom, how can you be so comfortable and resolved when you have lost someone you loved so deeply? Aren't you sad? You are gracious with these people that insist you go up to the casket with them and it makes me so mad." "Awe honey, I am fine," she said, "You know it is hard to see Daddy leave us, but I prayed so long for him to give his life to the Lord. He was so up and down in his faith bound by those cigarettes, and he did not feel worthy enough. God could have taken that habit away if daddy's faith had been strong. I wanted him to make it to Heaven more than I wanted him here," she went on, "So, I prayed. God, whatever it takes to save him, please do it. And God answered my prayer."

"What do you mean, Mom?" I asked, puzzled.

"Daddy had asked God into his life earlier, and I believe with all my heart he is in Heaven now," she explained as she hugged me.

"Honey, I know you are bitter, and I know things have not been easy. We caused some of that, and you had a lot on you, and I am sorry. We should have told you; we were wrong not to. Daddy would want you to let go of all of this now and move on with your life. He would want you to be happy, he loved you so much. God is not to blame for plans and dreams that change. I am so concerned about you and the way you are living. But I am just putting you in God's hands."

"I just do not trust God anymore," I said, "And now all of this and I will never get to have Dad tell me why he did what he did. It just does not make sense. And now he is gone, and you are telling me that you prayed that God would save him and take him from us?"

Mom blew out a breath and smiled at me. She sat there a minute and then said, "Gaye, I prayed that God would have His way, and save your dad. He felt so unworthy to be a Christian and I could not convince him that God loved him and would take the desire for unhealthy habits and his demons away if he only trusted. But Daddy was a hard shell to crack," she went on, "And so, I began to pray that God would save him regardless of what it took. Honey, Heaven is cheap at any cost. And I want Daddy there with me when this is all over. I hope you will understand this someday. And I pray you will be the person God intended you to be too. I will never stop praying for you," she finished then kissed my forehead and got up to return to the visitation. I sat there a little longer and my cousin came in to sit with me. He was one of my very favorites and had such a tender heart. We lost him not long ago while I was authoring this book, and it broke my heart. He and I sat there, and he tried to cheer me up in the peacefulness of that funeral chapel.

We cried together, and he reminded me that my dad, (his uncle Bun), loved me more than anything, and that he would not want me to grieve like this. I did not tell him that I had learned the truth about my relationship with my dad, I think he and everyone else in the family thought I knew the secret about my relationship with Dad, but that was not the case.

I do not remember the funeral; I was so upset and withdrawn. I just remember wanting everything to slow down, so Dad would not leave me. I remember my pain as I saw them put him in the back of the hearse the final time. I had rounded the corner just as they were settling him in and placing the flag over his coffin for his last ride. I do remember going to the National Cemetery in a big black limousine holding on to Bruce's hand for dear life. Mom and my siblings rode with us too. We passed a young man who was beside his motorcycle standing with his hand over his heart in an act of respect.

What You Can Become When Your Faith Grows Up

People were so kind that day when they saw the flag draped over Dad's casket. The motorcade of hearse and cars inched its way through the Ft. Oglethorpe Military Post where Dad had been in the 6th Cavalry as a young man. We eased along that route taking Dad for a little journey from his past on the way to the National Cemetery. I had remembered Dad taking us there on occasion when we visited during summers. He would tell us about events that occurred there, and he knew the stories behind the monuments that still stand today. By 1918, there were over 1600 buildings erected at that base and they surrounded the fort. It was the largest detention camp for German POW's (Dad's least favorite people), He never gave us reasons why. The 6th Cavalry had arrived with their horses (1500 of them), in 1919 after the end of WW1.

Pearl Harbor was attacked in 1941, and we entered WW11. The 6th Cavalry then joined General Patton in North Africa. My dad fought under Patton for several years and at several historic events. Dad had said the man was out of his mind, but there was no finer leader. I remember looking out the windows as we snaked around the familiar area and thought about Dad in his uniform, a young and handsome man who spent eighteen years in the military for his country. I thought I had cried all my tears, but they came in waves as we found our way into the cemetery.

The cemetery is the hardest part; it is then that you must leave that special person behind and try and move on with your life. There were flowers, and military personnel and flag folding. And, then someone in the distance played taps. I had heard a story about Dad that when he was young, he played taps at that very cemetery (The National Cemetery), in Chattanooga, on the little hill in the center of the cemetery where the flags are displayed. Those taps touched me so that day, and I was trying hard to hold it together for my mom. I could envision my dad, young and standing there proudly playing. And then, just like that, it is over, and people go back to their lives, and you are left to your memories and days when you think you cannot go on without them, fighting to pick up the pieces.

The devil wanted to destroy me. It is like I had witnessed a crime and needed to be quieted. I knew too much. Saw God's power in ways that most people had never experienced. I had been young in a time when Pentecost was at a level like no other. I witnessed miracles and experienced them firsthand. So, the devil just whittled away at my insecurities, my self-worth, and I was drowning in self-sabotage. My mom was there and even though I was angry, I loved her so much and even I had to admit that God alone had brought Bruce into my life. It was the two of them that got me through the grief and loss. I not only had lost a parent due to death, but it was as if I lost him twice. I knew I could not dwell on that, or I would slide further into despair. I had never told my family until the onset of this book about my dad. It still smarts, still hurts, and the idea of it all is raw and foreign, even after all these years. To know that

I wanted a daddy of my very own as a little girl and he was there all the time, I just never knew it, hurts so much. But whatever his reasons, if Dad made peace with God and is in Heaven, then that is more than enough satisfaction for me.

I went back to the cemetery alone that night before it closed. I needed more time. I knew exactly where Dad's grave was, the flowers were still pretty but tousled around the ground in their pretty containers, from the wind, and the grave was covered with fresh dirt. The strong smell of dirt mixed with the floral and near rain is a stench I can still smell when I close my eyes and remember standing there. I had taken a card I purchased that afternoon before I headed to the cemetery. I wrote all my feelings down, all the things I had not been able to say to him and I sealed the envelope before I drove there. Someone had told me once that it is cathartic to write down your feelings about a person or whatever, and then leave it someplace. You could toss it in the river or release it along with your emotions for the last time, and so I tried it. I had picked a rose from one of the arrangements and I laid the card down on the grave placing the rose on top. My dad loved tulips and roses.

It was getting dark by now and I knew they would be closing soon, but I did not want to leave quite yet. I did not want to leave my daddy. I felt like I had just found him. Rain began to dance around me and the word Dad I had written on the outside of the envelope had begun to fade. The rain kept splashing and beating it until the word was completely gone. The envelope was blank. As if Dad was never there in the first place.

How appropriate, I thought. You are here and then you are washed away forever. One of the only two people in the world that I was most intricately connected to was gone. It ate away at me. Everyone needs a connection, and I did not have it. What else didn't I know? I finally left as the rain began to flow more heavily and the wind blew me as if to move my daddy and thoughts of him farther away from me. I sat in the car as the gates closed behind me leaving my daddy alone in that cold wet ground.

CHAPTER SEVENTEEN

The only thing good about my life was that I had met Bruce. I did not want to go into a lot with him at the time, and unload everything I had been through just yet. I just wanted to bury my grief and the void it left and try and move on. Our lives collided in a bar of all places. When he drank for his own reasons and his own story to tell. And I was trying to forget my past and the betrayal in my life. We were constantly together, and our parents loved us both. In early August that same year, we decided to get married. Well, he said I picked him up in a bar and was now making him marry me. It was strange I must admit. We had only dated since March 1983, it was fast, but we knew it was right.

We have talked about it and how both of us had been saved early in life. I was raised Pentecostal and you had to be in church every Sunday whether you had been baptized or not. When Bruce was baptized in the Christian Church, his dad felt that once you were baptized you were OK, and you did not necessarily need church. But both of us had slipped away from God and the odds were so against us that we would remain married. But neither of us ever thought about that. It never once crossed my mind that we would not stay together and would finish our lives as one. And so, soon we were making wedding plans for November 19, 1983. It would be years later that Bruce would share things with me about chance meetings before we met, and we were both amazed. I had mentioned earlier that we would talk for hours on end about everything. I had told him about my little red Gremlin. I paid one thousand dollars for it in fifty-dollar increment payments, and I loved it. Except for when it rained, the floorboards would flood, and I would have to bail out water. And, he had told me about working at a furniture store early on when he first moved to Chattanooga. His dad was with Shell Oil and was transferred to Chattanooga from Indiana.

I would not find out until much later in our lives (I think in 2019), as we stopped at a red light on the other side of town that he shared this with me. He was holding my hand in the car like he usually does, and we had gone out to dinner. "See that spot over there," he said, pointing to a place by the exit from the freeway. "Yes, I guess." I had no idea what he was going to say. "One day, I was delivering furniture and you were at that spot trying to get across. It was a four-way stop then. The windows of your little red car were down, and your beautiful hair was flowing. People were looking at you, and you were laughing, probably at the attention, you were receiving. Everyone was waiting on each other for their turn to go through the stop. I was driving the truck, and I looked over to the guy with me and said, I am going to marry that girl." I was shocked and could not believe what I was hearing for a minute. We figured we were both nineteen at the time when this occurred.

And he went on, "When you had mentioned once the funny story that had happened a couple of years later about having furniture delivered and I realized it was from the same store I worked at, I put it all together. I was supposed to deliver that furniture to you, but I stayed back. But when the guys got back, they had told me all about the beautiful girl with the long dark hair they had delivered furniture to. I did not realize it at the time, but you were the girl." I said, "Yes, I was a couple of years older, I think twenty-two." I was thinking out loud. "Well, you were probably there when I came to purchase the furniture." "Yes, probably in the back." He smiled. I was so astounded, talk about God wink moments. "But why didn't we ever meet?" I asked. "Because it was not God's timing that is why," he replied.

There was never a doubt in my mind from then on that we were supposed to be together. All of this had transpired six years before we met. So, let's review the timeline so you can truly see how God worked. Bruce saw me first when we were nineteen at a four way stop and told his co-worker he was going to marry me. At twenty-two I bought furniture from the company he worked at, and he should have delivered it but had heard about me when the guys returned from the delivery. At twenty-four (he is five months younger than me), Bruce told his friends that he would be getting married that year in 1983. We met on my twenty-fifth birthday, March 12, 1983. And we were married on November 19, 1983.

One evening, we were sitting at the table with my mom making wedding plans and I got a little melancholy, and Bruce had noticed it. "I guess I'm just wishing Dad knew about our plans and he was here to give me away," I started. He looked at me. "He knows, I told him that day I met him that I was going to take care of you." And then Mom stopped what she was doing and said, "Daddy and I had talked, he was happy you had found Bruce. He never wanted to leave you in the state you were in before Bruce came along. Daddy had told me that he was content knowing Bruce was there." Another confirmation that this was right.

Our wedding was beautiful. My mother had worked her magic and no detail was left undone. She had made it all so special for us. Each step I took down that exceptionally long aisle, I was more certain than the last that this was the best decision I had ever made. I missed Dad though. That is always a sweet time between a dad and his little girl when he proudly escorts her down the aisle to her awaiting husband to be. But our neighbor who was a great friend of my dad walked with me. He always treated me like I was his daughter. He whispered in my ear right before we headed down the aisle that I was beautiful. And, that dad would be proud of me. I wasn't sure about that, but I sure hoped he would be.

We had decided to stay home and not take a honeymoon right away. I was tired after all the planning, and we were content to just stay in our cozy little rented home and eat left over cake for the time being.

I had only started a new job in December, after our November wedding but had settled in nicely with everyone. I was overseeing the insurance plan for the employees along with training, first aid and safety. I was becoming fast friends with our contact at a large local Insurance Company. I would authorize payment under our policy as a self-insured company, and the insurance company would adjudicate the claim from there. So, my contact and I were in touch often throughout the day. She would talk to me about coming there to work, and our sales representative who visited me at the plant, would also encourage me to put an application in to work there.

One night, I was in my office working and the Personnel Manager was in his office. The main door to our combined offices opened and the owner of the company walked into the area, spoke, and headed to the manager's office. I could hear everything. He was fired that evening for reasons I did not know. And, by Monday morning, another man was in his place in our offices. Just like that, he was replaced with someone new. The new manager was obnoxious and pushy, and thought he knew everything. I discerned early when we shook hands the first day, that he would be trouble.

He would call me pet names and I was not a fan of his condescending attitude. It did not take us long to realize we did not care for each other, nor could we work together. I left shortly after he arrived. I took time off from working after that for a while. Bruce and I took a trip to Walt Disney World in late May of 1984. We were going to be there for about four days, to just enjoy a little belated honeymoon. The day we arrived I did not feel quite right, but I could not think of any reason why. The next morning, I got up feeling uncomfortable with cramping while we were still in our room. But we were soon off to the Magic Kingdom. I have been many times and I loved getting there when the park first opens. By the time we had arrived near Fantasy Land, my abdomen was cramping horribly. I had thought I had eaten something that made my stomach hurt, and then I soon realized it was not that kind of cramping.

I went to the restroom and was in there for what seemed like an eternity trying to feel better. Nothing helped. It was hot outside, and the restroom was warm even with air conditioning. I can remember standing in that stall and feeling the most helpless I had ever felt. I was as broken as I had ever been. After a time, I held that little being in my hand, and I could not move. I was paralyzed. How could this be? My emotions were all over the place. I wanted to scream, I needed to cry, but I just stood there stunned. What do you do when you are far from home in the happiest place on earth, and you are devastated from something as horrible and dreadful as this? I felt so alone.

All the self-doubt and rejection hit me like a boulder hard and deep and cut to my heart. I was a mess. I could not even do this right. What did I say to Bruce waiting outside? How do you say, oh we were pregnant and now we are not so let's just go ride the rides. I had to get my bearings and it was difficult. Should I have shown Bruce? Wild thoughts went through my mind. When I finally came out, I told him something had happened to me in the restroom. I do not know if he could see how upset I was. I tried not to be, and to be in control, but I was crashing and burning inside. I could not say the words. But having experienced what I had shortly before, I thought I had a miscarriage.

We had no idea I could be pregnant; I had no symptoms. I remembered what my doctor had said that it would be difficult or maybe even impossible to have children due to the endometriosis. So, I was shocked. But it was an awful image that I can close my eyes even now all these years later and still see so clearly. We did not know what to say to each other. He asked if I needed a doctor or if I wanted to come back to Chattanooga, and I told him no, there was nothing we could do now. It was over just like that. We did not talk about it, and we never told anyone what happened not even my mother. We were not sure why or how it happened, but it was as if God had blocked it from my feelings. I was so fragile at that point, there was no way for me to handle that loss compounded with everything else. We just never really mentioned it. I did not want to relive it. I did not want to go there in my mind. I tried to remove it and the images I saw, and I guess both of us were in defense mode, so we never brought it up again.

I certainly could not discuss my feelings because I thought if I let myself dwell on it for any length of time, I would lose my mind. I could not take on any more pain. At that time, we were not prepared for children. I was not fit to be a mother; I was struggling just to make it day by day. When you are fighting God and you know you are out of his will for your life, it is a miserable place to be. I remember at night soon after, the devil came to me in a whispered breathy voice. He would remind me of the semblance of a baby that I had held in my hand, and his words made my spine tingle, "Where was God? Where was He when you cried your eyes out in the restroom of an amusement park, no less. He did not help you, did not come to your aid as you expelled your child from your body, where was He then? That baby rejected you like everyone else has except Bruce, and he will one day, just wait." Oh, how the devil loves to beat you when you are down, and you are easy prey. How he enjoys pointing out our inadequacies and weaknesses. He never forgets our shortcomings.

I was at a place in my life where I felt I was walking on thin glass. With each step I took, it would break a little more. I just knew that at some point, it would crash and everything I had wanted would be gone. The devil tried to tell me that Bruce would be gone too. And, now after what had just happened, I was not sure. Bruce had become the catalyst in my life that held my world together. It would be easier to put this memory in a safe place, tucked away in my heart and leave it there. But, looking back, I wish we had received counseling or at least told my mother or had prayer, but I was in a different place in my life. It is so strange, because there are times, I wonder what could have been. What if I had carried that little one to term, and what would he or she have been like. And I have secretly cried tears even now over what occurred that day. As the years have gone by, it bothers me more now wishing for three children. I do not understand what happened or why, but it still haunts me. It was God's sweet intervention for us to wait before we started a family. We do not know His reasoning, nor have I tried to analyze it. But it left me empty and sad for a long time. Bruce has reminded me that we will meet again in Heaven and that is a great comfort.

There is regret and I still feel loss. I do not think that ever goes away. I did see my doctor when I got back and he advised me that because of what had happened and my history with severe endometriosis for so long, I would need laparoscopic surgery to see what was going on and determine the extent of my condition.

After this procedure, it was evident that the endometriosis was much worse, and I was referred to a fertility specialist. We had not been married long at all. And now the burden of being forced to try for a family or limit our chances of never having one gave us no choice but to proceed with treatment. I felt even more pressure because Bruce was the last of the LaFoe family. He would want a child to continue the family name. But he never once forced me to undergo treatments, and never pressured me. He was the sweetest and most attentive person to walk down that road with.

I will tell you that this was an exceedingly tough time for me. It started with me taking fertility drugs that made my body extremely hot like I was melting from within. I had mood swings where I would just sit and cry, which, in my state of mind, did not help. Bruce was working second shift, so we did not see much of each other during those years. And, lucky for him. There were charts, graphs, shots, and pills. There were specimens and timing temperatures and days I had to drive to the doctor at the worst possible times, while trying to work. We even attempted artificial insemination, but nothing worked. No baby came. Every test we took was negative. I had started working at the insurance company.

Every time things looked hopeful, it turned out that I was not pregnant. I just wanted to throw up my hands and say *I quit*. After three long years of that constant torture day after day, I needed a break. And we stopped all forms of infertility testing. We both knew what the doctors had said. We needed to get pregnant as soon as we could because time was ticking and not in our favor. We moved again and then finally moved one last time to our first home that we purchased.

Along with making the decision to stop fertility testing after those long years, we also did not talk much about a family. I was so sad because I thought I had let Bruce down. He would just give me the sweetest smile and say, "It is going to happen, you will see." I could not do a normal thing like have a baby. I never told him, but there were times I wanted to tell him that he may want to move on with someone else that could give him children. We did not talk a lot about children before we married, but it was obvious he was the last of his family to carry on the name. And I did not want to keep that experience from him. It would not be fair. I had let him down. I wanted a child more for him than me.

I had not been around children often in my life, except the ones in children's church that I taught as a teen. And to be honest, little ones got on my nerves, hearing them cry or one having a meltdown. Mom always laughed and said, "Oh, but when you have your own, you will feel different." I was not so sure about that. Bruce's dad had come down for business and we had taken him to a Chinese restaurant for dinner around June 1988. He and I had drinks. Me more than him. We had kept up our partying lifestyle after we were married, and I was still drinking steadily. Bruce had changed my life in so many ways, but I was still dealing with a lot of baggage, and now this issue of having children compounded my stress.

He had stopped drinking after some things that are his own story to tell, and after God worked such miracles in his life. But we would still go out on the town and to the bars. It was a quick fix for me. I would forget for a few minutes about everything. And it was only by God's grace that I did not become an alcoholic. Somewhere in my mind, I would hear my daddy say, "I better never catch you drinking, it won't do a thing but bring you trouble." Oh Dad, you were so right. Bruce's dad had gone back to Indiana, and it was around the fourth of July 1988 that Mom and I planned to go shopping. Bruce worked most holidays. I was off work, and I loved spending time with her. We would laugh and window shop because unless I made her buy something or I got it for her, she spent zero money on herself. But long talks with my mom was just the ticket right about then, and I needed her counsel. I needed her to tell me everything was going to be ok. I had remembered how so often when life was hard that I would look to her for guidance. She and Bruce had also become close. And he loved that she always let him know she was praying for him.

I had gotten up that morning and I was as sick as I could be, but I did not want to miss spending time with her, so we went to the mall. I knew at any moment I was going to be sick; waves of nausea came and went the next worse than the last, but I tried not to let on to her. I could hardly put one foot in front of the other walking through the mall.

Mom told me that she needed to eat to take her medicine a couple of times. She was a diabetic and needed to eat at certain times to take her insulin. "Mom, I cannot even look at food, let alone eat anything," I said. She reminded me that she would need to eat lunch soon, so I sat with my head in my hands while she ate in the mall's food court. I could tell she kept studying me and finally I said, "What are you looking at me for?" I was agitated because she looked smugly at me. She had laughed and told me that she knew I was pregnant and that we needed to get a pregnancy test at the drug store on the corner by the mall entrance.

I got angry with her because she had known what the doctors had said that it would be difficult for me, and I may never be able to conceive. It had been four years now. But she insisted I had the look, whatever that meant. I guess an ob-gyn hospital nurse that had delivered babies in every place possible as a young nurse may know a thing or two, but I still did not believe her. I told her that we had tried everything, so it was not possible. After her coaching me a little longer, I gave in and bought two tests and took them home. She was so sure I was pregnant; she had even offered to pay for the tests.

While Bruce and I were waiting for the tests to tell us that evening, I was trying not to get excited. So many times before, we had thought it had happened only to be disappointed. But both tests were positive, and Bruce and I just looked at each other. I still thought it could not be happening, but he was excited and not at all surprised. The next morning, I called into work and told them I thought I had a virus and would not be coming in to work. I was still not believing I was pregnant. I then called my co-worker who was on maternity leave having just had a baby, and asked her which baby doctor she used, just in case. She was so excited at the thought of my being pregnant. She gave me her doctor's name and I called for an appointment. They got me in that day, and when I arrived, the waiting room was full of very pregnant women. I felt so uncomfortable, and so extremely sick I could hardly sit up. When the doctor came into the exam room, I will never forget how kind and sweet he was to me. "Well, congratulations you're going to have a baby!" he announced. I looked at him shocked and could not speak. I was waiting for him to say, oh, wait I am sorry. I made a mistake. It is the next room. But that did not happen.

He walked over to the examination table and placed his hand on my shoulder. "Do you not want a baby, Mrs. LaFoe?" he asked. And I began to cry and just blurted out everything about the infertility, and the timeline the doctors had given us. And that it had been so long, I had given up. And now, I was pregnant. I was so overwhelmed. I said, "Oh no!!! I have been drinking," and he laughed and told me it was time to quit. I was afraid I had hurt the baby, but he assured me all was well.

"You know you do not always have the answers. Only God can determine when a baby will come. And you can feel happy now because you are having one and everything looks great," the doctor concluded patting my back. I remember trying to walk out of his office. My legs were like rubber, and I was having difficulty standing. When I told Bruce, and then Mom and his folks, they were elated. And our journey into parenthood had begun.

From about my second visit to the doctor, I began having complications with the pregnancy. Initially, I experienced placenta previa early in my pregnancy which was rare. It usually occurs in the second trimester. It is a condition in which the placenta blocks the neck of the uterus. In cases like mine, you have horrible bleeding.

I would have to leave work when the bleeding started and go to the doctor's office. They would do an ultrasound to determine if the baby was all right. That went on for a couple of months and then I began to gain weight for no real reason because I had not eaten for the first eighteen weeks of my pregnancy. I had been so sick. And, I had no appetite even though I tried to eat for the baby even after that first eighteen weeks. I was just trying to keep down whatever I could. But my weight was really taking off. I had gone in for a routine visit and ultrasound and the doctor had said that I needed to see a specialist that dealt with babies in utero because the baby had characteristics of down syndrome.

Bruce and I went to this specialist for his evaluation. I just knew it was going to be sad news, but Bruce was his usual upbeat self. He never gave up. The doctor examined me and did a very extensive ultrasound with exhaustive measurements and said that indeed the baby had characteristics that would lean towards down syndrome. I was devastated. In my mind, I was thinking here we go God, dangling things in front of me and this is not going to go well. At first, they thought it had something to do with confusion about my blood type being listed wrong in the records. I have AB-Negative blood, but I had thought it was O Positive. However, they had resolved that issue before I came to see this doctor. As we talked, I became very disgruntled and as usual put my guard up. I said I did not want to bring a child into the world that would have issues. I was not strong enough to deal with that. And, I had gone on and on talking nervously while both the doctor and Bruce remained quiet.

He advised me that these children could be a blessing and that we needed to take time to decide together on moving forward. He also sent us to be counseled within the practice that day where a lady described down syndrome to us in detail. The woman had given us a sympathetic look and then produced a big smile like that was supposed to help me, but I did not want her literature, or her counseling or anything else. I wanted to run as far from there as I could. My heart could not hold what I was feeling.

On the way home, we were quiet. He had told us we would need to think about what we wanted to do, but that he would never suggest terminating the pregnancy. We had spent all afternoon in his office and so we stopped for dinner. I was getting my appetite back by now and I ate so much that night. The server had come over a couple of times and Bruce had finished eating and was just sitting back watching me.

He explained that I had just started eating again, and I was making up for lost time. He and the server laughed over that. We sat and talked for a while and I said, "I do not know what I was thinking in his office, saying I did not want to have this baby if he was going to have challenges." We had learned by now that we were having a little boy. "He must have thought I was a horrible person." And I began to cry. "I could never do anything to hurt our little boy, regardless of the outcome." He smiled at me, "Neither he nor I thought you were thinking straight. We knew you were upset." So, Bruce and I decided right then that no matter what happened, or what the outcome, we were having this baby and would deal with things as they came.

As I have stated, I began to gain weight and it was fast and I was gaining quite a bit at a time. I was watching what I ate and trying to take care of myself. But one day, I had gone in for my routine visit and my blood pressure was extremely high. I was instructed to go home on bed rest until it came down. However, it did not come down. It kept creeping up. I rotated through all three doctors in the practice because any one of them could deliver the baby, so they wanted you to see all of them. One of the doctors had really been unkind to me about my weight and had told me to stay off the cookies! And the only female of the three had stated that the baby was going to be extremely small. They all contradicted each other. But one thing for sure, I was not eating cookies.

I was still trying to work, and I had to park a considerable distance away in the large company parking lot downtown. It was uphill in the mornings. And I would often be out of breath. By now my ankles were huge and I had to wear tennis shoes with the laces undone to even walk. I would have the hardest time walking up that hill and then taking an elevator to the floor I worked on. By the time I got to my desk I was exhausted and would have the worst headaches.

It was the first of January 1989. I had been to see the doctor more as my visits became more frequent. It was one complication after another. When the doctor came in, my favorite, he told me that I needed to get to the hospital and that they would be waiting for me. I was to be admitted to the hospital. But he was so calm I did not think much about it. My blood pressure was unusually high the nurse had told me at check out. What she had failed to tell me was it was at convulsion levels, and they meant for me to get to the hospital right then. I was in full-blown eclampsia.

I had driven myself from work to the doctor, so I would have to drive to the hospital. But I got it in my head that I needed a few things if I was going to the hospital this early, so I went shopping before I got home. At the store, a clerk took one look at me and said, "Girl, you are not having this baby here are you?" Bruce was home from work when I got home about an hour later, and I told him we needed to go to the hospital that they were admitting me. I said, "Sure take a shower." And he did while I packed my things and we finally headed to the hospital. When we arrived through the emergency room, they were frantic. They had been waiting on me.

The emergency room staff had been in contact with the doctor, and everyone was anxious until I arrived. I was immediately placed on the obstetrics floor and hooked up to a monitor, IV's, and placed on my left side for what would be the duration of my pregnancy. The baby was not due until March 10, 1989! So, I was in for a prolonged stay. I was surprised at what took place when I arrived. It was quick and I was in a room and being closely monitored before I knew what had happened. People were scurrying everywhere like bugs when the light goes on. I was allowed visitors at first. My friends from work would come and hang out with me at lunch time or after work. Bruce would come in the evenings and mom was always in and out. It was fine for the first few days. But when days turned into weeks, it got old fast. At one point, because my blood pressure was so high, they plugged my telephone, placed a no visitor sign on my door and even monitored what I watched on television for fear I would start to convulse.

CHAPTER EIGHTEEN

On February ninth, the doctor performed an amniocentesis to see if the baby's lungs were developed enough should I go into labor or have other issues that would warrant an early emergency delivery. They would need this information so that they would know to have a ventilator ready if his lungs had not developed enough. It was as if everyone around me were walking on eggshells. I was not to be overly stimulated. Everyone was uncharacteristically calm around me, and it bothered me.

The procedure did show that the baby's lungs were not developed enough for delivery. So, it was critical that I remain calm and that they continue to monitor my high blood pressure so that I did not go into premature labor. Emergency steps were in place though, that if I started into labor on my own, they would go ahead and let me deliver even if it was early. And, if my blood pressure maintained at a certain elevated level for any length of time, they would immediately go in and take the baby.

One nurse came in constantly. As soon as I would just move to my back or my right side for a minute's reprieve from my left side, she would come in and tell me that I was not helping myself. "Mrs. LaFoe, you must stay on your left side," she would grind out with her voice that gave me chills, "Because baby needs oxygen," I would tell her that I had only moved for a second, but I knew she did not believe me.

It is true, there is something called the inferior vena cava (IVC), which is a large vein that runs down the right side of the spine and is responsible for sending blood from the bottom part of the body to the heart. When a pregnant woman is on her back or right side, a fetus can compress the vein, and stop the flow of blood which reduces the amount of oxygen to the baby. The mom's blood sends oxygen to the baby. So, it is a serious thing. Since I was on bed rest, I had to remain on my left side for the baby and good blood flow.

Mom had been attending the Assemblies of God; we only had one in town then that I recall. And her youth pastor had come to visit me on February tenth. He asked if he could pray and asked again if he could touch my stomach as if touching the baby. I told him that it was fine, and he began to pray the sweetest prayer that God would be with me, and with this child, and if they had to deliver him sooner than expected that he would be well and that his lungs would be perfect and developed.

I did not think much about it. It was kind of him to come, but it did not change how I felt about God. That evening one of Bruce's friends came to visit and he was there for a brief time when my water broke, and I went into labor. It was all hands on deck. Nurses were stirring around me, and everyone was on high alert.

I was taken to labor and delivery around ten that night and at first, I was treated like a normal ob-gyn patient. Bruce and I had attended natural childbirth classes at the hospital for the breathing techniques, but I was already in the hospital with complications in January when the class graduated. Again, I did not get to get my certificate, Bruce had to go get it for me.

Anyway, those breathing techniques went out the window. I had horrible Braxton-Hicks contractions all through my pregnancy to the point where I would have to stand still until one finished because I could not walk. And, now my contractions were just as intense from the beginning of labor at around ten the night of the tenth until now which was the eleventh. They were never easy and got more intense. The staff was monitoring my blood pressure every moment and soon the doctor arrived. It was the one that had been so hateful to me about my weight. He was on call that weekend. I was so angry. I had rotated back to him for a visit and was able to tell him how rude he had been and that my weight had been preeclampsia, and not from my eating cookies!

I remember saying, "No, I do not want you in here," that day in labor and delivery on February 11, 1989. He laughed, "Well, I am sorry, you are stuck with me." After a long night and day of labor, I received an epidural. I had tubes in every orifice of my body, and I looked over at Bruce who was sitting there just as content as he could be eating a huge meal of fried chicken they had brought up from the cafeteria. I could not believe it. There I was looking like a beached whale, with tubes everywhere and having contractions that felt like my stomach was being steamrolled, and he was eating chicken, without a care in the world. I said "Really? I am lying here with all these shenanigans going on and you felt the need to eat a chicken dinner in front of me?" He shrugged his shoulders. My mother jumped to his defense and let me know fast that her sweet Bruce needed to keep up his strength for what was ahead. I thought to myself, *what is going on here?* I was hungry, but could not have anything, not even ice chips. I knew right then she favored him over me.

It was about 3:35 p.m. when the baby went into distress. At first, the doctor thought it would pass, but they determined I developed cervical edema and they had to get the baby out quickly by a cesarean section. Of course, when he told me this, I said "Uh... no, no cesarean section for me; I'll just wait." I remember him rubbing my feet and saying, "Well dear, we are doing one in the next few minutes so get ready." "Bruce, I'm scared!" I said, and his look told me he was too.

He was whisked off to dress in scrubs and I could hear a nurse giving him instructions. I flew by on a stretcher and thundered into the freezing operating room where a flurry of movement was all around me. Nurses and anesthesiologists were hooking me up and talking in lingo only they understood, and everything was STAT, meaning *right now!* I was asking questions that were not being answered like, "Can you knock me out for this?" and "Hello, is anyone listening to me?"

And then finally the anesthesiologist leaned down by my ear and said, "Mrs. LaFoe, I will be monitoring you and as soon as the baby is out, the doctor wants me to put you to sleep." I remember the pressure on my stomach and trying to concentrate on Bruce who was sitting right beside me. It was the strangest thing to know that they had my stomach wide open, and I was awake through the entire thing. It seems so barbaric. I finally heard a little squeaky sound, not even a cry, and I went to sleep.

I remember waking up at times after, but I had no idea where I was or the time. Once, a nurse was in the room by my bed and nothing looked familiar to me. I asked where I was, and, if I had a baby. She got down close to my ear and said, "Mrs. LaFoe, you have a healthy little boy, but I am sorry, you are in our storage room. You are not well enough to be transferred to ICU, so we had to set this up for you." *What? ICU?*

They had not had many cases like mine; we learned much later. I do not recall saying anything else and I just drifted in and out of consciousness. Some of this was medically induced and the other was my body. At times, my eyes would open, and I would see nurses, or doctors or my mom praying over my bed. What was that about? "Mom? What are you doing?" And she would say, "Honey, I'm praying for you." That did not seem unusual so I would drift out again. I had no concept of time, and I did not fully understand where I was or the severity of my condition.

When they had first diagnosed me with preeclampsia back in January, my history did not lend itself to this disease, and my doctor had told me back then that the medical community does not know why some women are more predisposed to it than others. And, even most women that have it are often treated until their delivery through outpatient care. But my case was so severe at the onset that I had to be hospitalized. Things can change that quickly with this condition.

Pre-eclampsia leads to eclampsia, or as it is also called toxemia, and if it is not controlled it can lead to permanent damage to all the major organs, seizures that can lead to coma, stroke, or death. And, in some cases, the baby can die too.

I would wake at times and the pediatrician would be sitting by my bed. He was animated and funny and had the best bedside manner. He would tell me things about Jonathan's progress, but nothing really registered with me. Whoever came into the room always got down by my ear and told me who they were. I did not understand why but it was to keep me from trying to sit up and possibly cause a convulsion. Jonathan Chaz LaFoe stormed into the world at a mere 4.15 pounds and perfect in every way at 3:43 p.m. February 11, 1989. And, no ventilator was required. He was thriving in the NICU, and I was dying in labor and delivery.

Once, I remember my IV starting to hurt, and I had moved around to look at my arm. Immediately, a nurse flew into the room to see if I was ok. She advised me that I had salt going into my veins and she showed me how my skin glistened from the amount of salt in my body. Of course, I had no clue what she was talking about, but my arm would be so uncomfortable because that salt would build up outside the puncture sight and it would sting and hurt so badly. What they gave me was actually Magnesium Sulfate which is an inorganic form of salt. It is often used to help prevent irregular heart rhythm and also to prevent seizures in women with preeclampsia and eclampsia.

It was after they had drawn blood gases from me that they began evaluating my body for the impact on my organs. I was failing fast.

The eclampsia was at its worst. My doctor had moved into the doctor's lounge on the evening of the eleventh because my condition deteriorated after Jonathan was born. I did not know it during that time, but there was talk all over the hospital about the young woman in labor and delivery fighting for her life. Mom would tell me much later that she would go down to the cafeteria and people would stop her and ask about me and the baby. People she knew told other people and the nurses on the floor had told people throughout the hospital. They would tell mom that they were praying. I believe without a doubt that those prayers were instrumental in God touching me later.

Bruce and Mom were there every waking moment they could be with me. And I would wake up to see them sitting by my bed. I would be so glad to see their faces. Bruce spent time in NICU with Jonathan because I was not able to be there. I did not know he was doing that, but when I found out later, it was a comfort to me knowing he had been with our little boy. I had no idea what was happening around me.

Doctors that I was not familiar with would come in to see me and explain problems with my kidneys, or lungs, and I would shake my head like I understood, but I could not comprehend what they were saying. It was always something about problem areas and organs not functioning. I could hear myself grunt a reply, but I had no concept of my condition or the severity of it. I would be awake and then lose consciousness again. It was a constant state of in and out. I could look at someone who was talking to me and not understand a single thing they were saying. It is so difficult to describe that place between being consciously aware of your surroundings one minute and then quickly in a deep sleep. It was as if people were yawning when they talked to me. I saw things in slow motion. I remember waking up at one point and looking around at the shelves of supplies and wondering where my flowers were. Having been in the hospital for so long, I had a room full of beautiful flowers, balloons and anything people were kind enough to send that would make my stay isolated in a hospital room easier. But there were no flowers, just cold metal shelving, boxes of supplies and my bed.

I know that Bruce, Mom, and nurses had told me at times what was happening, but I could not recall anything from one moment to the next. And I would ask the same questions over and over. I had no control over it. At one point, a doctor came to my bedside and touched my arm, as if to wake me. I looked up and he smiled down at me and introduced himself. He was a cardiologist. He looked down at the floor, as if thinking what he was going to say, and I was trying hard not to go back into that deep sleep. He leaned down close to my face and began by saying, "Young lady we need to have a talk."

It was just he and I in the room, I think. I kept blinking my eyes as if that would help me stay coherent. And I said, "OK." "You may be aware," he said, "You have been struggling since the baby was born." Had I been? I cannot remember if I responded. I don't recall anywhere in the conversation that I said anything to him. "Your body continues to want to shut down." And, he said something about my major organs being a concern. He patted my arm again and said something that got my attention for the first time. He looked into my eyes and said, "We are trying to save your life, but we cannot give you any guarantees. Your body is dying. You are dying." Then he went on and said something about my having had an episode with my heart, but that even though it showed up in the blood gases, there was nothing remarkable about my heart or damage that he could see. Something to that effect.

This part is so difficult to write because I was in a fog the entire time after the birth, and it makes me so emotional. But I heard, we are trying to save your life. Your body is dying. I know that tears fell because I could feel them hot on my cheeks and puddling around my face. He told me to rest and that I was well cared for or something like that. And then he was gone. Normally, you receive that kind of news with your family members present as a source of support, but Bruce had to go home and check on our dogs and shower I think, and Mom needed more insulin or something because she was not there either. What do you do with that kind of news? I began to really cry, and a nurse came running into the room and listened to my heart, checked my vital signs, and told me I needed to be calm. My monitor was going off and the graphs were all over the place. How could anyone remain calm after that news?

When she thought I was safe to leave, she started to shut the door behind her, and I told her to leave it open. It had remained opened all the time, because they were right outside my door, but this time I was starting to feel closed in. I do not know whether it was the news I had received or whether I was coming around more but I was becoming more alert to my surroundings. I even remember that I tried to elevate myself a little in the bed. My arms were bruised and hurt from the IV's and the concoctions they were loading my body with. And I was feeling isolated and trapped. It felt like everything was closing in on me.

How do you start that conversation with yourself, or anyone, when someone says you are dying? I looked around at this room, this makeshift ICU and thought to myself, *today may be the day I die. So, this is how it could end. Nothing good or bad at this point in my life will matter after today if this is the day.* I had never felt so raw before. For some reason, I was not scared. It was as if I were resolved to the knowledge that I could not change my circumstances. I could not change the facts of my condition and how it had deteriorated. I could not argue all the testing done that gave this bleak outlook. No, there was nothing I could do. Who was I going to turn to? For over twelve years I had been full of bitterness and resentment.

I had railed out at God on more than one occasion. I had been so tired of being disappointed and thinking He dangled things, people, and career in front of me and then took them away. I was mad at Him for so long, and it is so difficult to admit that. I had grown up learning to trust Him for everything. I had faith that He would direct my life from the time I was a little girl. I trusted God for my healing when I had suffered so long, and I did not give up on Him then. I waited on Him. But when so many things went wrong in my life, I blamed God for all of it. The last straw was watching my dad die so horribly and in such pain. I could not do anything to help him, and everything I needed to know about myself died with him. I had gotten my eyes on people all too often. And people will let you down. They betray you and lie to you and I tossed God into that mix. I could not trust Him. But the older I got when my heart was broken, and the rejection and loss in my life with my dad occurred, I blamed God.

When things had not turned out like I thought they should, I decided I could manage on my own and turned my back on everything I had known and grew up to believe. How did I have the audacity to think that I, a mere human, could do things better than God could. How could I turn the tide in my life? I could not heal myself. I could not restore love or keep my dad from dying. I was not able to see the future to know which decisions were going to be the right ones in the end. I had been miserable, hopeless, and broken. I gathered up all the pieces of me and thought I could do a better job managing my life on my own. Wow, how arrogant and mixed up I was. I turned to alcohol to rid the memory of what I knew best. It would take me to a quiet place in my head for moments at a time, but never long enough to stop the hurt or the pain altogether.

Now, here I was in the most critical circumstances I had ever been in. I remembered my tiny son, somewhere in that hospital NICU needing a mother. I had not even seen him, and now the thought of never seeing him or watching him grow up was more than my heart could handle. I thought to myself, *I cannot even get this right.* You come to the hospital to have a baby. A very normal thing for a woman to do, but not me. No, I had to be one for the record books.

I began to think about my little boy and what would become of him. How would he thrive missing a mother's love? I know my husband would have been wonderful to him and would have given him a great life, but I wanted to be part of his life. I wanted to watch him grow, wanted to see him look back being assured I was there if he needed me. I did not want to miss him going off to college and to see him experience all the wonderful aspects of youth and falling in love. I wanted to be at his wedding. I needed to be there for all his good times and even the bad ones that we know would slip into his life. I longed to see the man he would become. But I was not promised tomorrow and, I was not even promised today. The doctor's words had been loud and clear, I may not make it past today.

The fogginess had cleared in my head, I had fought it hard, and I was left in a state of numbness. I was stunned and could not believe the situation I was in. Nothing that had happened in my past seemed to matter any longer and I was ashamed that I had held on to all those bad memories and all that hate. Nothing will wake you up faster than a slap in the face that you are dying. I looked around and saw where I was, and it registered to me that I was not in my room filled with flowers and balloons.

I saw metal shelves of supplies and boxes and machines connected to me that were purring along as if they were keeping time with each other. I did not immediately talk to the Lord. I felt like an unwanted visitor at some stranger's dinner table. How was I going to approach this with him? How do you start that conversation? "Hey God, it is me, Gaye, I know it has been a long time, and I have been horrible to you and all, but I may be dying later today or tomorrow. I just wanted to ask if You would save me. Thanks." But no, I could not do that. I was not in any shape to ask for anything, or to barter with God. I knew that if I died at that moment, I would be lost for all eternity. It was that simple. For all those years I had ignored His existence in my life. And now I would pay a price.

I began to think of Jonathan again, so little and such a miracle. We had gone through so much waiting and planning for him, and now this. As I lay there, expecting the worst, I remember saying, "God, it's me." I remembered saying that at night when I would get into bed as a child. If I had something on my mind or I was upset or scared, I would call out to Him, "Are you there Jesus?"

I was fully alert now, and oddly more so than I had been since before the delivery. No one had been in the room since the doctor had left except the nurse that one time. I said, "Thank you Lord, for our baby." And then it just all poured out of me:

"Lord, I don't even know what to say, you know the things I have done. You know my attitude, my thoughts, and my actions. I cannot ask You to forgive me because of the news I have received, that is cowardly.

I do not think it right to make a death bed confession, but I need You. I am asking for my child's sake. If you take me, will you please take care of my baby and his dad? I cannot bear to leave them, but I know it is not up to me. But, if You did see fit to spare me to raise him, I will do everything possible to ensure he knows who You are. I will take him to church, and I will be the best mother I know how to be. If you would do this, I cannot even begin to tell You how thankful I would be. I am so sorry for the way I have been. I am so sorry for doubting you."

I cannot fully describe what happened next. I felt a presence in the room that was familiar to me. I knew that God was in this place. It was immediate. If I could have been able to get out of that bed with all my tubes, I would have bowed before Him. His presence was so strong and heavy.

After I could soak in those moments for a minute, I said, "Jesus, thank You for all the happiness, happy times, I had tried to forget about. Thank You for showing me the joy and the faith I once had, and what has been missing from my life for so long. Thank You for holding on to me. It has been so dark where I have been. All this time, I have blamed You, but, in those situations, I know you really spared me from bad choices. Spared me from terrible things. You had better plans for me. Please forgive me. And, if this is my time to go, help me to be ready to meet You. And give me strength to leave my family, that precious little boy and my husband that I adore."

I cannot begin to share how God moved over me in those moments. I had been so broken, and my life had been in shambles. But now there was a peace that only God can give. God was waiting in the wings for me to realize that I needed Him, not only for my baby but for myself. He was quick to come. If everything had been up to me that day to save my life, it would not have happened because I was not in charge, I had no power. When I said I was so sorry, I was expecting thunder to clap or quick banishment. I had continued to let God down repeatedly. But it was not like that. God wanted me to remember about the good times and my life before all the chaos. He was not reminding me of all of my mistakes.

The devil placed a stamp on me that said return to sender. He wanted to finish me off. Shut me down. But God delivered me anyway! Praise His name! He had reminded me of happy times. There was nothing negative, just fond memories of happier times so long before. I remember lying there and feeling light suddenly as if a large burden had been taken from me. I cannot explain it and like so much in my life, I do not have a true way to express the emotions I was experiencing.

My mind began to clear so that I could put all the words together that I needed to say. Before that, I would not have been able to cry out to God, I had no idea where I was, or what was happening around me. I was dependent on other people's prayers because I was helpless to pray on my own at that time. But now, the atmosphere in that storage room had taken on a new energy and God had cleared my mind. There were no windows, but I could see light in the room without a doubt. It was as if curtains had been pulled back in a dark room and it flooded with bright lights. I will never forget it. My guilt and embarrassment had changed to a hunger to reconnect with my savior. It was not because I was scared to die, but He had shown me when He had brought Bruce into my life at just the right time, and my hard shell had started to crack. I knew without a doubt God had put us together. I was still in His care. He did that to prick my heart and let me know He had not left me. No one could have brought us together like that but God.

I did not want to die lost to eternal hell, but I wanted, no needed, to tell Him how sorry I was for not trusting, not having faith that He would take care of me and turn my life around for the good. I said, "Lord, I know you may take me, and it is so difficult to ask Your forgiveness after all I have done. But, if You would spare my life to raise my child, I will forever be grateful. I will serve You and I will raise my son to love You." And after all that time of being lost in the world alone, I was home. I am so grateful to the Lord that I swerved from the danger of my own carelessness and that He restored me.

There was no fanfare, no minutes that ticked away while He contemplated whether I was worth forgiving or not. It was just like we had talked all along. I had not spoken a word to him in over twelve years. And now I knew for sure He had never left my side. Even at my very worst. Rebellious, drinking and days wishing for death, God was right there all along. It was like coming home from a long journey to the things that are loved and familiar. His salvation was swift, no questions asked. I recommitted my life to him, and he sealed our bond with his blood.

I look back now, and it was like God planned for me to be alone when I got that horrible news from the doctor. I may never have had a chance to be intimate and raw with Him had everyone been around.

I may have been too cowardly to talk to Him with people coming and going. I could have been too self-conscious to share my heart with Him. But now, I knew for really the first time since I was a child, that my bond with the Lord was permanent. No more running, no more doubting that He cared for me. Oh, I knew I would experience times when I felt discouraged, but I could never deny His power in my life again. He had brought me back from death and had restored me. I was overwhelmed, beyond words, and just filled with relief. The heaviness of my burden was gone. I still did not know if God would take me home or not, but I was ready either way.

Later that evening or the next, I do not recall. The doctors determined it was time for me to see my baby. I was starting to stress from not being near him. So, one of my nurses was instructed to escort and stay with Bruce and I so that I could see my little one. I was very weak, still a little foggy, but I had come so far in a brief time. God had touched me both physically and spiritually and had saved my life. I do not really remember how long I was in that room, but it seemed like forever. One day I am told that I am dying. Then fast forward to the next evening. I find myself taken by wheelchair to the NICU. It was more than I could conceptualize. Everything about this process was unnerving and strange.

When we arrived, the NICU nurse handed Jonathan to me and shoved a bottle into my hand. I was still coming back from all the trauma, and I guess I did not comply with what she wanted because she was quite hateful. She gave me a look of disgust and said, "Well, feed your baby!" Apparently, there is no communication between labor and delivery and the NICU unit or she would have hopefully been more empathetic knowing my circumstances. Thoughts were swirling in my head, and I remember just looking at Bruce for help. But I held my baby boy for the first time. He was so small, and Bruce helped me check to see for myself that he had all his toes and fingers. He never cried, he just squeaked and that caught me off guard. Bruce had seen him often in the NICU, so he was used to him and his behavior. But I was new to this. His little squeaks and squirming were the cutest things and music to my ears. He was beautiful and perfect. I was in love immediately. No description from another person is like seeing your baby firsthand for yourself. His pediatrician and Bruce had described him to me, but it was nothing like I could have imagined. Holding him for the first time and smelling the sweetness of an innocent little baby was beyond what my heart could take.

I was only allowed with him for a few minutes so that I did not get overstimulated. Then they let me go back to the original room that had been waiting for me while I was in labor and delivery. When we entered, it smelled strongly of flowers. It did not matter to me what condition anything was in; I was glad to be back in a real room. Even if only for a trial period, And, hopefully, closer to finally going home. It is comforting when I think about that time. What a difference a couple of days makes in your life. God was waiting in the wings for me to realize that I needed Him, not only for my baby but for myself.

I could not breastfeed and had to remain quiet upon returning to my room. One of my doctors came in to check on me and saw the nurse had left a breast pump on my table and she became angry. She asked the nurse why she had done it and then proceeded to fling it to the floor. She explained that even though I was in a room I was being closely monitored. The last thing I needed to worry about was breastfeeding. She shook her head, "Heavens, we are trying to keep her alive." Then she patted my shoulder and told me to rest and that she was sorry. After a week of being in my room without any issues, I was allowed to go home. Jonathan had to remain in the hospital another week, so I could not take him home with me. Nothing was normal about this pregnancy, and I was upset when I realized

I would have to leave him in the hospital. However, the doctor reminded me that I had just had major surgery, and had been near death. I needed time to recover from what I had been through. And the real miracle was that none of my major organs were impacted. Even though they started to shut down, there was no long-range damage. I was well.

It was good to finally be back home in our house, and around anything but the four walls of a hospital room. I had been there for so long, so it was wonderful to see something different. The next morning early, I was up and moving slowly. I held on to the furniture to walk and keep balanced. But I was ready to go back to the hospital to be with our baby. Bruce told me it was too early, but my look let him know I was going one way or another. So, he got ready and took me back. I was in great pain still from the cesarean section, but so happy to finally see our little boy in the incubator. He was having ultraviolet treatments for jaundice so we could not hold him right away that morning. I began to look around at the paperwork by his little space. There was a little book that described him, talked about his habits, eating and everything related to his care. As I looked through it, I came to a place where it said, "Father has bonded with the child." And, then in big letters it said, "Mother has not bonded with the child."

I immediately felt horrible, and the worst guilt. Tears were coming fast, and Bruce saw how upset I had become when I handed him the book. When he saw the words, he tried to comfort me as he always did. But I felt like the worst mother ever. I was not there for my child when he needed me the very first days of his life to bond with him. Would I ever bond with him? I was so scared. When we finally got to bring him home, I was overjoyed. We were scared that day and I was so happy to see my mom. She had experience and had come to help us adjust to having a baby. And especially a tiny one. Believe me, we certainly needed her because that little life was now our responsibility. That is something that becomes soberingly fast for new parents.

When we were getting ready to take our little nugget home the social worker for the NICU told us that we would need clothes for a preemie baby. She offered some clothes that they kept at the hospital. People came from all over to have their babies treated at the NICU so they would need clothes and other items. We had thanked her, but we certainly were not taking clothes that someone else may need. She told us that preemie clothes would be difficult to find with the change of seasons we were in, so she advised us to get Cabbage Patch doll clothes. I thought it was so funny. But sure enough, we went to Toys R Us and got Cabbage Patch clothes for him. Most fit perfectly, but there were a few outfits that were too large for him.

CHAPTER NINETEEN

Jonathan was thriving. And although he was considered a premature baby, his trips to the doctor showed growth and no signs of problems. The hospital monitored his growth, eating, and all aspects of his cognitive skills. God had given us a perfect gift. A perfect little boy, healthy and beautiful. There were no signs of down syndrome. He was wide-eyed and took everything in. And everyone that saw him was amazed at how alert and contented he was.

My blood pressure was coming down slowly to within normal range during the eight weeks I was recuperating. But the time went quickly. Before I knew it, I was searching for a caregiver for our baby. We did not want to expose him to a daycare environment with many children. We opted for an individual that only had six children and she came highly recommended. When I went to interview her the first time, I had Jonathan in his carrier in one arm, and my briefcase in the other. We often laughed together later about the lengthy list of questions I pulled out to ask her. The funniest to her was the question about whether she had fluoridated water or not.

She would say, "Gaye LaFoe, in all my years of doing this, not one person asked me about the quality of my water." On the first day back to work, I dropped Jonathan off on the way. I can still remember the horrible things that weighed on my mind about leaving him.

What if someone came in with a gun and kidnapped him? What if he choked? Or if a child tried to pick him up and dropped him. Unfortunately, that had happened around that same time to someone Bruce knew. They were not able to save the baby. I was in knots with worry even though I was trying to have faith that God would take care of him. Our sitter assured me that she would watch him constantly and my body shook uncontrollably from nerves when I handed my little angel over to her.

He was too small for a real bottle, so we used a small cylinder to feed him and he would only take an ounce or so at a time and drift off to sleep. So, it seemed we were always feeding him. Every day, we fell more in love with him. He did the cutest things and had the brightest eyes. We tried to soak up every moment. I felt he was growing much too fast. Bruce did not think he was growing fast enough. He could not wait to play ball with his little man. I think that is the difference between moms and dads. Dads are ready to move things along so they can do things with their children. And moms want to hold on to every minute and keep them little as long as possible.

Our precious boy wore a little white tuxedo romper and a tiny yellow rose boutonniere in memory of my dad, his grandfather, on the day we dedicated him. We were at my mom's church and there was quite a fuss and shouts to the Lord that we were there after the miracles God had performed in our lives. It was truly a joyful day. Baby dedications always make me cry. I love when parents want to return their children back to the Lord in this symbolic act, with the promise that they will raise them in the ways of the Lord. And I love when the pastor takes that little one and prays over them. There were days as he grew that Jonathan would turn his head a certain way and I saw my dad in him. Oh, how I wished Dad could have seen him.

Jonathan's first birthday came so quickly, I could not believe time had passed that fast. And I planned a huge event (like any), event I plan. It had to be big. Everything was moving quickly, and I wanted to hold on to every moment, every memory and every first he demonstrated. The doctor had told me during a follow-up visit, that he could not advise me not to get pregnant again, nor could he have confidence that the same horrible things would not happen again. He did remind me that it was something we would really want to consider carefully, and to think about the possible risks. I was terrified to get pregnant again, so I had no problem putting having another child on the back burner.

I got up one morning months later with a horrible taste in my mouth that would not go away. No matter what I did that day, it stayed with me. I racked my brain, trying to remember where I had tasted that before. A strong metal taste and I smelled eggs or something like that odor with it. It was familiar to me, but I had not been sick recently, so nothing came to mind. And, then it hit me! I had that taste and smell when I was first pregnant with Jonathan. But this could not be, no not again! It was not a joyous occasion finding out I was having another child. At first, I was terrified. Everything that had happened the first time was very vivid in my memory.

I was immediately classified as a high-risk patient. The sweet doctor that I loved and trusted was genuinely concerned as well. He promised me that we would get through this pregnancy together, and so the journey began again. Bruce was overjoyed. He was not at all concerned, and I did not see how he could be this way after what we had experienced before. But he assured me that he had known another baby would be coming very soon and that things would be much easier this time for me.

I always looked to him for reassurance, so between that and trusting God, I began to feel better about bringing a new baby into our little family. Everyone was overjoyed with the news because of my history with infertility and the struggle we had having Jonathan. So, it was great having the support of our friends and our parents. And I absolutely loved being pregnant. Even as sick as I was with Jonathan, and all the complications throughout that pregnancy, I loved it. We had hoped for a little girl and were elated when it was confirmed. Our baby girl was due near the end of November, 1990. Jonathan was having a little sister, and all was well with the world.

The first few months of my pregnancy were easy. And I was dreaming of doing special things with both my little boy and girl. No real morning (or in my case with Jonathan), all day sickness. No problems at all and I was ready to breeze right through this pregnancy without any problems. I remember feeling the baby flutter just a tiny bit late in my fourth month, and not much else. In comparison to her brother who was active quickly, she was very chill and hardly moved. And, at my appointment I had mentioned that she was not moving. They scanned me and said that her heart rate was fine and strong, and I would begin to feel her movements later. But that never happened. Well into my sixth month, there was no movement. Again, the doctor scanned me and told us that her heart was strong, yet he could not explain why she was not active.

I had explained it all to my mom and she and I would pray about it, asking God to intervene and keep her safe. We had a name by now, Bethany Elyse LaFoe, and I would talk and sing to her. I would rub my ever-enlarging stomach to see if it would generate movement from her, or some response, but it did not. Jonathan was highly active at night, and I waited for Bethany to follow suit, but she did not. It was in my seventh month that I fell on the stairs leading to the basement and bounced down on my behind to the bottom, scraping up my arms and legs. We called the doctor and he advised us to go to the emergency room and he would meet us there. Ironically, it was the same doctor that had delivered Jonathan. When he had me hooked up to the monitor, he said, "You are in labor." I assured him that it was Braxton-Hicks contractions, because I had them consistently, and he was shocked that they were that intense.

They had monitored me part of the night, and then felt that it was safe to go home. Still no movement from the baby and with all the technology available in that huge training hospital, they could not tell me why she was not moving or kicking. The only relief I had was that during this pregnancy the endometriosis had been dormant. The doctors told me that if you can even get pregnant with this disease, it will calm during pregnancy and then return. After I had Jonathan, it had raised its ugly head again and I had been back to my long cycles. Losing so much blood, I had to be on extra iron and the pain had been excruciating. This reprieve from it had been wonderful. We had just turned off the porch light from Jonathan's first-time trick or treating as Mickey Mouse when I went into labor. He was so adorable. But we had to hurry because my contractions were strong and fast.

The pain was immediate and severe. I could barely move. We hurried to get ready because we thought we had time before she was due. Because I was a very high-risk patient, the plan was for me to have a scheduled cesarean section two weeks before my due date as soon as it was safe to take the baby. Our great plans of having time to do everything with ease was short lived. We dropped Jonathan off at his babysitter's house, as she had graciously asked to keep him while I was in the hospital. My mom's health had deteriorated, and Bruce had called his parents who had planned to come down to take care of Jonathan, so they were now on their way from Indiana. When we got to the hospital, they began to monitor me. My contractions were fast and intense. Our little sweet girl was not waiting any longer, she was coming.

My favorite doctor rushed by on his way to the operating room and I was relieved to see him. He had always given me a sense of calm. And right now, I needed that. Knowing he was there helped me tremendously to not be as scared. I knew a cesarean section was coming and I was uncertain what would happen to me or the baby. I was praying and I remember saying "Jesus, are you there?" This delivery was even scarier than Jonathan's was. I did not have any idea I was in such danger with him, but now, it was clear in my mind that this could go badly. This child, me, or both of us may not make it. Why couldn't I just deliver babies like other women, no I had to be dramatic?

When the bustling around the operating room quieted down, and the surgery commenced it was different. I felt tense, but it appeared that everyone else in the room was as well. Their controlled professional demeanor was cracking a little. I tried to look at Bruce for comfort but in my mind, I kept dwelling on what may occur, and my heart was racing. I remember at one point the anesthesiologist leaned down to my ear and said, "Mrs. LaFoe, I am going to give you a little something to calm you a bit." It was sounding much like the last time, and I was anxious. But what he gave me did not help.

I prayed and prayed, and I could feel horrible pressure, even worse than my previous delivery. I could hear the doctor ask questions in rapid-fire and when he would not get an immediate response, he became agitated. I was surprised when he inquired about my blood levels that had been ordered stat and began cursing at the nurse. I had never heard him do that. And it was alarming to me that he was that upset. He was the calmest man I knew, and he was rattled to the core. That was not a good sign. Something had to be wrong.

It seemed like forever, and I could hear instruments clanking and feel the pressure on my abdomen. Oh, and that horrible tugging sensation. Once, I thought my body would be lifted from the operating table it was so intense. And, then finally, after what seemed like an eternity, I heard a little cry. It was the sweetest cry. I was awake and getting to experience this, not like the last time when they knocked me out right after Jonathan was out of my body. I got to see her little face and hear her cry and we were both alive!!! What sheer joy. Bethany Elyse LaFoe was born on November 1, 1990, at 4:57 a.m. They had a specialist on standby and of course the pediatrician because we really did not know what we were facing with her not having moved through most of my pregnancy.

I wanted to pinch myself, because I was so grateful not to have had the complications like before. Bruce and I were just enjoying our little sweet girl when the doctor came in that evening. He looked exhausted and I commented on it. He had been delivering babies most of the day. He smiled but headed right over to the bassinet where Bethany was. She was small at 6.13 pounds with thin little arms and legs and a big cry. We knew we were in trouble the first time she was not happy. I remembered thinking something must have been wrong, he looked troubled standing over her now. When he leaned in and saw her, he broke out into the biggest smile.

He began telling us about my delivery. There was great concern that Bethany would not be born without complications. With no movement, the doctors were on high alert once she was born to do whatever necessary to save her life. There was fear of complications with me but mostly about her health. He went on to say that when my abdomen was finally open, and he was able to see inside he could not believe what he saw. "I have never seen anything like it." Of course, Bruce and I were listening intently, we had no idea what he had experienced. "This little girl was caught up in a web of adhesions. She was in a cocoon and that's the best way I can describe it to you," he said. By now, I could tell it had left an impression on him. He was very emotional. "You know, you had been through so much previously, and I kept thinking, I am going to have to tell this mother that her child is not going to make it. And if she does, and I can get her out of this mess, she may have a withered arm or leg," he went on.

I was tearing up by then as he just gazed at our beautiful healthy baby girl. "You were losing a lot of blood and I had tried to move quickly for your sake, but I could not move quickly for her sake." he told us.

"But God helped you," I said, and he agreed. "You are our hero; I hope you know that." I said to him, and he laughed.

"You've aged me twenty years with these two kids," he said, shaking his head.

We looked at our little girl with so much gratitude to the Lord for sparing us, but also for making her perfect in every way. Only God could have made her grow in utero with no place to move around, no way to spread her arms or legs. She was a definite miracle. Later I would dress her in little outfits and think about what he had said. The outcome could have been much different for her had it not been for God's healing. One thing that stuck in my mind when the doctor had visited us that evening was how the odds were against her. Restricted blood flow, no room to move around and yet she was perfect in every way.

That still amazes me when I look at her, even today. She was a few months old, and I had remembered my promise to God to get these babies in church. We decided that we would try a local Assemblies of God closer to us than Mom's church. They were popping up around town now and we set out one Sunday morning to visit. I had promised God that I would have them in church programs and we both had agreed to give them the best we could afford to do in anything they set out to do. We had two incredibly special children and we knew it. The Lord had been merciful to us and to me. When we arrived at church that morning, the place was a little storefront building. I thought no way. I told God I would give these children the best and I do not even want to go in there.

Bruce could tell what I was thinking, like always and he said, "Come on, we are already here let's go in." I could hear piano music coming from inside the room as we entered, when we headed inside this little makeshift church. Not like the Assemblies of God I had attended as a child. It had pews and a little platform and a podium out of wood. A man was up leading a song and maybe thirty people were in that room. New blood, yes, and young at that! Welcome! they must have thought.

When the service was over, people came up to introduce themselves and told us how glad they were that we had come. Bruce looked content. The older ladies liked him at the onset, and they drooled over our babies. I felt like I was at a grandma convention. Everyone was very much older than us, and I only saw two kids. One a teenager that we later found out was the pastor's daughter and another little girl.

I wanted to be gracious, but I was not planning to return. I had made promises to the Lord, and this was not what I had envisioned for my children and certainly not what I thought God would want for them. However, Bruce liked it and after much discussion, we did return the following week. During the service, the man that led the singing and his wife, the pianist, made the announcement that they would be leaving the following Sunday. Another good reason not to return, no music. But the pastor had zoned in on us and started asking questions after church and Bruce blurted out that I played the piano and sang beautifully. I was so mad at him. I thought well, two can play this game and I assured the pastor that Bruce was available for any and everything he needed assistance with.

The only problem was Bruce was eager to help. So, my revenge was not sweet. In fact, it required soul searching the following week to come to grips with these commitments. We both had demanding careers. He was up at four every morning and did not return until late in the evening. I had to be at work by 8:00 a.m. downtown after dropping off the two children at separate places. I brought work home often because my position was demanding, and my staff needed me throughout the day. We would finish dinner, and baths and finally get the children settled and I would work or scrapbook. I had difficulty sleeping at night due to my stress level. So, I knew very well we were taking on quite a bit with the addition of church responsibilities. I did not want to start something else and not give it the time it would require. People would be counting on us.

One of the afternoons coming home from work, I was talking to the Lord about this church and what we were getting in to. I had asked Him to spare me, and my children and I had promised that I would raise them to hear God's Word and to love the Lord. But this did not seem like the place for all of that. I could not imagine this being the right place God had for us. As I was driving that day, God spoke to me in my spirit and said, "I did not ask you to get them in the best church in town. The building does not matter, the facade is no indicator of what is inside. My promise to you is that if you do this with your whole heart, I will take care of your children." It still brings tears to my eyes even now, how the Lord gently rebuked me. I had only seen the outside, and I had been very judgmental. I had wanted what I thought God would want for my children instead of what he actually wanted.

So, I said, Lord, let's do this. That next Sunday morning, I was so anxious. I did not play the piano well and certainly not in front of anyone, and especially with leading the singing too. But there I was hitting those clunkers and the people sang and joined in like they did not even notice my blunders. I played in one or two keys, and nothing fancy. I played songs I knew because I could not read music and I did the special singing either playing the piano or by using a soundtrack or cassette tape. My palms sweated and my fingers shook but I was like Peter in the water, I was looking to Jesus! Cause I sure needed His help.

Soon, Bruce was opening for the pastor, taking the offering, praying over needs, and even speaking on occasion. I was overseeing the music, taking care of the kids (all four of them), on Wednesday nights, working on special programs for Christmas, and anything else. It was an older demographic, so any parties we had, Bruce and I took care of. We were making great money and we wanted to help the church. He was Santa, and we handed out gifts and cooked for one of our Christmas parties and we grew to love everyone there.

Bethany was dedicated at that little church. I think about funny times there.

I had written a Christmas play geared toward the four children, and Bethany had promised she would sing *Away in a Manger* during the program. The four children, Bruce and I had stayed all afternoon that Sunday of the program setting up and practicing.

The crowd was great that evening, around forty-five were in attendance. It came time for Bethany's solo, and she got up under the piano bench and refused to come out and sing. I ended up singing the song, but watching the tape much later, I was laughing hysterically at me getting angry at her for messing it up. You could see the curtain moving as I was up under the piano trying to get her out. Oh, the memories.

And, as we watched our little ones grow, they wanted to go down to the altar every service for prayer. I would be at the piano, and Daddy, Jonathan and Bethany would head down to the front of that little building, and those great church pillars who could pray heaven and earth together would pray over them. We had been attending for quite some time and our children were five and seven now. The pastor wanted to build a new building and moved forward in securing the land and starting the build. Bruce and I paid for some of the things inside the new church. We covered the cost of the new baptistry and gave offerings toward other expenses associated with the new building. I do not know what happened, but things were not the same after we moved to that new church.

The older folks did not take to it as well, and to be honest; we all liked the old storefront ourselves by then. But there we were in a new church just like the pastor had wanted. Bruce and I had kept up the pace for a long time as volunteers and we were becoming exhausted with our schedules. The pastor had a regular full-time job, so he was under a strain as well. Anyway, a lady came to the church with her family and decided that she wanted to lead the singing. That was music to our ears. Both Bruce and I needed help. She was willing, and that meant more to me than anything.

However, it caused a great divide. The congregation felt that she was taking that away somehow from us and they were not having it. We felt so bad for her. And we would exhaustively explain that we were completely fine with new workers coming into the church. We desperately needed the help. I had been in churches before where people did not step up and if you happen to offer to do something you were then bombarded with duties. There are never enough workers in a church, no matter the size.

One evening we were having a guest speaker at the church. Bethany was sick with a fever, and I had to stay home that day from work with her. Anything that happened after 5:00 a.m. until evening was my responsibility because Bruce was on the road. It was difficult to contact him, and it fell on me to manage. It is just what we had to do. But it put intense pressure on me to juggle my mommy duties along with being a professional. And, then the demands of the church. Bruce had called the pastor to advise him I could not be there.

That Sunday morning the pastor made comments about us not attending that service from the pulpit. And, how we had left them in need. I could feel the tension in the room as he shot arrows at us. Bruce and I had talked about it at lunch that day and had hoped that it had blown over by the time we returned for the evening service. He called us to his office above the sanctuary about fifteen minutes before the evening service. He proceeded to tell us that we were not committed to the church and questioned our dedication. He got angry and said some things to Bruce, causing me to become defensive and it did not turn out well. I questioned his lack of wisdom in railing out at us. It was all so unfortunate. The members overheard everything. The tension was so thick.

After the service was over, we hugged and kissed everyone and that was our last time at that church. I knew that night that our time there was finished. We had given it our best, our absolute best, but it was time to move on. The children had been there since they were tiny. They were sad, and Bruce and I were both numb and felt a loss for a long time afterward. Sadly, our children were not baptized in that beautiful baptistery we purchased.

We had friends that attended the Church of God, and we began attending there. As the children began to become involved in sports and academics, their abilities began to shine. Jonathan and Bethany were well liked by students and faculty at school and did extremely well in their studies. They excelled in every sport they participated in. It was amazing watching them both.

They were recognized in the community for distinguished achievements, and people would ask us how we had managed to have such fine children. One day, a very prominent man asked me how we had these brilliant children. They were successful in everything they touched. And he wanted to know our secret.

"Well, we give God all the glory for our children. The very fact that they are alive is a miracle and we gave them back to God early." I shared with him. After that conversation, I began to think about it. It did seem strange that both kids were exceptional at everything they touched. That is not just from a proud mother, I have the awards, the letters, and proof to show their accolades through the years.

I remember saying, "God, what is the story? I know it is not Christian school because they learned more bad things there than in public school." We had to move them to public school at one point because I was off work for a back injury. The Lord reminded me then of that little storefront church. Oh, I cringed thinking about my piano playing. "Do you remember what I promised you when you were deciding to work at that little church? I told you I would take care of your children.

Everything that they touch is a result of my favor for your obedience. Every Sunday when they went up for prayer, I was heaping favor into their lives. The decision you and Bruce made to work for the kingdom in that little church did not go unnoticed."

I was so humbled. We had stepped out in faith back then because we were both overwhelmed at doing things, we were not comfortable doing. Bruce did not like speaking in front of people and I was tormented by the piano. But that little church and those dear people meant the world to us. I thank God for that part of our lives and that He kept His promise to us and our children.

About six months after I had Bethany, I had to have a total hysterectomy. The endometriosis had spread into my abdomen, and there was also a large tumor that had to be removed.

It was by God's grace that we were able to have her before this had to be done. I woke up after surgery and Bruce smiled so big at me. Just seeing him made it all better. My skin was a dark gray and there had been an order placed for a blood transfusion. The nurse had arrived for me to sign paperwork for the blood, and I refused to sign it. No, I was not taking blood, I had two children and I was fearful of acquiring AIDS. It was prevalent then, and many people were affected by it. The head nurse had called my doctor and he instructed her to tell me he was on his way to the hospital. A few nurses had come in from time to time and would instruct me to not move around. They would say to lie as still as I could. But no one told me why. When my doctor arrived, he looked at me and said, "Gaye, you have no choice but to take this blood. You lost most of your blood in surgery."

I was still doubtful, but he went on to explain, "You see the color you are? You are gray, there is no blood reserve in your body right now. You should have already had this blood. Your hemoglobin is less than four and it should be in the high teens!" A fatal level of hemoglobin is less than five. If it is this low, it can cause heart failure or death. A normal hemoglobin for a woman is between 11.6 and 15. "If you move or break a stitch that causes the smallest amount of blood to flow, you will die. You will die! There is no blood in your body. Now whether you sign this paper or not, you are getting this blood right now!" He looked at Bruce who looked as stunned as I was. Minutes later, we all watched as the blood began to flow through my veins. It took time, but my color began to return. When I look at those photos of me that day, it is so disturbing that I was that close to death again. But God had spared my life.

We loved our church, and the children were thriving, and all was well with the world. Holidays were great fun and each one was memorable. One Christmas when the kids were small, Christmas morning had finally arrived. I had my usual desire to make everything perfect for them, and so the den was filled with presents. That is what I remembered as a child at Christmas, so I just did what I was comfortable with and what I had experienced. After they had been opening presents for awhile little Jonathan said, "Daddy, can we take a break from opening presents and do something else, I'm tired." Bruce gave me that look that I often get from him that said it all. Again, Gaye, you went overboard.

LaFoe events were the place to be. We could easily have seventy-five or more children at a birthday party. And holidays were the best. I did everything I could to make those precious memories for our family. I knew very well that giving our children so much may not be the best idea, but they were not spoiled by any means. They did chores, worked hard in school, and participated at church.

CHAPTER TWENTY

One Saturday morning, in early 1996, I had an accident. I was vacuuming, and I pulled the coffee table to vacuum under it and felt something pop in my right shoulder. When I was around eleven years of age, I had gone out to throw the ball with my brother. Some days I felt better than others and on occasion, I loved to get outside. After I had thrown the ball, I felt a pop in my right shoulder and had to be taken to the hospital. Of course, with me it is never something easy or simple. The ball and socket from my shoulder had become separated which caused the ball to slip out of the socket. The orthopedic surgeon I saw then had immobilized me for eleven weeks so that I could not use my arm. He had joked that when I got older, I would want to wear slinky dresses and he did not want me to have a large scar. So, he opted to not repair it hoping the immobilization would help it to heal without surgery.

He did caution that it could happen again, and I would need to have it repaired. So here I was now, all those years later with the same problem. The orthopedic surgeon at present, had also immobilized me for a brief time but said that surgery was necessary, but only when I could not stand the pain any longer. I had refused to have surgery right then. When you are a mom, your needs go on the back burner. So, during the next eighteen months, I took care of two little children, home, work, and church. And I started a night program to complete my degree. I had not been able earlier because of my dad's health, and I only needed a few credits to graduate so this was my best avenue to receive my degree. This plan was initiated before that Saturday when my shoulder injury reoccurred. My timing was always the best.

Along with all of this, my favorite boss and friend took on an office within our company that was struggling to stay open. I would have done anything for him, and he brought me out to the field to revamp the quality goals and bring the office from paper to automation. I managed everything while favoring my right arm and holding it close to my body. I typed and drove with caution and pain. Bruce was a terrific help with the children and things at home. His schedule had changed, and he was on the day shift so could get the children in the afternoons. My life was in motion 24/7. I attended classes on Monday evenings, and it would be late when I got home. I always felt so guilty not being there on those evenings to tuck my babies in but in the business world you must have a degree and besides that, I wanted to finish something I had started.

I cannot even begin to describe how painful my shoulder was at times. I would sit in my office and would feel so badly that I would want to be sick in my trashcan. Finally, I graduated. And once again, I missed my ceremony because I could not move my shoulder to dress for the occasion that day. It had frozen and I was terrified that it would be like that forever. But, late in the evening after medication and rest I began to have some range of motion. I received my diploma the next week in the mail. One more thing on my exceptionally long to do list was completed.

The children were resilient, and Bruce was my hero during all this time. He cooked and cleaned and oversaw sports and I did everything I could under the circumstances. My boss was wonderful, and the office had turned around. I was so satisfied that I had been there for him when he needed me and that he had confidence in me to take on this huge responsibility. One day, we were heading back from lunch, he, another manager, and myself and we stopped in front of the emergency room of a local hospital. "Get out!" he said. I was taken back and asked, "What do you mean?" "Listen do not come back to work until you get that shoulder taken care of. You have put up with this for nearly two years and everything's good now, so get it repaired." What started out to be less than a two hour procedure, a week or so later, had turned into an almost six-hour nightmare.

The surgeon came into my room smiling saying that my shoulder had been a mess. His words. I was not surprised. Wasn't everything I did a mess? There had to be significant repairs in several areas of the shoulder, and the ball and socket had to be restructured and put back in place. I had to be admitted to the hospital after my easy breezy outpatient surgery. Could I do anything right? No. When I left the hospital, I was sent home for eight weeks of being immobilized. Bruce would have to assist me with everything. My right arm was held to my chest like I was always saying the pledge of allegiance. And, then the outside of my body was wrapped holding it in place. And that is how I lived for those many weeks. It was summer and brutally hot. I would ride to the ball field with the family and sit and watch the kids play ball and I would be soaked from sweat.

Because I could not take my arm down to my side, I could only move it out in front of me long enough to wash or dress. I wore these huge, oversized shirts that covered my arm and hung to my knees. Being short and wearing something several sizes larger did not make for a good look. I would just put my ball cap on and give in to my lack of style and frumpiness. One day, Bethany was playing on one field and Jonathan had just finished playing and we were headed to the concession stand. Bruce was her assistant coach, and her game had just got started.

There were a few moms who came to the ballfield dressed to draw attention to themselves. And they succeeded. I never understood it. It was a child's ball field. Anyway, Jonathan and I were walking to the concession stand and I had to walk slowly and watch for kids running so that I did not lose my balance and fall. My new bionic arm could not be disturbed. And I certainly did not want to go back for any further repairs.

Jonathan had been observing people and said, "Mommy, people don't look at you like they do other mommies." I did not know where this was going, I could not have felt worse about myself already. But I tried to play it off by saying, "Well, that is OK buddy." He went on to say, "When you come to watch me play, you just look like a mommy, you got your mind on me." How powerful for a little boy to realize what was going on. And what a wonderful thing for a mommy to hear. He knew I was only there for him and his sister. I did not care how uncomfortable I was after that; I would not have missed his games.

I took extensive physical therapy for weeks. I think that having such a painful illness as a child and teen had prepared me to manage this pain somehow. And, finally, my shoulder healed and left its reminder, an exceptionally long scar.

The night we brought Bethany home from the hospital as a baby, our house was chaotic and full of people. Bruce's parents had been watching Jonathan and his mom had opened the door leading to the basement instead of our bedroom and had tumbled down the steps. My neighbors and Mom were at our house while Bruce's dad followed the ambulance to the hospital. Bruce dropped Bethany and I off and headed to the hospital to be with his parents. Not the kind of homecoming we had expected. A year or so later, she became paralyzed from the waist down, and I will always believe it was from that fall. So, we would travel to Walt Disney World on occasion, but most often we went to Indiana, to help his parents. Bruce and the children would help grandpa and I would cook and fill their freezer and refrigerators with food so that grandpa would not have to worry about cooking. It was quickly taking a toll on him being her caregiver, but there was never a more loving and caring man to his wife. Well. Besides his son to me.

We watched our children excel and when people patted us on the back, we quickly told them it was all God. We both knew what we had been through, and that the very presence of our children was a miracle beyond our understanding. We were always on the go with activities, and we loved every minute of it. Birthday parties were over the top, I was my mother's daughter. I learned from the best. But they came so fast. I wanted to stop our world and tuck them away where everything would stay the same. Where our children would be buffered from the world, and from outside influence. Jonathan was becoming a young man and could light up a room with his smile and personality. He was liked by everyone, and we never had a moment's trouble from him. He could get a little strong-willed at times, but he was first born, so he and I would lock horns on occasion. But we would quickly resolve the issue and he knew without a doubt that I loved him more than life.

Bethany, our stunning girl was more reserved like her daddy. She had asked her daddy one day when he picked them up after daycare, what a valedictorian was. They had discussed different awards that day at preschool. He explained to her that you had to have perfect grades in high school to achieve that most prestigious award. So, that little girl set her mind that she wanted to be valedictorian one day. From kindergarten on, she never made anything less than an A on anything. We tried to reason with her not to put pressure on herself, but she was driven. She had a goal, and she was going to reach it. We even explained that she needed great grades in high school and that she had so much time to just enjoy school, but we could not convince her. She was also difficult to teach. Everything was easy for her, and her teachers would ask me what to do to keep her stimulated. I had no answers, I was not a teacher. As soon as possible, she went into the gifted program, but that was not even enough to hold her attention for long and she was reading well past her grade. When school was over for the summer, it was never discussed again by Jonathan until the time to start the next year, but Bethany was already searching out school supplies for the next year when we went to the store. Jonathan made great grades, but he liked having fun and was not as serious as Bethany was. He was a lot like me. They competed in everything, who could be the best? But they had a strong bond that a parent loves to see between her children.

The happiest day for Bethany was when she would get her supply list and could color coordinate all her binders and supplies. She would be in her room for hours working on her folders and supplies. In comparison, I would say, "Jonathan, what do you want for school this year?" and he would say, "Paper and some pencils I guess." They were different in many ways, but they were both compassionate, loving and driven in the goals they set for themselves.

They knew that there was no question they would go to college. I drilled that into them all the time. We loved how they interacted with each other. They played well as kids together making forts in the den and drinking pop with crushed ice. Grandma had given it to them when they had the chicken pox and she had watched them for us. We could hear their belly laughs watching their favorite Kid Song videos on Saturdays, and, at night, we would listen to them talking and laughing together on the baby monitor. When Bethany got too big for her crib, we turned her nursery into a beautiful room for her. I was so proud of it, and Bruce and I made it a big production.

She had been sleeping on Jonathan's bottom bunk bed for a time. So, the day arrived, and we finally presented her with her lovely new big girl room. "It is so pretty, but I sleep with brother," she said. So that was that. My, it was challenging though. We both worked extremely hard in our jobs and juggled everything, but we were a team, and that time with them was the best time of our lives.

The children were in a private Christian school when they were small. And when volunteering for events came around, it would really bother me at times. Other moms would wander in leisurely with their coffee and in their jogging suits. I would be in a suit and heels feeling like the worst mom ever. Because I had to hurry to get to work on time. I wanted to be the classroom mom. I wanted to sit and visit with the teachers and plan the Christmas parties. I did sign up to volunteer when I could, but I had to plan vacation time well in advance for those days. Once, when Jonathan was in pre-K and had a field trip planned to see Rock City and the Christmas decor, I was less than enchanted. My feeling about that place is that you do not take large groups of small children to run between jagged rocks with deep cliffs that hung off a mountain, but who was I to question.

So, the morning arrived, and the groups were being divided. I noticed no one was coming to my group. The teacher with her "Bless your heart" look came up to me and said, "Mrs. LaFoe, we know that Jonathan likes a little girl in class, so we thought we would let you manage Jonathan and her for the day." I thought to myself, *what are you trying to pull here, lady? I manage many adults; I can surely watch children.* She smiled and patted my shoulder and the little angelic being was placed in my care. When we arrived at Rock City, this innocent cherub turned into a holy terror. She was up and down, running and climbing and it did not take long for me to know I was in trouble.

When we got to the rocks where you had to squeeze through sections, she would take off running from me and I would have to try and get past other people while holding onto Jonathan so that I did not lose him too. And the worst thing was that she decided she wanted to see over the cliffs and snuck off way too close to the edge numerous times. I could just envision her tumbling down the side of that high mountain. God gave me sufficient grace that day because I was so irritated with that child.

By the end of that exceptionally long day, I told the teacher I felt sorry for her having to deal with that every single day. I never wanted to see that kid again. Jonathan had been great, and I loved being with him. I was worn out and nervous after that experience and doubted I would ever volunteer again. However, I gave in, especially for Christmas events. I would talk with the homeroom mother on this occasion who explained in her best baby voice that most of the preferred jobs were taken but they did have an opening at the mall. The mall? I knew full well she and the other stay-at-home ladies took the prime jobs, but it was for my children. So, at around 7:30 a.m. I trudged off to the mall not having a clue what the mystery job would be. When I got there and found the spot, it was the worst assignment ever given to anyone. Wrapping people's presents, no! the horrors! If there is one thing about the holidays I dread the most it is wrapping presents. The idea was that paper and supplies had been donated and we were to wrap presents to get a good donation for the school. Oh Lord, I hoped I had brought my credit card that day because I knew I would be paying these people and not vice versa.

It was the longest day. I wrapped so many gifts I cannot even remember how much paper I used. There was one other lady from another school and me. That was it. About an hour in, I hated everyone at that school, and every person that told me they needed their gifts wrapped "You know, a little special." What did that even mean? I wanted to say, "Oh special, like getting enough paper on the thing to cover it. Is that special?" I always had a problem with that. I was forever cutting paper too small for presents at home and now there too. When they would come and set those huge bags on our table to wrap, I wanted to be sick. It was not fun. I would have rather just given the school a large donation in our children's names. But I was one of the working moms, so I needed to give my best to the school, to make up for not always being at the teacher's disposal.

Another time, I drove a van full of boys downtown, with a pregnant mom about to deliver, and another woman that complained about every single thing. We were headed to the auditorium downtown to see a play and by the time we arrived and found a parking place I was frazzled. After the longest play in the history of entertainment, the boys were sleeping, and we had to wake them. They were cranky and hungry. Who could blame them I was too? After many problems getting out of that place and finally getting everyone safely back to the school, I was exhausted. The highlight was watching my sweet little boy enjoy everything about the day. A smile never left his face. I crawled into the house that evening.

My mother was causing us concern in early 2000. She would take extra medications forgetting she had already taken them and would leave food heating on the stove. She adored our kids and they loved her so much. Watching her slowly deteriorate was so difficult for me. I was always getting calls at work about her and would have to leave to go and fix a problem or care for her. We brought her to our house to live for a time and she almost burnt the house down, so we knew she would need to go to an assisted living facility. I think knowing your parent is no longer the strong warrior that you knew so well is the worst kind of pain. She was on strong medications now and would often say things that hurt our feelings without realizing it.

I was trying to manage work, my mother's care, and trips with the children when I could. It seemed we were going in all directions. We started our days early and at night well past midnight I would still be washing clothes for the next ballgame the following day. Once Bethany and I went to the aquarium in Gatlinburg with her fifth-grade class. She was nauseated the entire trip from carsickness. Once we arrived, I had to clean bird poop off her head because, as soon as she exited the bus, one large bird did its noticeably large business on the top of her head. Her expression was priceless, but the day ended up being fun and relaxing.

She and I also drove to Atlanta for modeling when she got older. She made good money doing this, and one of the agents had set her up to work at the Masters in Augusta Georgia one year. They wanted a girl with a specific look and presence, and they selected Bethany for the job. She would have made great money and it was truly an honor to be asked to be a hostess, but I was hesitant for her to be around all those men, so we declined. However, they also submitted her for a beauty pageant and she and I packed our bags for a trip to Atlanta. She only agreed because the winner received a scholarship. When we arrived, there were young girls everywhere and I having never attended a beauty pageant, had no idea how cutthroat one could be.

Bethany was getting attention, and mothers were giving her looks up and down, and none were welcoming. And I thought to myself, what is going on? After a long first day, we headed to our room and then to dinner. We were exhausted. The second day was the finals. Bethany had not taken it all that seriously and had borrowed a dress from a friend to wear and vintage clothes from Bruce's mom's closet. She was soon realizing just how competitive this thing was and I could see her disenchantment. But she won Miss. Junior Teen Tennessee! And was heading to the final round, the Nationals to win it all that evening. She had learned from the seasoned pageant girls that there was no scholarship money after all and that was it for her. I could tell in her interviews, and the final competition that she had shut down. When it was over and another girl that had been in numerous pageants won, we were ready to get out of there. But it was so much fun being with my daughter on these excursions.

It was right before Christmas 2001, when the doctor and I had a conversation about moving Mom to a nursing home. I fought for as long as I could, but we had to proceed with the plan. She was unable to be in assisted living any longer and needed more skilled care. I knew very well that she would have to be monitored by us or she would not get the appropriate care she needed. It is just how it is. You want it to be better, you want them to love your loved one as you do, but it does not always happen. And there is always limited staffing. I knew that would be added pressure on me to deal with this. It was a sad time when we moved her in. The day was gloomy, rainy, and cold and my heart was breaking. She had begged us not to take her there, but we had no choice.

I will never forget. It was just a few days before the holidays when we moved mom to the nursing home, and I was beyond heart broken. I had dealt for some time with someone at work that had said horrible things to me and who had tried to manipulate me and cause problems, and I had kept all that to myself. I tried to stay positive for my staff and employees. But between that and dealing with my mother's situation it had drained the life out of me. I could barely motivate with the heaviness I felt.

The hardest part of life is being a caretaker. No one knows the struggle you face unless they have been in your shoes. It was just Bruce and me. We had no support team to fall back on. Every single day was difficult. I knew I was spreading myself too thin. But I could not stop working or neglect the other demands of family and overseeing my mother's care. It was my reality and I had to do my best with it. I relied on the Lord so much for everything. And I was really beginning to work my faith each day. I had no choice about most things in my life and I needed the Lord's strength and mercy.

I would leave work at lunch and often go to the nursing home a short distance away and just be with Mom. I could always feel the Lord's presence in her room. Some days when I was at my wit's end, I would lay my head on her chest, and she would pray over me. Those prayers would get me through the rest of the day. I was living on grace and not much else. I was over tired and slowly coming to the end of my rope with everything pulling at me. I had put a telephone in her room so she could call me, and I could check up on her between visits. But later, as she began to have increased medications due to the Parkinson's disease, it had become an unwise decision as she called me at all hours begging me to come to see her.

One day, she got it in her head that Jonathan needed her so she told the staff she would be leaving to see about him. She called a taxi service she had used for years when she was well, and they sent a car for her. Her room was right by the nurse's station, and I will never understand why no one saw her. She rolled her wheelchair outside the front doors and waited until the taxi arrived. Right in front of the building, she sat waiting for the taxi and not one person saw about her.

We had just built a new house, and she had not been there yet. But she told the driver to take her to the area we lived, and he assumed she would give him the address once they got closer to our home. After driving all around, he told his dispatcher that he did not think Mom thought she knew where she needed to go and she was confused. The dispatcher who was also the owner told the driver to take her for a little ride and then back to the home. I received a call at work, that Mom was missing from the home. They could not explain where she was or why, but that she was gone. There I was in the middle of a project that had to be completed under a deadline, and my mother was lost somewhere out in the city. At that time, I did not even know who she was with. When I could get away, I headed over to the nursing home and she had just arrived back in her room. "Mom! Where have you been?" I asked, worried. She acted like nothing was wrong, nor was she phased by all the commotion that transpired as the result of her little adventure, and said, "I thought Jonathan was calling me and I had to go help him." Bless her heart, I could not be angry at her. I was so relieved that she was OK. I called the taxi service and they told me that the bill was one hundred and twenty-five dollars, but they refused to let me pay it. The owner said, "We love your mom, she has always been a joy to work with, so it's fine."

I met with the administration of the nursing home. I wanted to know just exactly how not one person had seen her leave. How she had managed to get past the nurse's station, the reception desk and the busy lobby area and not be seen or questioned. They did not have answers for me other than they did not take her seriously when she said she was leaving. I warned that with my mother, you best take what she says to heart. If she told you something, it was bankable. I removed her room telephone, and they had to place a band on her ankle to keep up with her.

At times, Mom was coherent and fine and other times she did not know us. Well, she did not recognize me, but she always knew Bruce. He was her favorite of course; we both knew it. He could get her to eat, and she would tell him how much she loved him while I sat there like a visitor in the wrong room. Because the medications were so powerful, she had mood swings, and she would become confused. She railed out at Bethany one day saying her dress was too short, and once she accused Bruce of seeing another woman that sat outside her window. It was sad, but also funny at times. My emotions were up and down seeing her like this. She was all I had left. I had counted on her for so much. Especially her prayers. I never wanted to think of her leaving us either by losing her memory, or in death. She would often tell me, "I will not always be here to pray for you, you need to do your own praying. Once I am gone, it will be your responsibility to pray for the family."

When we went to visit, Jonathan would get one of her many Bibles and quiz her on scriptures. She did not know who we were at times, but he could give her a place in the Bible, and she would rattle off the scripture without stopping to think. The kids would get the biggest kick out of it. I would explain to them that Grandma had always told me to keep God's Word in my heart and that nothing would ever remove it. Not confusion, or old age, nothing will ever take God's Word from your heart. What a wonderful life lesson for my children to experience something like that. Mom's Bibles were well worn and filled with markings and comments. Oh, she knew her Bible well.

CHAPTER TWENTY-ONE

We juggled sporting events and school activities with our work schedules, and it was difficult and trying at times. I felt like I lived in my car. I would race from work downtown to get to the school for basketball or whatever they were involved in at the time. And Bruce would meet us there. Most nights I would not have time to get food so they would get pizza from the concession stand to hold them over until we got home.

I noticed children watching them eat and so I began to get pizzas to feed everyone. No child needed to participate in after school sports without something to eat. Many of these children had not eaten since lunch. And some kids did not even have lunch money, I learned later. So, I decided to start packing a large cooler with things that traveled well and were healthy. It got to be a tradition as the yellow cooler became popular. When I entered the gym children would yell to my two, "Your mother is here with the yellow cooler." Or sometimes, they would ask, "Is your mom coming tonight and is she bringing the cooler?" It gave me such joy to feed these babies.

A teacher came to sit with me in the stands one time during a game. One by one children would come and show me their progress reports. Or they would tell me about their day. And I always got the biggest hugs. And, then they would get what they wanted from the cooler. She finally said, "Mrs. LaFoe, what is in that cooler?" I said, "It is food. I feed these kids." Once in one of my children's classes, the teacher asked the students if they could have any other mother who would they choose. The class had responded "Mrs. LaFoe." It brought me to tears when

I heard that. I loved every one of those young people and I fed them until mine graduated.

In the spring of 2001, I woke up one morning and had what felt like a catch in my left side towards my back. I thought I had slept wrong, but as I began to move around and prepared for work, it became more intense. Our office had moved to an area closer to my home and thank goodness it was all flat land, with no hills and no stairs. I crept along in the parking lot that day, taking tiny baby steps getting into the building. Nothing relieved the pain. I made an appointment with my doctor, and he immediately sent me for tests and an MRI of my lower back. By now, the pain was excruciating, and anything that I tried to do was difficult. The children were older and took care of themselves for school, while I was hardly able to dress myself.

I went back to my doctor for the results, and he advised that I had damage between my lower vertebrae and a great deal of deterioration.

Along with that, I had extensive degeneration in my neck, and he was able to show me on the X-rays where there were actual visible holes in my neck, and the deterioration filtered down to the top of my spine. He sent me to an orthopedic surgeon that confirmed everything he had stated. Little could be done to restore the deterioration, but before he did surgery on my back, he sent me for minimal impact physical therapy. Heat and gentle manipulation only made it worse, so upon my return to him we opted for surgery of my lower back to repair the damage. I was frazzled to say the least. And the pain was intense and constant.

I remember sitting up at night because I could not lie down. I would pray for God's healing and that my condition would not get worse. We had built our home, and things seemed to be going well for a change. No issues, Mom was at a satisfactory level, and things had been good for a season it seemed. But now, I could not plan for this. I had no way of scheduling, or my usual type A behavior of list making. It was out of my control. I felt helpless, but I also had to keep reminding myself that God was not surprised or taken aback by my situation, and he would be with me.

I woke up after surgery in the worst pain I had ever experienced in my life. I had drains in my back, and no one had warned me about them, so I almost pulled one out as I was thrashing around in the bed. The medication pump they had given me was not even taking the edge off and my pain medications had to be increased. I could deal with pain, and had to most of my life, but this was excruciating.

The first time they tried to get me up I nearly fainted from the pain. It was not really depression that set in, but it became clear to me that I would have a long recovery and when the doctor came in to visit, he stated just that. So, I was troubled about my future, and our life. My back had to have extensive repair, and he could give me no clear answer as to why it had occurred suddenly in the manner it had. I had not injured myself. We did lift and tug huge manuals at work and it seemed we were always packing and unpacking up our offices, but I could not attribute it to anything specific I remembered doing that would have hurt me.

The recovery process was lengthy. I was trying to have work sent home to me to do while I was on short term disability. I knew I was not supposed to worry, but I did.

My administrative assistant would send me a big box every week or so, and I was constantly checking work emails and voicemails. Even though I had left one that stated I was out of the office due to illness, people still left messages that required a response. Day after day, I was stuck at home with no outlet, no one there or company except my dogs. I quickly tired of television and began to listen to music. My pain level was so great that I really could not concentrate on reading. I received calls from church folks and friends. It was always nice to hear from someone. The pastor and his wife checked in as well. The day we had our housewarming, I was stuck in a chair by the window as friends came to see our new home.

I had gone back to the doctor, and he had recommended additional surgery that would result in placing rods and steel braces in my back to stabilize it and more for the deterioration that had occurred. But I had researched that, and I was not prepared to go through it and only then as a last resort. I wanted to be well, healed. I had experienced healing in a miraculous way as a young girl of seventeen, why not now? After a time, my company began to pressure me to investigate long term disability. The department that managed that aspect of the business was in New York, and I was assigned a claim specialist to collaborate with me. I had advised them several times that I was not interested in disability, I wanted to be well to return to work and to my life. But time clicked away, and I wondered if I was going to be like this forever.

I was so tired of being in pain. It seemed that my entire life had been some type of illness or pain, and I was beyond over it all. I had hoped that the surgery would help or correct the problems, but it only seemed to make the pain worse.

Again, the pressure of all of this was taking a toll on my body and my emotional health. I was not able to see my mom in the nursing home, and she begged for me to come. The guilt was beyond what I could endure at times. Guilt is often worse than physical pain. The worst part was that I could not do one thing about it. I was fighting so many obstacles, my job, myself, our finances. Bruce and the children kept things going because I was useless. The medications would take the edge off the pain but would not really stop it and I would lie awake wondering if this would be my life. I had already suffered so much illness and now this. At times, I questioned the quality of my life and if it was worth it. Should I just give in and not fight? But that was not in my nature. I had experienced healing, I had been given a second chance at life and I was not going to stop fighting. It was difficult though. I missed my work, missed my friends, church and family time.

I sat in my chair day after day by the big window facing the back of our property. I prayed constantly, and I knew that God was there, but He did not answer. We had built this house because we both worked; we could afford it and now this illness jeopardized our home and everything else we had worked so hard for. One day, in my prayer time, I cried out to the Lord, "What are we going to do about this house, Lord? I'm not at full salary, and we have other obligations, and our children are in a private Christian school." It was not fair for them to sacrifice because of me. God began to show me tall buildings in my spirit. I saw them every time I prayed. At one point, I yelled out, "What are you showing me this for?"

And then more gently, "What does this have to do with me and my situation?" One day, I had finished my devotion time and the Lord spoke in my spirit and said, "How badly do you want to keep this house? How strong is your faith?"

I had to laugh. I said, "Well, Lord, my faith could be better right about now."

"Get up and go march around this house seven times."

I thought it must be the pain medication; no way could I march around this house or any house, I could hardly walk. I could hardly make it to the restroom. Again, in my spirit I heard, "Go outside and walk around this house seven times." I knew then, I had to be in myself thinking this because surely God had not instructed me to do it. He knew my condition. On the odd chance it was the Lord, I said, "Listen, God, how am I supposed to do this? This house is long and there is no way I can even walk to the restroom without problems, let alone go outside. What if I fall?"

What if this and what if that. You know how we often try and reason with God when he gives us clear instructions.

I felt a tightness in my chest, and I thought standing up would help relieve it and when I struggled to stand, I felt God moving me to go. I baby stepped my way to the front door and then peered out at the three steps leading down to the walkway as if they were large mountains I had to climb down. Everything went through my mind and even telling this now it seems so bizarre. I gradually eased myself down each step which seemed like an eternity, and, finally, I was on the sidewalk. I had made it that far but looking out at the sides of the house and the uneven ground in areas, I did not see how I was going to do this. My head was saying go back inside, you look ridiculous. But I was scared not to be obedient.

We live in a secluded area where there are few houses and only minimal traffic, but I still felt extremely uncomfortable even attempting this for fear of what my neighbors would think seeing me.

And I knew beyond a doubt that I could not do it on my own. I could not understand why the Lord had instructed me to do this. I know there is a reference in the Bible about the Israelite's marching around the walls of Jericho for seven days and the walls came down. That is found in the Bible in Joshua 6:1-27, but what exactly did this have to do with me now? I started to go around the side of the house which faces a large area we refer to as the pasture and it is flat there. I began to panic being so far from the front door and I stood there in fear. I did not feel I could go back, and I could not force myself to go forward. There is not much traffic on our private road. But I noticed a lot of traffic going by our house. I was sure people watching thought I was insane. This is so difficult to talk about and I know there are people that will read this and doubt it but that is OK. God and I know what happened that day and that is all that matters.

I began to cry. "Lord I cannot go on. I am scared. What if I fall? What if I get around back and I cannot get back inside?" A strange sense of calmness overtook the fear, and I felt in my spirit, "You will never know until you take a step. That is what faith is, Gaye." Strangely, my faith had been deeper since that day in the hospital when God had spared me. In the past, I would have railed out at Him with what I was going through now. But, now even with no real hope in sight, I had not reacted that way. God had brought me through so much and I was determined to trust him now. I was becoming more grown up in my walk with the Lord. I had learned that regardless of what came or went I needed him more than anything in my life. And as silly as it sounded to me, I knew in the deep of my heart that God was taking time with me to get me through even tougher times ahead.

I had nothing to hold on to, but I eased myself one baby step at a time to the back of the house, where a little hill loomed ahead of me. *Lord! What now?* I knew it was there, but it seemed larger than the last time I had seen it. There was no way down but to walk down this mound, so, with my usual panic, I began to ease myself along. I did nearly lose my balance but quickly caught myself. My back was throbbing to the extent that I could feel it down to my feet and up through my neck. I had no choice I had to move on. This was only my first trip around the house, and I have no idea how long I had spent getting to this point, but I was only at the halfway point by then.

The land levels off directly behind the house, so I was able to walk with a little ease. And, then it was up the other side. With each step that was more difficult than the one before, I asked the Lord to help me. This had not been my idea and I did not understand what He was teaching me but, after what seemed like an eternity, I made it to the front and was on the driveway. Not only was I in horrible pain, but I was exhausted. I was sweating and my body shivered in fear from the experience. It is not easy to barter with the Lord. When He gives you clear instructions and you then try and finagle a way out, it does not work.

As I stood there, I had to make a choice. Was I going to ease myself inside the house, or go another time around this huge house as the lord had instructed me? It was as if one part of me was giving up and the other was saying you have one more in you. Whatever I was supposed to learn from going through this I hoped to learn it quickly. Whatever he was teaching me, I was open to His instruction. I wanted to do anything to stop this madness. I just wanted my life back. But I knew God had a plan. At a crossroads in my faith, I made the decision that I would try again. Something inside me gave me more desire to forge ahead than to retreat. I audibly told the devil to move out of the way, I was coming through. By the time I was back to the driveway on the other side of the house, it seemed like my feet had moved more easily, I was a little more limber and the pain although still great, was tolerable. So, again, without pondering it, I headed out again. By my third time around, I was beginning to concentrate more on talking with the lord than being concerned about making it around the house.

I was pouring out my heart to him and sharing the concerns I had about life ahead and the wellbeing of my family. When I made it halfway on my fourth attempt, I was praising the Lord! I had my hands in the air, and something had occurred inside me. There was a freedom, a supernatural freedom of my body that let me walk without concentrating on each step. My fear was replaced with joy to see what I was accomplishing. What an undertaking it was to walk, let alone walk around my house so many times. But that is exactly what I did. By my sixth time around, it was getting dusk outside. I had been outside a good part of the day. I had not eaten, had not had a drink of water, and even though I was in pain, I was smiling at what I felt. Such a release of emotions and frustrations that had bound me were leaving my body and mind.

I had begun singing and singing loudly. Songs of praise and worship filled my mouth and my soul. And, then I had made it back to my front steps after the seventh time around my house. The Lord had instructed me to walk seven times around. I felt that, because of my prayers, He would restore me, we would keep our home, and He would allow us to be able to send our kids to college. I had no promises from Him; it was all faith on my part. Those were my two greatest concerns. The children were still young but having them go to college was my biggest concern. I knew that would require a substantial amount of money and, with my current situation, we would not be prepared. I had to trust God. I stood outside at the foot of those three stairs leading up to our front door for a bit. I was amazed that I had done what God had told me to do, but I had received such a blessing by doing it.

When I finally climbed those stairs and went inside, I was tired and in pain, but I felt that I had been on another journey with the Lord and that I was well cared for all along the way. I had to trust Him now.

I remember having to use my 401K money for Bethany's braces, and other things. And when we had to take the children out of private school, I had cried for days; it was all my fault. I had fought placing them in public education and the time came when Bruce said we must do it. It was not because I felt better than other people, I had heard so many stories about how dangerous public schools were. And I was concerned about the education my children would receive there. On registration day, I insisted on going and we took Bethany first to her elementary school where she would be in fifth grade. I was shaking with dread as if I were turning her over to a horrible place filled with toxic people. I had trouble walking but I was determined to be there to see for myself. We met the nicest people and found that her teacher was a Holy Ghost filled Christian that we loved from the beginning.

We took Jonathan next to his middle school where he was in the seventh grade and the first person we met was a Christian. We had talked like we knew each other all our lives. Both children not only thrived but loved their schools. I had been so wrong to worry about moving them. And after all, God had them in his care so I should have known they would be taken care of.

I continued to sit in my chair day after day. It was two years of this, and it was beyond taking a toll on me. I would put on gospel videos and listen to praise music. I would pray and cry out to God for help. And it seemed like nothing was happening. The time was just clicking on like a train going nowhere. One day, I said "Lord, what is happening? I am so desperate and so lonely being in this house while life just passes me by." I still struggled with movement and range of motion. The pain was still great, and, without another surgery, there was nothing more that could be done.

I cried out, "Can't you hear me? Why won't you listen to my prayers? I am sick of this!" It was quiet and, as I sat there, the Lord spoke to my spirit and said, "Your prayers are heard by Me, but there is something you must learn." I was beyond frustrated at this point, and I remember how angry I got. I yelled, "What do you want from me? I walked around this house; I have prayed everything I can pray. I do not get it anymore." I just sat there for a little while feeling defeated, and I really don't know how much time passed. But then I felt in my spirit that in all the times God was faithful to me, there was still something I was missing in my connection with Him. I could not understand what it was he was trying to show me. I learned after much reflection and communion with him that he desired the sacrifice of my praise. I said, "Lord, I do praise You. What am I not doing? How am I not praising You?"

He showed me that one of my greatest gifts to honor him is my praise. My sacrificial gift of praise. The kind that continues even when my heart is grieving. It is learning to praise him when you think you cannot go on. It is shouting your praises to him when you feel the worst or defeated. It is praising Him when you cannot see past your circumstances. It is honoring Him with your voice and your heart and your mind. It is lifting your hands when you are not able to because you are self-conscious, but you do it anyway. When you see no hope in sight, but you still praise God. Praise is not looking for something in return, it is given freely. You praise because of who He is, not because of what your desires are.

It is reverence, honor and glory that belong to God no matter what happens. And, I had to learn this. How had I not seen this before? My praise was not conditional on my needs or wants.

God was gently rebuking me for my behavior. If I needed something, I ran to Him, blurted out my request and desire and moved on. If He did not answer quickly enough for my liking, I would get mad and question His love and promises. But not once did I understand that praise was sacrificial on my part. It hit me hard that I had not seen it before. It was so simple. God requires our praise in the good times, in the tough times, and all the time. It is not contingent on whether He does anything additional for me or heals me. It is not about Him doing something for me and then I will serve him better. No. The very fact that He died for me and took my sins away is enough reason to praise Him continuously. There it was! Sacrificial praise. That is what God wanted from me. And so that is where I began.

I began praising Him more when I was hurting the most. When I was the loneliest, I praised Him with my whole heart. When the days were long, and the nights were longer, I praised him anyway. And, when I did not see anything good happening ahead of me, I praised Him.

The company was pressuring me even greater now to take long term disability so that they could get my salary off the books. I was forced to file for disability and was denied the first time. It always happens that way. The attorneys for the company had indicated that it was a normal process and would take refiling. Most disability cases are denied initially. So again, time went by. It was two years into this nightmare, and I woke up one Sunday morning and asked Bruce to help me get ready for church. I wanted to go to church. It had been so long since I had attended. He was not sure it was the best idea but helped me anyway. I felt dry and needed refilling. I missed my church family. I knew it was going to be difficult and uncomfortable, but I needed to go and be part of a service. I was praising God that I was even able to attempt going to church that morning. I remember we eased into the back of the sanctuary and sat in the first available pew. So, unlike me, I always liked to sit near the front. Bruce prefers sitting in the back.

I was really in pain by the time we arrived and even the walk into the building seemed more than I had anticipated. I was tired and uncomfortable thinking I had taken on more than I could manage. It was a regular service, nothing out of the ordinary and I remember that during the worship part of the service, I was trying to sing but could not concentrate on the words. I love worship, so it was difficult for me to not participate. I did not feel like I could stand for long, but the pastor asked those that needed prayer to come, and I held on to each pew as I headed down to the front. Bruce had offered to walk with me, and I told him I could do it alone. It was unusual for a Sunday morning service to have prayer for the sick during the worship and singing, but pastor was obedient that morning.

I got back to my pew after prayer and immediately, one of the ladies of the church came to me and got on her knees in the pew in front of me and began to pray. At the time, I did not know her well, but I remember her sweet prayer. She went back to her seat and as I continued to stand thoughts of praise began to fill me. I remember thinking, *God, this is what You were teaching me. The praise that comes regardless of what you will or will not do on my behalf. It is the praise that comes when our faith is weak, and our pain is great. It is the unknown, but no, the assurance that You are with me regardless of the outcome. I am going to praise You today because of who You are, not because of what I need. You are worthy of my praise regardless of my situation. And whether I am healed or not today or whenever, I am going to praise you with my whole heart.* As I began to exercise that praise to the Lord, at a point, I raised my hands and began to sway back and forth (Bruce has told me), I do not remember doing this. I felt like I was at the very tip of a high cliff looking down into a dark abyss. And I began to laugh.

The more I laughed, the more a cool breeze covered me. I could almost feel it moving my hair and gently surrounding me from my head to my feet. It was a gentle breeze. That is the best way I can describe it. I do not know how long I stood there, three or four minutes, but I could hear myself laughing, it just seemed far away. It was like I was looking down into that dark space or hole and the more I studied it, the more I laughed. At one point, the pastor told me later that he explained to the congregation that I was laughing in the spirit for those that may not have understood my behavior. Bruce said that people began to laugh at my laughing not out of irreverence but because of the atmosphere change in the room. It was light and even he laughed a little. I remember coming too or waking up whatever it was and looking around.

Almost immediately, I was disappointed that I had returned from wherever I had been. I saw my husband and children looking at me. I did not really know how to grasp what had just occurred. But something miraculous had happened to me. I cannot explain it even today. Shortly after this, the pastor concluded the service and there was no preaching that morning. The Holy Spirit had done all the work necessary. When it was time to leave, Bruce started to help me up and I told him no, I was fine. I did not need assistance. The children asked if I was OK, and I assured them I had no pain. Absolutely no pain! I knew I had been changed, that God had healed me. I was beginning to understand that things were different when I walked back to our vehicle with no pain. In fact, we went out to lunch that day.

We had not done that in a few years. I had been bound to this injury, bound to a chair and had not been anywhere except the doctor's office. All afternoon I was peppered with questions, did I feel OK? Was I in any pain? My family was just as surprised and happy as I was.

I was trying to take it all in. Trying to wrap my head around being without pain and I knew that God had delivered me fully. The next day I felt good, and the following day I felt even better. And I became stronger in my body. I began to understand the fullness of his glory and the miracle that had happened in my life. When God heals you, you know it. There is a touch like no other. There is a power that is like no other when he releases you from suffering. About two weeks after God healed my back, I received a notice in the mail that I was to attend a hearing in front of a Social Security judge in a couple of days. The New York attorney would be joining us for that court date. The Sunday evening before my court date, I was at church and the minister who had come to preach for the evening service came up to me during prayer time at the altar. He had called the congregation down to the altar for prayer. I had never met this man before. He came up beside me and said to me, "God has your back sister! He will go before you." I needed that confirmation from the Lord because I was concerned about attending that meeting.

My life had been radically changed once again. My faith was the strongest it had been, and I had decided that no matter what happened I would be content in my situation. So, when God healed me, I was even more pumped and excited about taking back my life. The attorney called me the day before to advise me of the schedule and with his New York accent, he stressed that we would need to meet that morning prior to court. Bruce came with me that day, and he was as excited as I was that God had healed me. I dressed myself, and we headed to meet the attorney early in the morning. We met him at the International House of Pancakes restaurant near the Social Security office. He was just as I envisioned. Slick in his tailored suit and talked fast and confident in his New York accent. But he was nice enough, and I was surprised when he started coaching me on what to say and not say before the judge.

At one point, I stopped him and said, "Listen, I need to explain something to you that you may not fully understand, but God has healed my back. I am no longer in pain; He has completely healed me." He waived me off like I was dismissed and continued to coach me. Again, I said, "I cannot go before this judge and lie that I want this disability when I am not disabled any longer." At this point, we had continued our conversation outside the Social Security building. He stopped and leaned against the stone wall behind us outside the court offices and I told him my testimony. Bruce interjected on occasion and when I had finished, he just stood and looked at me. He did not know what to do because he knew I was not backing down. So, he said, "Well, you decide when you get in front of the judge what you want to do, but you are ruining this case and your ability to get the money you deserve. We have worked so hard for this."

I reminded him that I had not been the one seeking this and that I was forced to do so. When we arrived inside the courtroom there were people that I did not know sitting on either side of long tables. They were there to talk for or against my case. The judge was elevated above us, behind a large desk. The only person I knew was Bruce, so I was a little unnerved at first. The judge proceeded to ask me a few basic questions and after that, I said I had something to say. And I asked the judge if I could address everyone. He agreed and I began.

Keep in mind that all of this was under oath and recorded as part of my long-term case file. "Your Honor, I am no longer disabled and have no desire to pursue this case," I stated. My flashy attorney's head slumped down in defeat. The more I spoke, the more I felt empowered. The great judge was not in front of me, but the one I served in God the Father. As I began to give my testimony, the people ready to argue for and against me closed their materials and sat back to listen. I looked at the people at the table. Some looked uncomfortable, a few looked stunned. And one or two gave me a big smile. I went on further, "I do not want this money, I never wanted to seek disability; it would be a lie for me to accept it, because God has healed me." When I finished, the judge took a minute or two and then he began to speak. "Never in my career has someone come before me not wanting something, Mrs. LaFoe," the judge said, astonished, "I cannot explain what has occurred in your life, but I am so happy for you." And then, he told the court reporter to take his next comments off the record. "Because of your honesty today, I am awarding you a settlement for back pay. Go on a cruise, or have some fun, you deserve it."

I was not expecting anything and did not want anything more than to give my testimony. I was so satisfied and happy as the people began to leave the room. Bruce and I were elated that I had been given the opportunity to share my testimony. The attorney walked out with Bruce and me. He shook his head, "I don't really know what to say, you are so brave and one of the most honest people I have ever met, and that is rare." We took the moments left with him to tell him about the Lord. I hope we planted the seed of God's hope in him that day.

Now, you would think that everything was wonderful after that. But you would be so wrong. I was naive enough to think I could go back to work in some capacity with my company to keep my seniority, but that was not the case. They fought me every step of the way. One day, soon after my court hearing, I received a box from my assistant. She had warned me that something inside would be upsetting. Inside the box on top, was a copy of an email that had been distributed to the management team and God knows who else. It stated, "If we do away with Gaye's salary, what will it do for our budget?" Talk about kicking a person when they are down. I was not surprised; having dealt with the lack of professionalism and cutthroat behavior I witnessed previously in the office. But I was heartbroken, and I felt violated. I do not know why I thought it would be OK and things would go back to normal. So much time had gone by.

I was looking for work there every day after that and it had consumed me. The company finally advised me that one of the contingencies of my receiving my severance package was that I would have to come into the office. I would need to sit at a physical desk for two weeks to look for jobs before they would release me and give me my severance. So, every day for two weeks I went into an empty office where I sat for seven and a half hours at a computer and applied for positions within the company. I knew from the onset it was a waste of time, I would not get another position at the company. I do not even know if people knew I was there or what they had been told. I can only imagine. It was the worst experience and I felt so disappointed by everyone. I felt like I was being punished for having had an illness I had no control over.

I had worked there for over seventeen years and given my absolute best, (which my appraisals reflected), but, in the end, it did not matter. It chipped away at my self-worth, and I became so frustrated at myself that all of this had happened. I hired an attorney, and she began to work tirelessly to determine why I was not rehired even at a lower position just so that I could keep my seniority. I was not even looking for my old position back. Finally, as more time went by, she subpoenaed human resource staff. I had to sit through depositions with people that I genuinely liked and still think the world of today. There was only one person in the entire company whom I had a conflict with. So, I never had a problem facing anyone. I knew what had transpired, and I had done nothing to anyone. I have no regrets and no ill will towards anyone. There was a new hire from the company that attended each day. He was part of the HR department now. When we would go to break, he would talk with me. One day, he said, "Gaye, I am so sorry about all of this, I can tell these people think the world of you and you them."

We knew we had a legitimate case, and all the facts were in. It was a waiting game, and a year went by. I just knew I would be going back to work there, and any thought of going elsewhere was not in my plan. God had healed me and even the doctors were baffled as to what happened knowing that my back was strong with no signs of the pain I had once experienced. It could not be explained in human terms, it was God and only God's work.

I still had degeneration in my neck. But my lower back was completely healed.

CHAPTER TWENTY-TWO

One day during all of this, I received a call that my mother had been taken to the hospital for a heart related issue. The nursing home had taken her, and I was to meet her there. I was leaving to go when I received a call from a cardiologist's office stating Mom would need a pacemaker put in immediately. I told the woman on the phone that I was on my way and would be there within minutes and would need to speak with the doctor before the procedure.

Up to that time, Mom had been fine. She had only one mild heart attack when I was little. When Bruce and I arrived at the hospital we made our way to the nurses' station to ask for Mom's room number. The nurse advised me that they had already taken my mother to surgery and when I asked who had signed for her to have the procedure, they stated that they had her sign. I was furious. The nurse had implied that it was not an emergency, but that the doctor was there and wanted to proceed. I told her that my mother was not in any physical or mental condition to sign for this procedure and that I would be taking this up with the doctor when he had completed the procedure.

That man never got with us after the surgery was over like any reputable surgeon would have. To have had the fine name he had in the medical community for his great care was a mystery to me. I wanted to face this doctor and tell him what I thought about him. He had an elderly woman who did not fully understand what was happening, sign for a procedure under duress. I should have sought an attorney that day and pressed charges. My mother was not always capable of making decisions because of her illness. But he did not want to be inconvenienced waiting on me to get there. The next morning, the nursing home called me to say that Mom was discharged from the hospital and was heading back to the nursing home via ambulance. I got ready and headed over to sit with her once she arrived. When I saw her, I thought she looked pale. And when I touched her face, she was warm. I immediately called the nurse, and we took her temperature which confirmed a fever.

I told the nurse that something was wrong, and that we needed to get her to the hospital. We tried to get Mom back to the hospital where she had the procedure, but there were no available beds. So, we ended up taking her to another hospital. At first, I was concerned because I thought she had been in the best hospital in the city. I soon learned that was not the case. I was able to talk with Mom for a time and she was alert. She had told me that she was not in any pain, but her fever was really spiking by now. The doctor that came to see me at the hospital was a kind young man. He was an infectious disease specialist and would be managing my mother's case. He stated they had begun testing to determine what kind of infection was occurring, and the extent of it in her body.

He advised me that elderly individuals can get infections easily and that they would hopefully isolate the infection quickly and begin treatment. I was relieved that Mom was in his care. I wanted the best for her. I sat beside her bed day and night. Only leaving her to shower and dress in the adjoining restroom. I kept her Bible open and read scriptures and prayed over her. Often the doctor would come in and give me a report that they were still searching for the problem, but I was beginning to panic at the amount of time it was taking.

He came in late one evening and said, "Mrs. LaFoe, we think we have isolated the infection..." Before he could even get it out, I blurted out, "It is the pacemaker, isn't it?" He told me that the infection had begun behind the pacemaker and that staph bacteria had been isolated. They were immediately placing her on more antibiotics specific to this bacteria with hopes that it would remove it from her body. I remember the horrible thoughts that went through my mind. I wanted to do physical harm to this doctor for his negligence. He was aware that my mother was a diabetic and he offered no antibiotics to anticipate or offset infection. The staph was due to instruments or other items used in the operating room that were unclean or not sterilized properly, most likely. I cried out to the Lord to take care of her and to please heal her if it was his will.

The next morning, the doctor returned with more news. Along with the staph infection they had found, Mom had acquired sepsis and it was traveling through her body. There are three stages of sepsis. Sepsis, severe sepsis, and septic shock. Mom's body was moving towards septic shock rapidly. Typically, only forty percent of people survive this advanced stage of septic shock. Mom was no longer alert. She was in deep sleep most of the time. I could not get a response from her. I remember crying and asking if there was anything else they could do. The doctor warned that sepsis moved quickly and even with medications to offset it, he could not guarantee it would stop the growth. I knew I was losing her.

He told me how sorry he was and even said that I had a good case against the doctor should I want to take those steps. I have never heard a doctor speak against another one before, but it gave me something to think about. To fight the sepsis, they had to give Mom medication orally that turned her mouth blue. It was in large doses, and I was concerned she would choke. I do not understand why they give oral medications to someone who is not alert. It is beyond my understanding. The next afternoon the doctor and a geriatric care specialist came to see me. They advised me that my mother only had a brief time left. They had done all they could for her. It was tragic. So senseless and may have turned out differently had the surgeon been competent. I would never know now. When they left the room, I begged God to get me through this. I was so glad that I had Him in my life to help me. I remembered the awful time I was away from God. I would have never made it then had this occurred. But I had changed for the good the day I had my son. And my faith in God was strong. This time I ran to him for comfort.

I cannot even describe how my heart broke hearing this. I knew she could not communicate with me now but being with her gave me comfort and I could not even think about not having her here. Bruce had come and I do not remember if the children came to say goodbye or not. He asked me if I was planning to call my brother and I said no I had no plans to do that. My husband has wisdom that I do not always have, and he convinced me that my brother needed to say his goodbyes and that he and I needed each other right now. I am so glad I listened to him. We did contact him, and he immediately began planning a flight home. It amazes me that doctors can give you the near timing your loved one will die based on body sounds and look.

They had told me it was coming and soon and based on their examination, it would be that day. They can usually tell by a drop in blood pressure, weak pulse, discoloring, and often what is called a death rattle. A death rattle is when the body can no longer swallow and remove saliva on its own. My mother had started to experience this. Both doctors had told me how deeply sorry they were, and one even got down on one knee beside me and hugged me. I remember that early evening I was brushing Mom's soft white hair and singing *One Day Jesus Will Call My Name* to her.

I was telling her how much I loved her and that I needed her to fight and stay with me. The tears would not stop, and I was broken and raw. They say that one of the last senses that leaves the body is hearing. People are not often aware of that. So, I wanted her to hear every word I said. I wanted her to know how much she meant to me and that I appreciated her for always being in my corner, and her prayers. I told her I did not want her to leave me, and I would whisper in her ear "Please, please fight, Mom. I need you."

All at once while I was singing to her, she breathed in this big breath, let it out and then she was gone. "Mom! Mom! I screamed out to her." I buzzed the nurses' station, yelling for them to come. Quickly, the room filled with people. A nurse grabbed me and hugged me tightly while the others were working on Mom and documenting things. As she held me, I remember my legs starting to slip to the floor. She pulled me up and said, "You can do this honey." She held me and rocked me back and forth as I sobbed into her chest. At some point, she left the room, and one of the other nurses told me that the nurse had just returned from leave. She had lost her own mother and this night was her first back to work. God sent her to me. She knew exactly what I was going through. I will never forget the comfort she gave me on that awful evening.

I called Bruce and he called our pastor. They both arrived quickly. Mom went to be with the Lord on January 31, 2004. My sweet brother had not made it home in time to say goodbye. I will always be grateful to my pastor for being there. He and his dear wife had been such a blessing to our little family through the years.

I remember when the funeral home came to take my mommy away. It was cold and dreary outside that night. We were in the hall when they came out of the room. My little Mom was in a black bag on the stretcher. She was so small on that stretcher. I wanted to stop them. There had to be a mistake. She would not leave me like this. There was no white sheet to cover her, I can still see that, and it makes me cry just having to relive this now. We were watching in the hall when the funeral staff moved past us. I wanted to say Stop! Do you know who you have there? That is the best mom, best friend, and the greatest person you will ever have the privilege of being close to. So, manage her gently. Take care of her. But at death, you are downgraded to a plastic bag. You are rolled out in the frosty night stripped of everything you have ever known. And stripped of everything you have ever been. Only a number identifies you now.

How quickly life can change. That is the stark reality. The most wonderful people in the world leave the same way as the worst villain. How could it be that I would not have her with me any longer? My mother was the only real stability in my life. Never once did she waiver in her belief in God, never shook her fist at Him or called Him out for the hand she had been dealt. Never one time did she deny the Lord or give up. I was bobbing in life. I would gasp for air feeling like I was going under. Without her love and prayers, I would not have made it. She was the only real family I had known in my life.

I would never want her back in this awful place. This miserable chaotic world. But I really did not know how I was going to make it without her. The woman that had shown me how to be independent. She had taught me to speak my mind gently. Something I never quite learned. She put family first and loved with her whole heart. Her gifts were limitless, and her servant's heart was beyond any I have ever seen. And she loved Jesus more than anyone I have ever known. I was past missing her already and had moved on to longing for her presence, and we had not even had her funeral yet. I was an orphan now. It is a realization that hits you hard no matter what age you are. When your last parent leaves this earth, you are technically an orphan.

How many times had that drifted in and out of my mind? She was gone. What could I have done differently for her? Maybe spent more time with her, I do not know? I was always struggling with doing what everyone else needed from me, but I failed her in the end. At that moment, I hated everyone that ever took my time from her. Guilt seeped into my heart. Life had so many commitments and I never took all the time I should have with her.

All the months I was struggling with my back issues I missed being with her. And now she was gone. As much as I loved Bruce and our children, I felt lost like no other time in my life. The cold outside was no worse than what I felt in my heart. I was alone now. Even though I had my little family that loved me, and whom I adored. It was not the same. I know everyone feels the tremendous loss when they lose a parent, but I had only really had Mom my entire life. She was the only one I connected with. There was no one else. Maybe things would have been different with my dad, and I would have had a better connection with him had he told me the truth earlier. I do not know. I dreaded going to the funeral home for those awful arrangements. Yes, we want this, no we do not want that, expensive, cheap, what did it matter? She is not here now, and I could have cared less. But I had to press on because I wanted it to be as nice as possible. I owed her more than I could ever give her now and doing this last thing for her was the last tribute I could give her.

Because she loved my singing, I went with friends and recorded songs for the service. I wrote the eulogy and a poem to add to the program. There was no one else that had shared more time with her than I had. As difficult as I knew it would be, I needed to give her the praise she deserved. I wanted to honor her one last time. Mom always talked about making Heaven her goal, and she would say I cannot wait to get there. I cannot even imagine her excitement when she saw Jesus.

I Made It!

My heart can sing a victory song
My tiring journey and race is done
No more to suffer life's painful tests
I pleasure now on Heaven's best. I made it!

No more to worry, fret or grieve
The trials here, I gladly leave
Secure in knowing I have safely crossed
To heaven's home, was worth the cost
I made it!

> I hate to leave you all behind
> but soon I will see you in God's time
>
> Do not cry for me
> I am where I longed to be
> With Jesus, happy for eternity
> I made it!
> Gaye LaFoe 2/2005

We had looked and looked for the right outfit and I would not stop until I found the perfect dress for her. She would have cringed at the price, but the color was so like her, lovely lavender. It had faint sparkles so unlike the simpleness that she would have wanted but overall, it was a gorgeous dress and one that I felt proud for her to wear when she met Jesus face to face.

We gathered before everyone, and I could not fathom we were there to say our goodbyes. What a fighter she had always been. I tried to remember that God wanted her to come home. It really does not matter how we die. We all will at some point. But it hurt so badly. My heart ached. Oh, there were times as her caretaker as she aged, that it was extremely difficult for me to deal with her. It happens. But there would be a void in my life without her. I really had to try not to hate that doctor, and everyone associated with causing this. But it hurt so badly. I looked at her in that casket and it was as if she would sit up any minute and say, *now stop all this, I am fine*. But it did not happen. Nothing was fine.

The crowd was large for the viewing, but there should have been more at her funeral. More people to say thank you for everything you did for me. Thank you for the sacrifices you made to help me. But they were not there. My mother did so much for so many. The funeral was difficult, it always is. I did not want the time to end, and I certainly was not ready to take her to the cemetery. That must be the absolute worst part. I could hear Jonathan crying moments leading up to the eulogy and I was not sure I could proceed, but I owed it to her. I loved having my brother home. It was as if we had picked up where we left off. He was such a comfort.

We edged along to the National Cemetery where Dad is buried for her last ride. I cannot even remember what took place there at the burial. That evening pastor and his wife came and brought dinner and we visited with them so they could meet my brother. And the next day he was off to head home, and everyone would go back to their lives, and I would be without her.

A couple of days went by, and I was starting to work my way through the process of grief. I had experienced something similar when my dad had died, but it was not the same. I loved him but did not have the bond with him that I had with my mother. The experts say you experience various stages as you proceed through the process of losing someone dear to you. I knew that Mom was gone. I had no doubt that she was in Heaven. So, I moved through the first stage of *denial*. I did pick up the phone to call and check on her once or twice like I had so many times before. I went in a couple of days after the funeral to clean out her room at the nursing home. Mom was in a private room. We wanted her to not be disturbed, and to have the things that were familiar to her so that she was comfortable.

When I opened her door juggling some of the boxes, I had brought with me, her room was completely bare. There was no sign that she had even been there. All that was inside was a bed. Her bed. At first, I was shocked at the bareness and the unexpectedness of it, and then I was overcome with anger. Who gave them the right to go through her things, pack them up and take them away? It had only been a couple of days, and we had paid the rent through the end of the next month. I remember going to the nurses' station and demanding to know where my mother's things were and who had made the decision to remove them. I was told that since she was not coming back, they decided to make room for a new client. I think the worst side of me showed that day because I told everyone just exactly what I thought. They advised me that I could come another day or make an appointment to pick up her things. I made it clear that I would be taking them that day. And I made them parade every box to my vehicle, outside the main entrance.

They had robbed me of that bit of closure I needed. I had spent some good times and challenging times in that room with my mother, and now I could not go through her things, and take time with them. If for no other reason, I needed that time to remember. I needed to touch them, feel her clothes, and be with my memories before I packed them away. And that experience was taken away from me.

The second stage of grief is *anger*. It is blaming the person for leaving you. Or it could be towards God, blaming him for taking them away. I have witnessed individuals passing in their nineties and family members will say, there just was not enough time with them. It is never enough time. The anger comes from them leaving you behind.

Bargaining sets in as the third stage of grief. Promising you will do better if you could have them back for even one more day. It is not realistic and irrational but, when you are grieving, your emotions are all over the place. Nothing about any of this seemed rational to me. I was desperate not to be separated from my mom. It had just been us for so many years. I had tried so hard to hold on to my joy. I knew she was with the lord and that had been her only desire for as long as I could remember. But my rope was frazzled and wearing thin. I felt the burden of grief so heavily on my shoulders.

Depression is the fourth stage of the grief process and a complex one. I do not honestly think I was clinically depressed, but I was not diagnosed either. I know I was so downhearted. I felt brokenness, and that I should have done more. I could have somehow protected her more. As with everything in my life, I internalized it and accepted the blame. I had thought long and hard about pressing charges against the doctor and the hospital. He had made her sign the papers for the surgery when she was not in her right mind. And the unsterile instruments resulted in the infection. But we would have needed an autopsy, and it would have delayed her burial. She had been through so much; I just could not bear to have her body go through more. I did send him a fiery letter stating that his negligence had contributed to her death. And that would have to be enough. Had I not been a believer, or had this happened earlier in my life, it may have been different. But I had the hope of knowing I will see mom again if I live for the Lord.

There is a final and fifth stage of grief, *acceptance*. But I was nowhere near that place. All these stages mingle with each other and there is no stopping and starting a new one. Every day, I experienced a little of each. It broke my heart to remember our times together. My mother had carried the torch for me through the darkest of times. And she never gave up on me. She had held on to God for me with all her might and her powerful prayers, and there was no doubt in her mind that God would receive me back someday. She had known that at least. I was reminded repeatedly by her that God had started a work in me at an early age and He would not let me go too far from Him.

Months had come and gone, and I was still in the throes of grief. But somehow it was more like an oppressive covering now. It was as if grief hovered around me, stalked me, and was trying to drain my joy. I could not sleep, eat, or enjoy everyday events with my family and friends. I could not find my way from it, could not hide it, or leave it behind. It was a heaviness, and it was constant. I had talked to different ones for counseling, and I knew people were praying for me, but no one had known the extent the oppression had on me. I was dealing with it and trying to get back to work. I knew full well we needed the money. My position contributed to the family finances. But I would not let myself give up on returning to my company.

My attorney had done a tremendous job in pleading my case. And after the depositions, and all the paperwork was complete, we waited for the arbitrator, to make a final decision. We hoped it went our way. Weeks went by, and I finally received a call from the attorney. She sounded so defeated on the phone. "Mrs. LaFoe were you aware that the arbitrator's office, and the company's law offices are in the same complex? she asked. This was out of state.

"No," I replied, "I had no idea." She sighed and told me that the attorneys for the company in that office had gotten to the arbitrator and somehow swayed him. We had more than enough evidence, testimonies, paperwork, computer evidence and everything else. But the arbitrator had now refused to hear our case after committing to hear it. "And we cannot force him to tell us why?" I asked in disbelief. I could not believe what she was saying. "Well, isn't he a judge? Doesn't he have to hear the case?" "No, sadly he does not." She replied. "And we can't make him tell us why he changed his mind?" "Nope, we cannot" she sighed. We talked a little longer, and I hung up the phone. I felt so defeated myself by now that right and good had not prevailed.

That, and the grief from my mother's death was more than I could bear. I was just raging inside.

The past feelings of not measuring up began to revisit me and settle in my mind. I needed my mother's encouragement and counsel. I missed her terribly. Only God really knew how I was suffering. I cried for no reason, and nothing filled the void. I tried to remember that God was in control, and I put my faith in Him, but it was a daily struggle. I knew that He saw all of this. He knew my heart, and he knew the things that transpired behind the scenes in secret against me. He knew my enemies. I had to just hold on to him and not lose my faith.

CHAPTER TWENTY-THREE

It had been a little over a year since my mother's death. Some days it felt like it had just happened it was still so fresh and raw for me. It was a Saturday afternoon, Bruce, the children, and I were in the kitchen. Something came up about me not working. I remember Bruce becoming angry, animated even, and railed out at me to "Get a job!" It did not matter what I did, he just wanted me to find something. He was tired of carrying the load. His words ripped through me and cut me to the core. I knew the pressure he was under. I understood his feelings and I did not blame him. We are different in that I share my feelings and then I am done with it. But he keeps his feelings inside until they build, and he becomes combustible. He was right, but it hurt. Especially, in front of our children. We had minimal confrontations in our marriage. I knew we would get past this, but I had no idea how or when.

I did not know what to do and I could not help myself. He had every right to be angry. I had lived on a pipe dream of going back to my work and I had thought so earnestly that I would be able to. I had lost sight of time and everything around me. With my mother's death, it had made things worse and more magnified, and I was just drifting without a purpose. I did not know how to dig myself out of the grief to move on. I had lost so much, and I did not have the strength to move forward. Even as I prayed desperately for God to intervene and bring me back from the loss of my mom and the job I loved. I did not blame God for my back injury, we never even knew why it had occurred. No one was to blame.

Sunday morning, I got up early, dressed quietly and headed for church alone. I did not want to be around anyone at home. I was embarrassed and lost, so I did not want to face my family. Especially my children. *What kind of mother was I being to them?* I had become a selfish bundle of empty space with no real value. That is how I perceived myself to be. We had a guest minister that day. I had no idea who he was or that he was coming. I do not remember the service. But at the end of the service, he asked everyone to come for prayer. As everyone was praying, he walked among them and prayed with some. I was standing at the front pew getting ready to go back to my seat and he came and stood in front of me. He stretched his hand out to me and said "Today, you will get your victory."

I did not know exactly what he was referring to but something inside me came alive; I began to feel strong and determined. I stopped at my seat long enough to grab my purse and hurried out of the building. As I was leaving, a friend was also leaving and asked me where I was going in such a hurry. I told her I was going to face my demons. She said she would be praying for me.

I got into my vehicle and headed towards the National Cemetery. I had not been there since the day we took my mother. I could not go; it was still too raw. But today, I found myself driving to that place with no idea why, other than what the preacher had told me. *Was this where my victory was?* I did not know, but I had to do something and even if nothing was there but the memory of my mother, I needed to be close to her grave. She was the only one other than God, who knew my heart and my intentions. She read me so well and understood me. I struggled with sharing this next part. Only my husband, children, and Pastor Glenn knew this. It is not up for debate. It happened just like I am sharing it.

The closer I got to the cemetery; I began to feel nauseated. And I began to sweat. It was not hot that day, and I had air conditioning which I turned up high, but I was sweating horribly. I began to hear the devil whisper, "You do not want to go there. You know you do not want to go there. It will break your heart if you go there." I tried to put these thoughts out of my mind and continued to the main gate. By then, I was shaking, and my head was jerking like I was having a spasm. I could not get my bearings and had no idea where to go.

I saw a little kiosk at the side of the road inside the gate and I pulled near it and stopped. Walking toward it my legs felt weak and I was afraid I could not stand. I had become scared that my body was reacting in such a way, not sure if I was having a heart attack or something. I could still hear whispers saying, "Do not do this." I put in my mother's information and a map popped out with my parents' names, dates of death, and where they were buried in the cemetery. Seeing both of their names on this map made me want to cry, but I remember taking a big breath and getting back into my vehicle for the journey to their grave. No one seemed to be around; it was still early in the day, around 12:30 p.m.

I had not remembered the big magnolia tree close to their grave. I had not remembered much about that place. But there it stood. I had to walk around to locate their gravesite. I stood steps away from my parent's grave. My pain was so great, that I began to sob uncontrollably. I do not think I had ever felt so alone as I did that day. I was a failure, my family thought I was, and the only person that really believed in me was gone. Dad had been gone many years now. I had been there mere seconds when I heard someone behind me say "Do you need a hug?" I was startled. There stood a beautiful African American woman in a gray silk suit with a huge cross around her neck. It had a dark stone like an onyx and was stunning as the sun beamed off it. I immediately fell into her arms. I was not afraid or inhibited, I was hurting, and she drew me in. It was as if God had sent Maude to me after all these years. I had the wonderful comfort from the nurse the night my mother died, and now this. How strange it was.

She said, "Child, why do you stand at this grave and weep, your mother is not here?" I did not think about it then, but she would not have known why I was there. How would she have known that I was there because of my mother? I was steps away from the grave site blocking her view and she was behind me near the roadside. I began to tell her everything that had occurred about my job, that God had healed my back and that I was not able to let my mother go. It just all flowed out of me like water down a spout. I told her I was a mess and had ruined my life and everything for which I had worked. I poured out my heart to her.

"Your mother told you that you have worth, she was your biggest fan." She said whispering in my ear. I thought how strange that she knew this. "She told you often that everything was going to be ok, and you needed to hear that from her today. Even though she is not here. Your mother doesn't want you to feel this way, she is with the Lord." She began to squeeze me into her with her arm around my shoulder. Then she leaned her head back laughing with a huge smile on her face. "Oh child, she is so happy." I asked her why she stopped and if she had seen me from the road. She smiled and touched my face with her hand. "I was on my way to lunch, and I was told you must go and see about her. Do you know how special you are to God that he would send me, to you?" "No, I know I am not special to anyone that's for sure," I said half laughing.

"Oh, but you are child," she went on, "I was told I would find you in the cemetery. I wanted to eat but I had to be obedient and come to you. I do not get to come often. God knows your troubles child."

I thought that was such a strange statement. *Come from where? What was she talking about?* I asked her if she lived nearby or saw me on her way home from church and she said, "No." I asked her name and she smiled but did not respond. There was a small tree that I had not noticed, to the side of the grave. I guess I had not noticed anything the day my mother was buried. None of this was familiar to me. As she was talking to me, there were three large black crows that had dove into that tree and were making loud squawking noises. I was listening to her, but

I would glance up at them from the shear noise they were making that drew my attention. I remember her taking my face into her hands and saying, "Look at me, they will be gone soon." When she said this, she turned her head and her eyes darted up at them and they scrambled out of the tree. They flew away so fast. I had a feeling come over me that I was with someone with authority or power. I cannot explain it. I was becoming alarmed that she and I were alone in that part of the cemetery.

Who was this woman? I asked her again who she was, and she said, "I told you, I was sent to you. Your mother was your caretaker. She was your strength and you relied on her, but she is happy where she is, she is home now." I had lowered my head and the tears were falling down the front of my suit. She lifted my head with her hand and said softly, moving as close as she could get to my face. "God wants to be everything to you, and I am here to tell you that. Oh, how special you are to Him. He knows you are here weeping. You have a family, children and a husband who need you." I thought to myself, *how on earth do you know all of this?* "Who told you about me, someone had to have told you?" I asked quizzingly and she just smiled.

"You came here today to be with her," she said and looked at my parents' grave, "but she isn't here, she is with the Lord, and your life must go on. Whatever your reason for coming here, whatever you need from your mother, God wants you to know how much He loves you, and He alone is who you need. Your mother does not want you to be sad. She wants your faith to be strong. I came to see about you. I do not know what the plan is for your job or the future. That is in God's hands. You are not to worry about those things. But he has been trying to get your attention through this. He has healed you before, you are special to Him. You must understand me. It is all going to be all right, child, you will see."

I remember shaking my head. "You are so loved, child." She finished as she stroked my wet face. We were walking closer to the grave by now, and we stopped. She looked at me and said, "I cannot prophesy over you if there is any doubt. You must believe what I am telling you." It had begun to sprinkle rain and I was getting wet. She had her hand on my arm and I said, "Please, tell me your name." "My name is Janice. And I am here because of you. I do not get to go much, but today it was my time to come." It was so damp and wet now, and even though it was the middle of the day it was darker than when I had arrived earlier. But her clothes were not spotted with the rain; she looked like she was fresh and undaunted by the weather around us. Her light gray suit was without any water droplets from the rain. However, I was feeling the rain start to penetrate my clothes. Again, I asked if she lived nearby and there was no response. She held my hand and said, "There is much for you to do but you are bound by this grief."

She closed her eyes while putting her hands gently on either side of my face. She began to talk as if she was speaking to someone. I can still see her shaking her head and saying, "Yes, yes." as if she was responding. I could not hear anyone else but her. I could not move from her hands. And I was not certain what was taking place. But I stood there with my eyes on her face and watching her every move. Then she released my face from her hands, opened her eyes and stepped back.

"God wants to be everything to you, and you are to remember that and that He loves you. Now, you must leave this place and never return. There is nothing for you here. No more will you feel this pain." And she spoke with such authority that I was taken back a little. In that instant, she took my arm and started leading me to where my vehicle was. I stopped and said, "No, I think I would like to stay a little longer." But she took my arm gently but with a little force and said, "No! you cannot stay here. You are to leave this place and never return!" She repeated forcefully.

As we were walking towards my car, I was asking questions, but she looked straight ahead. I started to turn around and she said, "No! Keep walking." I was afraid to look back then.

"Janice, I have so many questions, please Janice, please tell me. Please talk to me about this, I don't understand." I was blurting out questions and I did not know what to do. I could not let her leave. There was so much to say and understand. And I felt so close to my mother around her. There was a peace that covered me in her presence. I can hardly write this the tears are falling fast and hard. You will never know what I felt that day with her there. I could not imagine her leaving me now that she was here. When she touched me, I felt so safe and content. We couldn't leave now. I was beginning to understand the magnitude of her visit. She looked down at me in my car and said, "This is all you need to know at this time. You have much to do and you must leave this sorrow and the past behind. God wants you to know He loves you. You need to trust Him with strong faith. You must go now; life will be good to you," she finished and shut my car door. I watched her walk behind me to an exceptionally large silver colored car. The rain was falling by now, and my vehicle was ugly from dirt smudges and the wetness. But I looked behind me and her car was not touched by the rain. Not one drop was on her vehicle that I could see.

I watched her drive by, and her head was down like she was not watching where she was going in that sparkling car. *What just happened to me?* I thought about it, and I could hardly breathe. I watched her drive to the gate. My parents' grave site is near the back gate facing a busy road. She had turned to leave through the gate, but I never saw her car go to the left or right. As God as my witness, I have never seen anything like it. I remember jumping out of my car and running to that gate. I guess I could have driven, but I was not rational right then. There was a car coming in and I said, "Stop! Did you see a silver car go by, which way did it turn?" The man looked at me like I was insane. I asked again, "Which way?"

And he shook his head and said he saw no car. I could see through the fence and the car was nowhere to be found on that busy street.

I ran back and jumped in my car and grabbed that map and began writing everything I could remember that she had said. I still have it. I did not want to forget anything. I took off out of there, thinking I would see her along the way, but I never saw that car.

All the way home, I was giddy with excitement and a heightened sense of awareness of everything around me. I could not explain what had happened to me and I was sure no one would or could ever believe me, *and why would they?* This was odd, out of the ordinary. And it bordered on the unbelievable. I had difficulty comprehending what had just happened. My body tingled from the cold and wetness of my clothes. It was the only thing that made me sure I had not been dreaming. I ran into the house where Bruce and the children were, and I was blurting out everything that had happened. He was apologetic about our encounter from the day before and I was well past that explaining the encounter I had just had. Something had happened to me. I left that cemetery without that heaviness of grief I had carried for more than a year since my mother's death. It was no longer with me, covering me or weighing me down. It was gone! God had taken it away.

I was free from it, free from the bondage of oppression and sorrow. God had sent someone, a being, I do not know. I could never explain it and that is why I have not told anyone until now. You do not have to believe me. I am not concerned about whether I am believed. I know what happened that day and I know beyond a doubt that Janice was special. She was special to God, and she became special to me. She had been instrumental in removing the pain from me. I did not know what to do at first. Bruce told me to call the pastor to see if he could explain it. Talking to Pastor Glenn that afternoon, I explained in detail what had happened.

"Gaye, I believe you have had a heavenly visitation. I believe God sent an angel to minister to you," he explained. The time with this being, Janice, played over and over in my mind. I did not want to wash my face from where she had touched me. Or change my wet clothes. What I had experienced was supernatural and beyond my human capabilities. My finite mind could not comprehend any of it.

I do not recall how much time we were together that day, it seemed like a second and a lifetime all at once. I cannot explain any of this in the words it deserves. I have never shared this experience with anyone except my husband, children, and pastor. It was a sacred and intimate time that I did not want to be scrutinized or belittled for what happened. And I only share it now because it is a very important part of my story and my journey. I have not shared that day's events with anyone because it was mine alone to hold on to. And, I have relived that time repeatedly when times were difficult. God knew my circumstances so well and was so familiar to my need that he sent someone to bring me back from the darkness of grief and loss. A grief that was not healthy, not safe and beyond the normal stages one would experience after a death. I could have never found my way out of it. Nor could I have explained the oppressiveness that controlled me. But I do know without a doubt that I was released from it that day, February 13, 2005.

I have never experienced that grief again. Oh, I remember my mother and the many fond memories we shared together. I loved her more than anyone will ever know. Memories come at holidays or when we have a special family event and tears are joined by those thoughts of her. But I am content that she is with the Father in heaven rejoicing. Janice has never returned to me, but I will always remember that day with her. I have never returned to the cemetery to visit my parents' grave. I am sure their souls are with the Lord and will rejoin their bodies when Jesus returns. I struggled with sharing this experience, but I believe that with every word noted here, God has directed my steps, and my words. My hope is that it will build your faith and strengthen your walk with the Lord. If He did all this for me, He could do it for you. What does it say about me, well nothing, what does it say about God? Everything.

CHAPTER TWENTY-FOUR

Even the quiet in my life was so loud at times. I had no peace, and I had been existing and not living fully that last year or so. And now my life had changed. I had a new awareness of who I am with God. And, for the first time in my life, I came to grips with that. I may not be significant to anyone else, but I am significant to God. I am not a misfit begging to belong, I do not need to spare my feelings or harbor them inside to protect everyone else's. I am not weak nor a mistake. I am God's child! The very thought that He had met me at so many low places in my life and continued to mold me without me even knowing was beyond grace and mercy. I was not worth fighting for, and that is a lie of the devil. Never ever allow yourself to feel less than to God. He loves us. The idea that he knew I felt lost and alone and sent someone to me was beyond anything I could have ever imagined.

My DNA, the blood that courses through my veins, and the very makeup of my body shows me that my creator cared for me and delicately formed me. As a child, I started my walk with the Lord early, and exercising faith was a key factor in my journey with Him. But time and circumstances caused me to become jaded when I got older. Did God give up on me? No never. God will never lead you where He cannot keep you. But situations occurred and I became focused on people and everything but God. But even in those times, He redirected my steps. His hand kept me when I was a little girl trying to find where I fit in. When my heart was broken from loss and rejection, He was there. When I felt like an island to myself most of my life, I was never alone. He was with me whether I knew it or felt it. His eyes watched me in places I did not belong and protected me in my vulnerabilities. And His love kept me when I was dying in a makeshift ICU hospital room. People will always have an opinion about you. Some are for good and others to try and destroy you.

You will never be enough for most. But I have learned to trust only one voice. My father's voice is what I listen for. I'm so grateful that I swerved from the danger of my life and that He covered me when I was helpless and fragmented. Even during all the chaos, He watched and listened for me. Oh, the devil had my number, and not only did he try and take my life, but he has also blocked me every way possible in authoring this book. But! I will not be stopped, nor will God's work be thwarted.

I have scars, we all do. God removes the pain and changes the situations, but He leaves the scars. He leaves them as a reminder of where we have been and what His compassion has brought us through. If you want to talk to me about your walk, I need to see your scars. I need to hear your testimony.

I consider most of the things that have happened in my life to be miracles. The healings and the visitation. But I think that as believers, we do not truly believe in the marvel of God in our own lives. But God works with us individually. What is unique to me may not be to you. My needs are different than yours. But God sees each of us as we are, and deals with us accordingly. Oh, we may pray for a miracle but how many will honestly say that they genuinely believe in the deep of their heart that God is still working miracles today? Well, I believe the supernatural happenings of God still occur today. They are not just old stories from the Bible. A life with Christ can be filled with miracles. The very fact that we can wake up each morning is a miracle. So, I thought I would share some of what I have learned about miracles, needing one, and the plan to receive one in your life.

Have you ever planned a dinner party? If you have, you know the detailed work that goes into every minute of the preparations—the right mix of guests selected, your best dishes and decor are prepared for the evening. The perfect centerpiece and scrumptious food menu is thought out carefully for your special event. All the planning and effort pays off when you see guests enjoying the evening and your hospitality. That same concept can be applied to waiting on something from God. You prepare yourself for God's blessings. A miracle is an event or happening that would contradict natural law, but that shows God's power to eyes of faith in the believer. If you have ever experienced a miracle or known someone who has, there is little doubt that something unexplainable has occurred. It is much easier to comprehend the idea of a miracle when you see it firsthand. We read in the scriptures and various references about miracles. Why do we see Jesus performing them in the Bible? He wanted the knowledge of God's power to be witnessed and communicated to the masses. And, the Word was provided for us to have a map to follow in our journey with him. He gave sight to the blind, the lame walked again with just a touch from the savior, and deaf ears were opened.

Jesus was confirming the power of miracles and the fulfillment of His promises. He did those early works to show nonbelievers. Throughout the Bible, we see His miracles. Some logical, some unorthodox, but all amazing.

Jesus did not single out the rich, the handsome or the talented. He sought out those who had a need. The very dredges of society were as special and worthy to His caring eyes as any man of means. The main thread of all the miracles performed was based on a single five-letter word: F A I T H.

Why do I feel the need to write on miracles and faith? Not because I profess to be a great theologian, far from that. It is because I have experienced them in my own life. I believe that God opened my eyes to a process of preparation for things to happen in my life. Preparations for miracles. My afflictions happened to be physical. I strongly believe that my physical issues, some that I deal with even today, in 2022, have become my way of staying close to the Lord. If I did not have a reason to trust him each day for my life, I may become careless, and think I can make it on my own. That is completely false and a lie of the devil. So, I deal with afflictions and pain daily. And I am totally dependent on God for my health. Let me share some thoughts that may help in your journey towards your own miracle.

I have counseled Christians about what they needed from the Lord. They know bits and pieces of my testimony and have asked for guidance in seeking their own miracle. Often, I have heard statements like, *Am I worthy to even ask God to fix this or change my situation?* And I have even heard, *I think this may be more than God would want to take on.* Can you imagine? No wonder we do not receive from God; we tie His hands with our doubt.

My comeback is usually, *are you and I worthy in the least for God's provisions?* No, we are not. But God cannot lie; therefore, His promises and miracles from centuries ago are available today. If God said it, then it still works today. As a child of God, the covenant He made with us at the time of our salvation is one that cannot be broken by anyone but us. We have free will, and freedom to separate from God. But He will not tire of us and the many problems we bring to Him. If that were the case, He would have been tired of me long ago. Our free will can cause us to lose out on salvation, on faith and on receiving a miracle, but it will never be the result of God giving up on us. Our problems are anything but big to God. Although I grew up in church and knew the lingo and the buzz words, I lacked in faith and in understanding when it came to my own needs as an adult. So, it was during my life that God showed me many factors about worship and a true knowledge of His work that I was able to apply to my life. Some of this I will share with hope that it will help strengthen your faith and help you work toward your own miracles.

The initial step in preparation for a miracle is *salvation*. The cleansing of sin from our lives is key for us to communicate with the Lord. God speaks to nonbelievers to draw them to conviction and subsequent salvation. He will not communicate with those who are not in communion with Him or that reject his offering of salvation. *Reflection* is what God showed me next regarding my search for a miracle. How did I get to this place? Often, we lack discernment and wisdom. People would say to me, God must be teaching you a lesson, or just do not claim it. As if God was punishing me, or just not claiming my illness was going to just take it away. We do more harm than good to people who are hurting when we lack wisdom. I believe that there are times when God allows a crisis or illness to come to a believer to do a necessary work in their life. Thank God He did it for me! Those times in my life when I could not see past my problems or the physical pain, God was using it to mold me and to increase my faith. Not only that, but those around you may need to see the work you are willing to do to be healed, or, to see your circumstances change. It is not always about us. Some things we go through are to encourage someone else. Often, we go through things that our family, friends or even strangers observe to see how we deal with it. God may allow an illness or crisis to happen to soften someone's heart around you, that would lead them to salvation. Reflection helps us to delve into our own relationship with God. And with his help, to see where we need work to get to a place for our miracle.

My mother would say, "Do not be so heavenly minded; you are no earthly good." When someone is struggling with faith for healing or deliverance, the last thing they need to hear is contrite remarks from a fellow Christian. My prayer life for many years was what I called superficial praying. A quick prayer for traveling mercies, or to get me through the next meeting. I said a prayer at bedtime. And through the day I would say a quick prayer here and there. But my life was moving in all directions. I was busy. Often too busy to tarry and listen to God for answers or to just commune with him. I barked my needs to Him, but seldom did I sit still and listen to Him talk to me. It was not until my back problem that my relationship with God rose to a new peak. It was as if He said, *now that I have your attention, there are some things I want you to know. I've done so much in your life, and as the result of all of that you trust Me enough now to hear my instruction. I have missed you. Let's talk.* With my back injury, I learned to communicate with the Lord on a more intimate level.

He had my undivided attention. The hurt of excruciating physical pain, isolation, and loneliness as life moved on without me, brought me to a crossroad. Blaming God was not the answer; and only bonding with Him and becoming closer to Him was the key to making it through the tough times. I held on to God instead of pulling away like I had done in the past. The promise of this enduring for only a season was my strength, and I did not know what God had planned for me. But one thing was sure, I was focused, and I was ready for the journey. I knew that although I was saved and had a relationship with Him, I needed more. I would need to put more time into my prayer life to not only make it through this desert, but to be victorious in the end.

Mom said, "It's putting legs on your prayers." I knew I was lacking. I fully understood what I needed to do to get closer to the Lord. Not just for my healing, but because I simply needed a closer walk with Him.

Evaluation is a daily aspect of my life that I learned. What can I do? What do I need to do better, Lord? I became hungry for that undisturbed time with the father. As with death, facing a debilitating illness can cause you to move through a series of phases. It is so difficult to see yourself powerless and without control. I went through a time of shock, madness, sadness, denial, and acceptance. Acceptance only in the fact that I knew what I was dealing with and had begun to trust the Lord to make it each day. Not that I accepted this sickness and had given into it, but that I was tolerant of my situation enough to place myself in God's hands until my healing came.

One of my favorite scriptures is Psalms 103:14 NIV, "For he knows how we are formed, he remembers that we are dust." God more than anyone else knows our limitations. Psalms 142:3 NIV says, "When my spirit grows faint within me, it is you who know my way." No man, but Jesus understood my anxious heart and my fears of becoming unable to take care of myself. Believe me, I felt at times that it was more than I could face. But as I look back, each time I was at my most desperate, something would happen great or small that would confirm God had not forgotten me. Those times would push me on to the next day of the same pain, but also the same trust in Him. There are times in life when all you have left is that little bit of faith you can muster up.

There is a scene in the great movie classic *Miracle on 34th Street*, when Natalie Wood is trying to let herself be convinced that the kind old gentleman Mr. Kringle is really Santa. She closes her eyes tightly and says repeatedly, "I believe, I believe." Almost as if saying it repeatedly was going to make the doubt disappear. I spent much of my illness saying something similar. No matter what happened, I tried to hold onto God's promises. I can remember friends calling to check on me (some believers, some not.) They would make comments like, why would God make you go through this? It is not fair. That's right I was kind to others and did not harm small animals, so why me? I would almost slip and get caught in that trap of self-pity. But I would quickly remind myself of what a privilege it was to have God work with me individually. In the back of my mind, I would say, "*I believe, I believe.*"

Waiting is the most tiring process. We need answers when we are seeking, and I was the worst to be impatient. But God's timing was not mine. However, I had to remember that the wait may be for reasons we cannot see with our human eyes. Not only was I in need of a miracle, but He surrounded me with individuals who were also in need. Psalms 18:21 NIV says, "For I have kept the ways of the Lord and have not wickedly departed from my God." Earlier in my life I did the exact opposite. When things got bad and one problem compounded on to the next, my life seemed to snowball out of control, and I lost my way. I blamed God for things that did not turn out as planned, for broken dreams and opportunities that slipped through my fingers. He was responsible for my broken heart when I thought trusting a fellow Christian was enough. Boy, I was mistaken. I blamed God for this when I should have been grateful, He stopped me before I ruined my life. Having gone through that heartbreak prepared my heart for what was coming. The real gift God had for me in Bruce. My mother would always say, "You have to spend summer and winter with someone before you marry them." Meaning, you need to see them in all situations before you commit yourself to them forever. And regardless of whether someone is in the church or not, does not mean they are where they need to be with the Lord. I would advise any young person to use caution when you give your heart away. God wants only the best for you. I was mad at God, for rejection and loss in my life that constantly had me searching for answers I could not find. I blamed Him for feelings of inferiority. It was as if I measured Him the same way I measured every other man that let me down in my life. I lumped Him together with all the garbage and lies. I did not grab my chance. I did not have the confidence I needed, so I made excuses instead of trusting Him. Yes, I faced obstacles that conflicted with my plans, but I used those to rail out at God.

During my back illness, I began to open my heart to God's discipline. I was not in charge, and I had to come to that realization. I certainly do not believe my illness was the result of God's judgment or punishment, but I had rough edges to smooth and barriers that needed to come down. My heart and ears needed to be keen to His call, and I had difficulty giving up control to anyone before this illness occurred. What had started as a tragedy became an opportunity for me.

What I learned next and most critical to my healing miracle was *Sacrificial Praise*. It is absolutely the most important aspect of my journey to healing. I am convinced, that had I not obeyed the Lord the day of my healing would not have come. I remember how at times when I was so full of emotions and miserable from the pain that I could not put together a complete prayer. I could not always concentrate on making it pretty or poetic. So, I would just begin to praise the Lord at the worst of times.

God had shown me that with everything He had done in my life to that point, I had not yet learned how critical sacrificial praise was to my victory. God had healed me before, but He knew that down the road I would need to learn this principle. Sometimes in our life we are not as open to God's teaching as others. Now I was ready to know all that God had for me. Answers did not always come when I asked. I would put on gospel music and begin to thank Him audibly for what He had already done in my life. Because I could not go to church at the time, this had become my church. When I began to praise the Lord, it was a like a tonic to me. The more I praised Him, the more I needed to do it. The cobwebs were swept away, and God began molding me. I was able to really comprehend more clearly the importance of praise in a renewed and heightened interaction with Him.

Praise opens doors of communion; it humbles the soul to see his glory through submission. When you praise the Lord with your full heart and soul, you are saying, *God, here I am.* Regardless of what you do or do not do for me, you are worthy of my praise. The miracle at that point is just the icing on top. It is in seeking that you really find what you need from God. I have told myself this for years. It is not always about the destination, but more importantly, about what we learn on the journey.

In my mind, I visualize that when we begin to praise God, He hushes the angels in Heaven so that He can hear our praise. I envision that our praise is ushered before the throne and is sweet to God's ears. We get God's attention when we offer Him our complete and sincere praise, just because He is worthy.

I reminded God of his word, and his promise to me one very dark day soon after surgery. I had opened my Bible, and, through my tears, I read Jeremiah 29:11-14 NIV, "For I know the plans I have for you," declares the Lord, "Plans to prosper you and not harm you, plans to give you hope and a future. Then you will call on me and come and pray to me, and I will listen to you. You will seek me and find me when you seek me with all your heart. I will be found by you." That promise became my hope. I still get emotional when I hear that scripture. Romans 8:28 NIV says, "And we know that in all things, God works for the good of those who love him, who have been called according to his purpose." It does not say one or two things will work to our good, nor does it say that God will pick and choose what will work in our favor. No, it says in all things. It is not easy to wait, not when you are facing an illness that is chipping away at the very quality of your life or separating you from those you love. It surely is not easy to digest that God has a plan that may involve suffering for a time.

Faith is critical for every step, but difficult to exercise when everything around you is crashing and burning. It is in those times when you need it the most. Victory came for me, and I received my complete healing. It can come at an unlikely time. It is not always about fan fair or a big production. The times I received healing in my body were when I was in my church pew. At seventeen, I was standing at the pew. When God healed my back much later in life, I had fought my body to make my way to the front for prayer and did not receive immediate healing until I returned to my seat. If we read the Word, we know that God used unlikely and unusual situations to bring victory to people. He used a bush, burning fires, dead people, and even animals to bring victory. He called out to Lazarus who had already been dead four days.

When God says move, then move. I could not understand why He told me to walk around my house seven times. But as difficult as it was I did it. I did not have an immediate answer or miracle. I had been worried that my illness would impact us financially in keeping our home and hindering our children from attending college. Years later, our children finished college, received a great education, and have exceptional careers today. We are still in that house that has been long since paid for. So, obedience works! Be ready in faith to be obedient if He tells you to do something unorthodox. It will never be dangerous, or bring harm to you, but it will test your faith.

From the day of my back healing, I never took another medication, never had pain again in my back nor did I require additional surgery for it. It was complete healing. As the victory came, so did the devil with his lies. Why would God did this for you and not some child who is dying of a disease? I would often wake in the night and these thoughts would cover me with guilt. Even people that I knew and loved had not received their miracle, so why me? I was the least in the kingdom and one carrying so much baggage. Why me? As I began to study about miracles, I realized that I may never know God's plan or why. I did not deserve it, but I did not deserve salvation either, but He gave that to me freely, not once but twice in my life.

I decided one way I could give back to God for his faithfulness to me was to begin to pray more diligently for those around me who were in need. I began to ask God every time I leave my house to put someone in my path that I can share the hope of Jesus with. I am determined to use my testimony to make a difference for someone else. When victory comes, do not let the devil try to foil it by blanketing your blessing with a cloud of doubt or guilt. He does not want it to get out that God is still in the miracle business. I can guarantee that when the time is right, no matter how long the trial, God will bring victory, so hold on. If you prepare for a miracle, it will come into your life.

I will share this about my miracle process, and some may not agree, but I believe this in my life. Although God is not one to give and then take away, I strongly believe that I must *remain in tuned with Him* to keep my healing, my miracle. I had no idea when I woke up that day with a catch in my back that I was going into training. I had no idea what was in store for me. It was a long challenging time in my life. But I learned so much about myself and the God I serve, it made it all worth it.

Having been helpless and even in a wheelchair the few times I left the house during that time, and the threat as a young girl with being in one, I learned to be more conscious of those around me. I have been lonely; I have been helpless. And I am keenly aware of what people face. It is simple, we cannot be too busy to be Christ to someone in need. We cannot walk through life with our eyes shut and our head down. Look around you, there is need everywhere. I know that we will be held accountable for those times we did not heed the call to service. I apply this to my life every day.

When your need is greater than your pride, you are in a position to hear from God. You will do the work because you are desperate for a touch from Him. I have done some strange things. I could not even walk to the front of the church because my back was so bad and it was painful to walk, but I did it. I held onto every pew going down that long aisle because I wanted to show God, I was serious. I needed something and I was not going to give up or give in until He touched me. How badly do you need a miracle in your life? Does your sacrificial praise mean lifting your hands, clapping your hands in worship, not caring who sees you or who is judging you? Will it require you making the walk to the front in an act of obedience and humbleness? We must get to the place where we can say Lord, I am all in. I cannot go another step without your help. That is the perfect place to be, and exactly where God can begin to work. You must get to the point where you cannot make it another day without God's touch. You are vulnerable and ready to hear from him. When you become broken and are clinging to Him for your very life, he shows up. He is the perfect guest, invite him. You can count on Him to be there in your time of need!

"Glorious and majestic are his deeds, and his righteousness endures forever. He has caused his wonders to be remembered; the Lord is gracious and compassionate. He provides food for those who fear him; he remembers his covenant forever. The fear of the Lord is the beginning of wisdom; all who follow his precepts have good understanding. To him belongs eternal praise." Psalms 111: 3-5, 10 NIV.

I was talking with a homeless woman not long ago and I met her physical needs for warmth and food. I will stop right here. You cannot talk to someone about how much God loves them if they are hungry and cold. Meet the need and then share Christ with them. My mom always said, "Feed their bellies first before you feed them the Word of God." So, this woman said, "I have tried to live for God, but I always go back to my old ways. I always slip up." I knew exactly how she felt. "I struggle too," I said. When I look around and see how things are, I start to question God. I start to get caught up in the world's sadness and hopelessness. But I do not let myself stay there long. I cry out to my father to help me. No matter what comes, it cannot take my joy. That joy comes from Him alone. We all stumble.

I asked her if she remembered in the Bible when God only fed the people for the day but not the next. How He ministered to someone's need at a particular time, but He did not give them a week's worth or a month's supply in every situation. He gave them enough for the day. If He gave us enough to sustain us for an extended period, we would have no need to go to Him, to cry out for help. I explained that walking with the Lord is a daily walk. We get up each day, serve Him and try to do better than we did yesterday. We make mistakes, but we pick ourselves up, ask forgiveness and start again. That is all that He requires of us is that step of faith. If we had a storehouse, we would not need His daily provisions. Do not limit what God can do in your life.

I need God every single day of my life. We must understand as believers that the church is not the four walls that shelter saints with familiarity and freedom to worship. The church is outside those walls, where people just like us are hurting and in need of a savior. Of course, we gather because we need strength from like believers, and the Lord made it clear we are to assemble. But my heart has become so restless knowing that our time is short here, and there is so much left to do before Jesus returns. There are so many souls to reach. Our world needs a healer. I know firsthand what God can do in a life. I was battling something so much bigger than I could handle alone. We are so comfortable where we are. We are so contented to just be ministered to and let other people go reach souls. We have been churched to death. Saturated in our beliefs and ministered to until we have become stagnant and overbearing. God help us! Our eyes need to be opened. The church is beyond the walls. On Monday and Tuesday and every other day of the week, our eyes and ears need to be keenly aware of needs around us and opportunities to minister.

Finally, *Testimony* is critical once you have received something from God. Tell people what God did for you! Share your testimony. It encourages you and strengthens your faith as you speak about it. And it will definitely help someone else to not give up.

The Bible says we are overcomers by our testimony. The book of Revelation is filled with references for us on being overcomers in the faith. The Greek word for overcomer means to carry off the victory. To me that means we are in a battle. Every time you share your testimony you are fighting the devil. You are exercising your faith. And you are telling others that God can do the same for them! We live in a world where even most Christians are skeptical that God still performs miracles today. How can we believe that God has stopped working when the very breath we breathe each day comes from him? I could not understand why He had instructed me to author this book. It was foreign to me, and I was extremely uncomfortable in this unknown territory. But, in my spirit and with several confirmations from others, I knew I had to proceed in faith.

God had done amazing things in my life. He would want me to remind you the reader, that He has not changed. He is still faithful, and still works miracles. The God of old is the God of now. He is still the same today. The Bible says, "Jesus Christ is the same yesterday, today and forever." Hebrews 13:8 NIV. His grace was beyond my comprehension. His love was abundant and given freely to me. How could I not tell people that are hurting just like I was that the answer to their life questions is Jesus Christ?

CHAPTER TWENTY-FIVE

Several years ago, Bruce's dad came to live with us. Bruce's mother had died in August 2007. At first, it was wonderful, and we loved having him in our home. But as his health began to deteriorate, we were faced with many challenges. He and I both were under the care of a neurologist. He for an illness and me for my neck issues. I began to experience anxiety. I was alone with him most of the time while Bruce was out of town, and I was always fearful that something horrible would happen while he was in my care. The most challenging times were during the night when he would scream out my name and I would stumble around trying to help him back to bed. He became blind and lost his hearing. It was extremely difficult for us to communicate with him.

The doctor began to see changes in my health and decided to place me on some medications that would offset the anxiety of dealing with my father-in-law's illness and my lack of sleep. Little did I know that these drugs would impact my life so negatively. I was on extremely low doses, but the changes in me were becoming not only visible but harmful. When Bruce's dad finally went to be with the Lord, I started having serious complications.

My neurologist had left his practice due to his own father's death, and I had to seek out another neurologist locally. When I went to her the first time, she saw symptoms in me that were symptomatic of what is called medical Parkinson's disease that is induced by medications. My mother had Parkinson's disease, so I was keenly aware of how the body reacted to it. And I was terrified. As a young adult, it would have thrown my world into a fast spin. I was trying to hold on to

God to keep it at bay. She further explained that it was due to the medications I was taking. She was fearful of my coming off of them even though they were causing these symptoms. Who really knows the true impact of any medication long term? My previous neurologist had not said anything about the potential of Parkinson's disease in correlation with these medications.

I remember feeling too paranoid to leave my home. I was scared to get into the car, and I would constantly ask how long it would take to get somewhere and back to the safety of my house when we did go out. When we went to see Jonathan and his family the trip made me nervous and anxious. I feared being killed in traffic, and he saw the changes in me immediately. Visiting my daughter was the same way. In fact, when I was well after being off of the medications finally, one of my gag gifts from her for Christmas was a framed photo of a map. It gave the distance from her house in Birmingham to all the major restaurants and stores we frequented when we were there. They have since moved to Tennessee.

My husband saw me change from an outgoing, funny person that loved life, to a zombie. I had no idea I had changed that drastically. I would go for hours not saying a word, so unlike me. My children were concerned for me. Bruce had to take me to doctor appointments, and church. I felt safe in church, but I did not interact with others. We came in and left before I had to talk to anyone. And that went on for a long time. I was so bound by that medication. It was such a joy to finally participate and meet people at my wonderful church. They thought we had just started visiting there. But we had been there for quite a while. I was bound by these medications. I did not even see myself like others saw me, but I knew I was constantly anxious and afraid. Ironically, the reasons I was placed on the medications in the first place.

I made the decision that I would come off the medications which was a drastic and dangerous thing to do. It caused me to spiral into a nervous and highly agitated state. I remember telling the doctor at one visit that I did not care what happened, I had to stop these drugs. She had warned that I would need to be weaned from one under her supervision, but thought it was in my best interest to stay on the other drug indefinitely.

My body still did not react differently with just the one medication. In fact, things were worse; I still experienced the dread and the horrible side effects. I gained over twenty pounds, which was one of many side effects of the medications, and I hardly slept. I was fearful that something would happen when I was asleep. I became an insomniac. Bruce took me one day to my primary care physician and I told him I had to have help. I had prayed for God to help me, and I was trying to listen to my doctors. I made the decision along with my primary care physician to stop the other medication without the neurologist's approval. It took six months for the effects of those drugs to start to leave my body. And it took over a year to be back to normal or, whatever normal is for me.

Each time I have an appointment with him he still mentions that terrible time and how proud he is that I got my life back. It took a lot of time and a lot of faith.

I immediately dropped the weight and even decided I would drive one day. Just like that, I wanted to get out of the house. My head was clear, and my anxiety was gone. The Lord and I went on a little trip to the bookstore. I had not been out alone in such a long time. I will never forget how I prayed aloud during that drive for God's help. God cleared my head and removed the haze from the medication that had overtaken my body. I held onto the steering wheel so firmly that when I finally arrived at my destination my hands were throbbing. But God had gone with me. We had gone on an adventure after I had been a prisoner to this medication. Happily, I had no further problems. God had walked beside me during that time, and I am forever grateful to Him. It took great faith to step out that day. And sometimes that is all it takes.

As long as we are on this earth, we will face obstacles and things that test our faith. Even a drug that starts out to help you can rapidly reduce you to an invalid. But God's grace is sufficient for me! He got me through that time. I have shared all of this to let you know that no problem, and no burden is too great for God. I would tell my young self to stay close to the cross, and never give up on God. Never go out into the world to seek help or comfort because it is not there. The times I stumbled were the worst times in my life. I was disconnected from the Lord and that is the most dangerous place to be.

Do I face problems today? Yes, I do. Is it always rosy? No, it is not, far from it. But I have learned that God will remove it or will move me through it. He will take me over or under, but I always come out on top with Him. My mountains are just as difficult to climb but I do not climb alone. I have shared myself, my secrets, and my sufferings because I want you to know you do not have to climb your mountains alone either. I would much rather talk with someone who says, hey, I have been there and here is what you must do to get through it. Our testimony is a declaration, a confirmation of something that has occurred. It is me saying, let me show you, my scars. It is my hope to keep you from making a mistake and to help you understand to not put limits on God or His ability to meet your need. There is not one question in my life that God is not the answer to.

I know where I would be without his mercy. When I drank so heavily, I could not remember where I was, or where I needed to be. Most of my early 20's is a blur. I would end up in my car in a parking lot alone and cold and wonder where I was. I would wake up in my driveway and not have a clue as to how I got there. Never once did someone try to hurt me, rob me, or cause problems for me. Thank God I never hurt anyone. God was my shield, my strength, and my protector during those awful times. When I needed a touch physically, He came through. The only sad thing about awful habits is the problems do not go away. When you wake up or come to, they are still there.

I could not help myself, and there was no way I could get back from the destruction. But God saw through all of it. He saw past my inability to trust Him, my bitterness, and the hurt that I was holding close to my heart. He delivered me! He took it all away, drained the bitterness, the horrible rejection and fought the devil for my life. He restored me to a more abundant life than I could have ever dreamed of. I grew up with dysfunction in my family. As much as my mother tried to be everything to us, and tried to pray to hold us all together, we dealt with some tough stuff. There was pain, we had sadness and my siblings each had their own issues. I wish it had not been that way. We were happy, but there was conflict and hidden secrets. It was not perfect by any means. But my mother tried hard. And I know that both she and dad had difficult times growing up. I was determined when God blessed us with children that they would never have to question where they fit in. Never doubt my love or my intent to give them stability and a close family that loved each other. I did not know my story so I wanted them, no, needed them, to know theirs. God gave that satisfaction to me. It is all I ever wanted. I am so grateful that today, I can look back on my childhood and see so many happy times. I know how hard my parents worked to provide and love us. No matter how we grow up, it can help make us who we are. And God has gently reminded me on many occasions just how blessed I was.

I love the story of Lazarus in John 11:1-44 NIV. I so relate to his sisters, Mary, and Martha. They and Lazarus had been close friends of Jesus and he often came to Bethany where they lived to rest away from the crowds. Lazarus had become ill the Bible says. The two sisters sent notice to Jesus who was a distance away in Jerusalem at the time and asked Him to come because Lazarus was sick. But Jesus did not come right away. In fact, He stayed where He was for another two days. Now, the sisters are watching Lazarus decline to near death, and they are struggling with the fact that Jesus had not shown up.

We do know that Jesus arrived on the fourth day. Just inside the city limits, Martha met him and questioned him, just like I would have. "If you had been here, my brother would not have died," verse twenty-one says. Jesus told her that Lazarus would rise again. Did she doubt? She said, sure, Lord, at the resurrection, he will, I am paraphrasing. Then Jesus gave her a soft rebuke in verse 25 saying, "I am the resurrection and the life." That would have made me stop and think a minute. Martha then, ran to get her sister, Mary, who questioned Jesus delay like her sister had.

The sisters had a following of Jews who were there to give comfort to them. These skeptics were watching everything unfold. When Jesus saw the sisters' tears, it touched Him, and He instructed them to show Him where Lazarus was buried. The Bible says "Jesus wept" in John 11:35, the smallest scripture in the Bible. Jesus was not crying because things were hopeless, and Lazarus was gone. He was crying because the ones He loved were hurting. He knew exactly what the outcome was going to be, and he had stated it when he was still in Jerusalem. The people around Him remind me of us today; *didn't you do miracles before Jesus? Wasn't he the one that healed the blind? Why didn't he stop Lazarus from dying?* Gossipers and naysayers, sadly even in the church today.

The Jews believed that the soul of a dead body hovered around the body for three days after death. So, when we wonder why Jesus showed up late, He did not. He was right on time. He could have healed Lazarus from where He was in Jerusalem; He could have healed Lazarus on the way into town. But he wanted God to be glorified. So instead of raising him earlier, it would have been in the three-day period the Jews believed the soul hovered around the body and of course they would have questioned any miracle performed during that time. But when the fourth day came! Now, there was a miracle, and it was coming their way!

Only Jesus could bring someone back to life in front of all these people and He would do it on the fourth day so that there would be no question or doubt as to who did it! He told Martha to move the stone away. Martha was hesitant telling the Lord there would be an odor after four days. But Jesus reminded her in a powerful scripture found in John 11:40 NIV, "Did I not tell you that if you believe, you will see the glory of God?" And Jesus gave thanks to God in front of the people, the doubters. And He called Lazarus to come forth. The Bible says that Lazarus was bound by his feet and his hands when he came out of that grave. I can just imagine the shock from the crowd.

There have been times in my life when I let thoughts of not succeeding or becoming a failure take away my dreams. I have started things I did not finish because I got in the way. I let the devil take credit for the things that could have been. But no longer. His bill has come due. I will not live in fear! I will not stop until I have done all that God has for me. But it has taken me all my life to get to this place.

There were so many times when I thought God was late. Times when I wondered why He did not hear me when He knew I was about to go over a cliff. But in those trying times, He was never late once. He fought the devil for me and held me while I kicked and screamed that He had abandoned me. Behind the scenes, He was working on my behalf. When my body was racked with pain, when I was told I would not have children, when I was dying, He was there every time. When I was reckless and rejected, He was by my side. If I had not gone through all these things, I would not know how to really trust Him now. I cannot live on someone else's miracles. I can rejoice for them, but I need my own strength. I need God to do a work in me.

God turned my trials and testing into a testimony and my failures into victory. You and I are over comers by the word of our testimony. The more I share my testimony of God's deliverance I become stronger. When I talk about His healing and His abundance in my life with others, they are encouraged to seek this savior I serve. God does not let us go through a trial without a reason. It is always to teach us something, or to teach someone else around us something. It gets attention when you say, "Hey, look what God did for me!" We are carriers of His grace. I am and you are. God brought me out when I was hopeless and had given up. But when I tell someone what He did for me, they may not understand it all; I do not either. But they are encouraged that He can do the same for them. It is not just what He did in Bible times; look around, people are touched by God, and miracles take place every single day. He is no respecter of persons. We are all loved the same way, but our trials may be different.

I have known people who have never experienced the things I went through. They have maintained, gone to church and have never experienced doubt or the heartbreak that I have. Or not yet anyway. So, I cannot relate well to those people. I am happy for them, but I cannot relate to them. I need someone around me that says let me tell you what God did for me! How He carried me, picked me up and dusted me off. How He set me on the right path. Let me show you, my scars. Because when you are on the brink of self-destruction, and your balance is tilted to the negative because you have given up, it is the worst place to find yourself. But thank the Lord, He sought me out, He was relentless in holding on to me. If I had never been to that place in my life, I would have never truly known the power of God that redeemed me and brought me back. I would have never appreciated His power and His mightiness.

Days that stand out in my mind, are the day that I as a little girl walked down the long center aisle to the altar to ask Jesus into my life. And the day He spared my life in that hospital bed. I see God's hand in both of those scenarios. How He claimed that child and ordered her steps. Oh, I experienced loss, disappointment, and rejection repeatedly. And I was arrogant enough to go out on my own, thinking God had let me down. But He watched over me like a parent does when their child first learns to walk. They must let go of them and let them take those initial steps independently. But that child will always look back to see if the parent is still there, still watching, in case they need them.

Faith is stepping out but knowing God has you. We can pray and pray for a miracle, and we can even conjure up enough faith at times to really believe He will answer. But if He does not respond or answer when we think He should, we gather up the shattered pieces of our life and try to fix it ourselves. How often had I made things so much worse by setting out on my own? This is not a race I have to beat others for to finish a winner. It is an individual journey between the Lord and me. It takes work every single day to serve the Lord. Do I get discouraged? Yes, I do. Do I get frustrated? Yes, more often than I should. I am not made of metal or bricks; I am a dust and water girl. Molded for the temporary. I was not created to last forever here on this earth. This is not my home. When my time on Earth is over, I want to go home. Home where Jesus is. A place where not measuring up, rejection and heartache cannot find me any longer. Home where I am safe with my father and removed from sickness, death, and disappointment. Tears will no longer be shed in that place by you or me.

Our time on Earth is fleeting, transient and swift. Every minute counts. Every work we do and every person we minister to further prepares us for our next test and for Heaven. I think if we look at faith, we may wonder why God put it in the form of a mustard seed. I can just imagine people and church leaders back in the days when Christ was on the earth, trying to analyze and ponder how much faith was really needed by a person.

"Do we need a cupful, Lord?" "No, more than that," from someone in the crowd. "Well, do we need a mountain's worth, Lord? Or two cups worth?" God sees us as we are, and He understands how finite our minds are. No, you need the faith of a mustard seed; that is all you need. A tiny little mustard seed of faith is all that is required. It seems like such a small and insignificant amount until you need to exercise it. The mustard seed is discussed in Matthew 17:20. Jesus used it to show that something so small could create something large like the mustard bush. It is often thought to be a tree because of its large size. Jesus equates faith the same way. It just takes a small amount. A little faith can create a large miracle. When you really need faith to move in a situation, even producing a mustard seed size amount of faith is difficult, trust me I know. I am sure those that were around the Lord thought, well, that is nothing; we can surely have that much faith. Not always.

CHAPTER TWENTY-SIX

Faith becomes stronger the more you use it in your life. Back in the Spring of 2022, I went to church one Sunday morning feeling terrible. I have so many problems with fibromyalgia and neck degeneration, and it can be debilitating. I am in pain most every day. I cannot even get going in the morning a lot of days. It takes me often until afternoon to even be able to move my neck and body enough to dress and do the things I need to complete that day. That Sunday it was so much worse. I could hardly concentrate on the service. I said to myself, *if pastor opens the service for prayer for the sick, I am going down for prayer.*

It certainly is not that I do not think God cannot heal me in my seat. Of course, He can, and He has twice. But there are times God wants us to step out. When the pastor opened the altars for prayer, I was the first one down there, I think. I needed a touch from the Lord, and I had no doubt in my mind that I would get one. The difference between hope and faith is that hope is *wanting* something to happen, whereas faith is *waiting* on it to happen. Anticipating victory, waiting on your healing. I went to the altar, expecting a touch and I received one to last me the rest of that day.

I needed another touch the next day, and I will continue to need a touch until the Lord heals me again, and I know He will when He is ready. So, I rest in the knowledge that my miracle will be coming anytime.

When I went to the altar that day, I needed something from God. And I knew He would meet me there. Often, when you step out, it opens the door for someone else to feel comfortable going for prayer as well. It just takes a step in the right direction. I did not feel I could stay at my seat. God needed to see me humble myself and go the altar. The altar is the center of God's hospital. That is what church is; it is God's hospital for us and for those seeking. It is the place we come for strength, for fellowship, and to hear the Word. My heart is always full when I see people seeking at the altar. It is a place of reverence, of healing, of renewal.

Looking back at my life, my faith as a little child was driven by wanting to emulate my mother's faith in God. I wanted what she had. Later, I struggled with faith not because God had changed, but because I had changed. The world pulls and stretches us. It keeps us wondering and causes us to fear. If I could not trust God now, I would not even get out of bed. I would cover my head and never get up.

I had experienced so much that I put limits on Him. But you cannot put God in a box or limit His work in your life. God broke the chains in my life and set me free. Not everything works out the way we want it to as a believer. You cannot give God instructions on what you want or pick from a menu on how he should work things out. That is where faith comes in. We must trust that He knows best for us. There will be problems, lost relationships, and God never promised it would be easy. Through the course of an exceptionally prolonged illness and back problem, God had taught me not only about faith and trusting Him for every need in my life, but He also gave me a better understanding of how praise can work to my advantage. How praising Him can untie his hands to work in my life and how, even in the darkest times, praising God brings such joy. The very fact that my big problems are nothing to God gives me hope to continue.

In this season of my life, I have such strong faith. Faith that may not know the outcome or the reasons. Oh, I struggle at times with pain or hurt, but I have grown up with the Lord. I am mature in my walk with Him now. No more do I question His love for me, and no more am I carrying my burden alone. I can honestly say that without the issues I experienced in my life, I would not be the person I am today. Had God not reached down and touched my life and changed me for the good, I do not know where I would have ended up. I slip up on occasion and that is what mercy and grace are for. I get up, gather myself and start again.

I will be out somewhere, and people will ask me where I get my smile, and I will say from my father. I get it from my father. Of course, they think it is from my dad, and I explain from my heavenly father. It opens a door to minister to them. They cannot understand anyone smiling or humming the way things are today. But if they only knew my story. If I am humming or sing in a store, or smile at everyone, it is because of the sheer joy in my life. It certainly is not because of how I am feeling. But I can separate physical pain from the joy God gives me. I am living and breathing my life by faith, one miracle at a time. When I thought God had wanted me to have a music career and it did not happen when I thought it should, I felt He had betrayed me. I did not understand that my mission at that time was in taking care of my parents. I had prepared myself for that life on the road and His will. But that was not His will at the time; being at home was.

What I looked at as broken dreams was God saying, *no, not right now*. I thought if I didn't do it, I would be out of His will. So, I was so torn. But God had to show me that everything was just postponed for a season. I was mistaking my will for his. I do not understand why all of the preparations were made. Or the album was recorded? Things were moving only to stop. But I do not worry about that now.

Oh, I sing. I sing in the car, I serenade my husband, and someday if God convicts me, I will resume my singing ministry. When I am a little down, God gives me a song. So, I have never stopped singing, and lately He has given me the gift of writing songs again. It has been so long since I sat at the piano. I had to laugh at my first attempt in what had been many years. But it is all coming back now. I believe in renewal. God restores the very things the devil tries to rob us of.

God gave me so much more than what the devil dangled in front of me. A true and pure love that I share with my husband. We have been married 39 years November 2022, and I love him more now than ever. Our children are wonderfully blessed, healthy, and happy. And our grandchildren give us so much joy. Gone are the feelings of rejection and trying to figure out where I stood with my dad. I know he loved me, and God has given me the peace to accept that. Through authoring this book, I have finally let it all go. My having been obedient to God's call to tell my story has helped me release all the things I had carried for so long. I am free from it all now. All that matters is that Dad is in Heaven, and I will see him again. The loss and the tragedy of my childhood no longer plays a part in my life performance. I have swept everything under the blood of Jesus.

I can remember my mother telling me once that if she had not known me, she would never know the girl I had become. The bitterness and a heart of stone had taken over my life. I knew she never stopped praying for me. The prayers of a loving and Godly parent are a powerful thing. And, after God removed all of that from my life, she hugged me one day and said, "My girl is back. The girl that has a heart for worship and love for the lord."

My prayer is that my testimony will bring hope and deliverance. To lift you above your circumstances into total victory and increased faith in God. Authoring my story has been cathartic in ways and extremely difficult in others. It makes my heart heavy to think I ever gave up on God. There are days when I cannot even move for the pain. The devil is always ready and waiting to whisper, "Today is going to be a bad one, Gaye. Where is God now?" I must laugh at his persistence. And I will get up and say, "Not today, Devil! I may be weary, but God's got this." My healing may not come for this current condition, and that is OK. I know who my healer is. If I am not healed here, I will be once I reach Heaven. The miracles I have experienced are not for me to understand or to dissect. I cannot explain how or why God did these works in my life, but I give Him all the glory for his faithfulness to me.

He is my deliverer, my healer, and my only hope. He is my provider, my coming king, and my strength. Each beat of my heart is a reminder of how He brought me back. How He reestablished me into the kingdom and how I am to live my life. When I felt forsaken, He had not forsaken me. When my heart was broken, He covered me. When I was in pain, He held on to me and when I was lost, He sustained and protected me. If anyone has a testimony of the abundance of God, it is me!

We serve God by faith. I can ask God all day for a miracle, but, without faith, it will not happen. Every step we take in our walk with Him is by faith. Not in just seeking, but believing that He will do the impossible, the magnificent and the indescribable. Do not put limitations on what God can do for you.

I know now what truly walking with the Lord means. Each day is a new opportunity for me to have influence, to change the atmosphere around me and for others. There is a saying that is often attributed to St. Francis of Assisi, but it has never been proven that he said it. "Preach the gospel always, when necessary, use words." What that says to me is live your life before people. They can feel the Lord, they can see it in your demeanor and your actions more so than any words you will ever say.

Be Christ to those you see along the way. I refuse to give in to the devil when he puts doubt in my mind. Even the writing of this book required great faith. I thought it was the most ludicrous thing I had ever heard when I felt God's call. One day on one of the two prayer routes I drive when I need direction from the Lord, I said, "God, no one wants to read my story. Nobody knows me or cares." And, God said in my spirit, "I gave you that testimony; share it." God had said to do it, and I am being obedient.

People were asking me to author my autobiography, but, ironically, they did not even know my whole story. But God placed it in their hearts to plant the seeds as confirmation for me. God challenged me, "Share my goodness and my faithfulness with others. Remind them that I am still the miracle worker, still the hope for this world. I have not changed." If we ever needed to know this, it is now. But I would have rather not shared the details of my life, my weaknesses, and running from the Lord. But God gave me peace one day when I was looking at my screen debating to delete everything I had written to that point. I have thought often about that day when He came to me in that makeshift ICU room. I was not living right, and He could easily have hurled me into eternity lost. But that is not the God I know. He is the God of judgment, and He could have easily not had mercy on me. He could have whispered in my ear; *you have had more chances than most and I am tired of your disobedience.* But He did not. He filled that room with his sweet presence and took a young woman that fought herself and was battered from life and He gave me another chance. Another chance to know His grace and His love to the fullest.

So, when I began drafting this book mid-2021, the devil was after me. My laptop software crashed, and my printer started making horrible sounds. I developed the worst tendonitis in both arms and in my right shoulder. The pain made it so that I could not type or even write down my thoughts. Although I knew that God wanted me to write my story, the devil tried to stop me at every turn. It took me only five months to author the book, but all the rest of the time I spent being stopped by the devil for sickness, or technical problems. So many times, I had to have people pray for me so that I could keep going. I still face self-doubt. I lacked confidence that He genuinely wanted me to do this work and I was leery to share my deepest imperfections. But in my heart, I know I had to be obedient to His call.

I knew exactly why the devil was attacking me. He would not want a story of victory in Jesus out there. One that talks about faith and miracles that have happened now and not just biblical accounts. And the absolute radical changes God has made in my life. No, he wanted to thwart this plan God had for me to tell it.

And, for weeks I battled tendonitis and cried day and night because the pain was so intense. And believe me, I know pain! I decided one day to walk through my house and pray in each room. And, especially in my office. My mother always said, "When the devil comes in the window, throw him out the door!" So, I prayed, and I rebuked Satan and told him to get out of my house, out of my body and out of this book! I am not one that gives up easily. I do not throw up my hands and surrender like I used to. The devil knows that about me now. This fight we fight here on Earth is real.

In writing these snapshots of events, I am satisfied that God restored memories and conversations so that I could give a glimpse into His grace to me. I often wanted to hit delete and wipe the screen clean from what I had written and just give up. I wanted to quit. I felt out of my element and not worthy to author any book. I would tell God that he would need to send it down in tablets because I did not even know how to begin to write it. I still face self-doubt if I let myself. If I touch one person though, I have done my job. I have done what God instructed.

When your burden gets too heavy, give it to God. When you cannot see past the sickness and your outcome looks hopeless, give it to God. When you have lost your way, or you cannot face tomorrow, give it to God. When your marriage is rocky, when your funds are depleted, and when you do not know which road to take, take the one that leads to the cross. Give it all to God. I promise that when you do, he will become everything to you. It took most of my life to get me to this point, having faith for the speed bumps of life. Having faith to get me through each day, each problem and each time life pulls the rug out. But I am stronger and more prepared than before. The journey will continue to take me on roads I am not comfortable traveling. When I cannot see the next curve the devil sends my way. Or the next hill I must climb. But if I have the Lord with me, I will not be afraid. I will continue to walk with Him.

I have lived through enough that I know without a doubt that Jesus will take care of me. And although there is still work to do in my life, I am better prepared for what the devil tries to do. I am no longer someone that is seeking. I have found the answer for my life and that is Jesus Christ. I am steady and focused, and I see with eyes of understanding and wisdom. I am no longer a child wandering here and there in my relationship with the Lord. I am established in my faith and focused on my walk with the Lord.

Do not ever think that your problem is so big that God cannot hold back the sea for you; He will always be your life preserver. Peter and the others doubted that night on the raging water and Jesus was right in the boat with them. Jesus reminded Peter to keep his eyes on Him and if he did, he would not sink in the water. There was nothing special about Peter or the others; they were earthly men. Men who had problems, had pasts, and yet Jesus selected them to walk with Him and learn from Him. When I start to lose sight of what God has done for me, I think about the disciples. They walked with Jesus every day, saw His works and miracles, and still doubted!

I do not fight my battles alone; God fights them for me. I am not bound by my circumstances or by what a doctor has to say. I go to the healer, right to the source. Our world needs a healer. We need Jesus Christ in our homes, our churches, our workplaces, and schools. And we need Him, especially in our government. I will stand before my father one day, and the tapestry of my life will be held up before the light. There will be dark places where I let God down, and there will be worn places where I struggled, tossed, and turned. But there will be spotless places where I surrendered everything I had to Him.

And, after that day, I will no longer remember the sadness of this world. The things of this life will be over. The pain will be gone, and I will stand before Him a new creature. And I pray that every person I have ever ministered to will be there with me. There are those who have told me, "I do not see God changing my situation, and surely not giving me a miracle. My faith is not strong enough." Listen, the very fact that you believe in a God that you cannot see is faith. You are already there. Now, it is time to exercise that faith. Begin to praise the Lord, stay in constant praise, and speak your need to Him. Remind Him of the promises provided in the Word. Your miracle is there, but you may need to do work to receive it. I did. There may be rough edges that need smoothed in your life, things that need to be addressed. Ask God to reveal those things.

I have shared my heart and have talked about uncomfortable things in this book. But my desire is that for every reader, God will open your eyes to what is available to you when you pray. When you praise and when you ask and expect something from God. Your miracle may be different from mine. Your needs may be different. But we are all in need of a touch from the master. We are all hungry for a work in our lives and to see God move. If I had to relive everything in my life to get me to this place again, I would do it without hesitation. Because I have more faith, more direction, and more peace than I have ever experienced before.

When I pray, I know my prayers are heard by my father. When I ask, I know my miracle is coming. And when I seek him for answers He lets me know what to do. This relationship does not come without sacrifice. God has required much from me to get me to this point. But I see through mature eyes. It is liberating, and I am free from what bound me for so long. He has placed in my heart a desire and passion for others. The restlessness I experience now is for those that are hurting, those that need healing, those that need salvation and those that are weak in their faith. The victory is ours! The battle has been won! We know how our story ends. Jesus is the victor! We WIN in the end.

Now get what you need from God! I have fulfilled my promise to Him, and you know my story and the journey God has taken me on. I wish I had learned sooner. Had trusted God sooner, listened to Him more intently, and followed more closely. But it has brought me to this place, where I know without a doubt to whom I belong. Through the writing of this book, God gave me total recall of times, events, and conversations that I thought I had long forgotten. I followed His lead through this entire process.

There were times I had to get up and leave my laptop because my memory brought back to me things that I had hidden so far away. And I had never wanted to think about them again. I would need some air or to wipe my eyes from the tears that clouded my vision. And, I had to take breaks and regroup from it. Every time I left my laptop I wondered if I was making the right decision to lay my life open for others to see. But then a new faith, stronger than before, would come over me. I am sixty-four years old as I write this. I am no longer concerned about how I measure up with people. I try to be a friend to all, but I do not have the need to be accepted any longer like I did as a child and as a young adult. I have a keen sense of where I belong. I know now where I stand with God, and He alone will measure my deeds and my life.

I would tell young people and my own children and grandchildren not to set your pace to the people around you or to circumstances that come your way. Keep your mind and your heart on the things of God. When you are young, Satan will try everything he can to destroy you. He will place people in your life to sway you. He will cause you to doubt and be led astray. He will tell you that you are not good enough and you do not measure up. He will tease you with thoughts of depression and giving up. He will make your life miserable if given half a chance. But do not let him!

I have accepted God's call to share my testimony. And I have no great aspirations other than to give Him all the glory and honor for what He has done for me. Writing this has taken me on a roller coaster of emotions. My heart is as attached to this book as much as my fingerprints are to my fingers. I cannot share the mysteries of God because I do not know what they are. But I know what I believe, I know what I have experienced, and I know that my foundation is solid, and my direction is set.

I had limitless potential as a child. We all do. But things occur, and situations arise as we grow that are captured in our minds like photographs inside our brains. And these memories mold us later. The decisions we make, and the life we live are choices, and often those choices are not the best for us but arise because of earlier issues we experienced but never dealt with. I struggled all my life with acceptance. I felt different, and I questioned my place in my family. I needed to know where I fit in with my dad, but those answers will never come. But once I gave it all to the Lord, I knew I belonged to Him, and he filled that void.

When I became a young adult, I began to see more clearly that there were deeper things of God that would catapult my life into a new direction, and a stronger faith. I wanted more and I needed more of God. But that happened only after I had made a complete mess out of my life. And only God could have changed me.

There is a difference between liking the idea of God, and a relationship with God. To have a relationship, it requires both of us giving to each other. It means that God takes care of me, and I, in turn, follow His leading. It is a bond, unlike all others. I love my family, but I love God more than anything. The pieces of brokenness that I carried from my childhood and the inadequacies I felt were not the result of my upbringing; I had a wonderful childhood. It was the devil that set his eyes on me. He knew that the day would come when this believer would tell her story and God would be glorified. He knew that God had done amazing things in my life, and he wanted me to be afraid to proclaim it to others. There is a battle going on between God and the devil for each of our lives.

But here I am. After all the pain and sickness, after everything, I am still standing and that is only because of God's mercy to me. The title of this book, "What You Can Become When Your Faith Grows Up," means that every foundational step we take can lead us to a better knowledge of God as we grow in Him. But it is a choice. I choose to live by faith. I have been a recipient of God's miracles, love, protection, and favor. And I will proclaim His goodness and His faithfulness until the day He calls me home.

May you also make the choice to follow Jesus, to live by faith and to receive all God has for you. Your miracle is coming! Just have faith to believe it!

EPILOGUE

When I completed this book in June of 2022 and began the final stages with my publisher, I faced another health crisis. It came out fine, Thank the Lord. But I remember sitting down and crying out to God, "Why? I have done everything You have asked of me. I have told my story, left no stone unturned, and laid my life open for everyone to see. And yet, I am facing more." In this stillness of my frustration, I heard a whisper in my heart. "When you plant a beautiful flower, you must do the work so that it will thrive and bring enjoyment. So, you remove all the debris and pull the weeds around it, so it flourishes and grows. You are that flower. Through the process of authoring this book, I have helped you remove the weeds from your heart and mind that hindered your growth in Me. Those things needed to come to the surface to be dealt with. Never waiver in your trust in Me. Never doubt My attention to your life. This book has caused growth in you, and it has removed everything that has been harbored for so long. It will touch lives."

Thank you, Jesus

"May the God of hope fill you with all joy and peace as you trust in him, so that you may overflow with hope by the power of the Holy Spirit." Romans 15:13 NIV

FROM MY HEART

Album Cover

Mom   My Daddy   Paternal Grandparents. Edna and Plessy Will (papa)

Dad and me   seven or eight months later   Trip to J.L. Hudson's

Candy and me   Junior League of Mercy when I was older   Junior League of Mercy

Debut Solo

Dad and me in Petoskey

Candy striper days

One of my favorite photos of my mom.

Singing at the Piano

Our Wedding 11.19.1983

My babies

One of the last photos of mom

My brother, the day after mom's funeral

Family time

My handsome Jonathan

Love of my life, Bruce

My gorgeous Bethany

letting loose on the turkey

US

DON'T QUIT

WHEN THINGS GO WRONG, AS THEY SOMETIMES WILL,
WHEN THE ROAD YOU'RE TRUDGING SEEMS ALL UPHILL,
WHEN THE FUNDS ARE LOW AND THE DEBTS ARE HIGH,
AND YOU WANT TO SMILE, BUT YOU HAVE TO SIGH,
WHEN CARE IS PRESSING YOU DOWN A BIT,
REST IF YOU MUST, BUT DON'T YOU QUIT.
LIFE IS STRANGE WITH IT'S TWISTS AND TURNS,
AS EVERY ONE OF US SOMETIMES LEARNS,
AND MANY A FAILURE COMES ABOUT,
WHEN ME MIGHT HAVE WON HAD HE STUCK IT OUT.
DON'T GIVE UP THOUGH THE PACE SEEMS SLOW-
YOU MAY SUCCEED WITH ANOTHER BLOW.
SUCCESS IS FAILURE TURNED INSIDE OUT-
THE SILVER TINT OF THE CLOUDS OF DOUBT,
AND YOU NEVER CAN TELL HOW CLOSE YOU ARE,
IT MAY BE NEAR WHEN IT SEEMS SO FAR,
SO, STICK TO THE FIGHT WHEN YOU'RE HARDEST HIT,
IT'S WHEN THINGS SEEM WORST THAT YOU MUST NOT QUIT.

There is some question as to who authored this poem. Some say that John Greenleaf Whittier penned it in the early 1800's; however, Edgar A. Guest is also attributed to writing it in early 1920.

HELPFUL REFERENCE SCRIPTURES REGARDING FAITH

Therefore, I tell you, whatever you ask for in prayer, believe that you have received it, and it will be yours. **Mark 11:24 NIV**

I pray that out of his glorious riches, he may strengthen you with power through his Spirit in your inner being, so that Christ may dwell in your hearts through faith. And I pray that you, being rooted and established in love. **Ephesians 3:16-17 NIV**

Now faith is confidence in what we hope for and assurance about what we do not see. **Hebrews 11:1 NIV**

For we live by faith, not by sight. **2 Corinthians 5:7 NIV**

But when you ask, you must believe and not doubt, because the one who doubts is like a wave of the sea, blown and tossed by the wind. **James 1:6 NIV**

And, without faith, it is impossible to please God because anyone who comes to him must believe that he exists and that he rewards those who earnestly seek him. **Hebrews 11:6 NIV**

Then Jesus said, "Did I not tell you that if you believe, you will see the glory of God?" **John 11:40 NIV**

"If you can?" said Jesus. "Everything is possible for one who believes." **Mark 9:23 NIV**

Because you know that the testing of your faith produces perseverance. **James 1:3 NIV**

Though you have not seen him, you love him; and even though you do not see him now, you believe in him and are filled with an inexpressible and glorious joy, for you are receiving the end results of your faith, the salvation of your souls. **1 Peter 1:8-9 NIV**

Jesus said to her, "I am the resurrection and the life. The one who believes in me will live, even though they die, and whoever lives by believing in me will never die. Do you believe this?" **John 11:25-26 NIV**

For everyone born of God overcomes the world. This is the victory that has overcome the world, even our faith. **1 John 5:4 NIV**

If you believe, you will receive whatever you ask for in prayer. **Matthew 21:22 NIV**

But you, man of God, flee from all this, and pursue righteousness, godliness, faith, love, endurance, and gentleness. **1 Timothy 6:11 NIV**

"Go," said Jesus, "Your faith has healed you." Immediately he received his sight and followed Jesus along the road. **Mark 10:52 NIV**

If I have the gift of prophecy and can fathom all mysteries and all knowledge, and if I have a faith that can move mountains, but do not have love, I am nothing. **1 Corinthians 13:2 NIV**

Then Jesus declared, "I am the bread of life. Whoever comes to me will never go hungry, and whoever believes in me will never be thirsty." **John 6:35 NIV**

I have chosen the way of faithfulness; I have set my heart on your laws. **Psalm 119:30 NIV**

For it is with your heart that you believe and are justified, and it is with your mouth that you profess your faith and are served. **Romans 10:10 NIV**

And by faith even Sarah, who was past childbearing age, was enabled to bear children because she considered him faithful who had made the promise. **Hebrews 11:11 NIV**

Be on your guard; stand firm in the faith; be courageous; be strong. **1 Corinthians 16:13 NIV**

For in the gospel the righteousness of God is revealed—a righteousness that is by faith from first to last, just as it is written: "The righteous will live by faith." **Romans 1:17 NIV**

Is anyone among you sick? Let them call the elders of the church to pray over them and anoint them with oil in the name of the Lord. And the prayer offered in faith will make the sick person well; the Lord will raise them up. If they have sinned, they will be forgiven. **James 5:14-15 NIV**

In the same way, faith by itself if it is not accompanied by action, is dead. **James 2:17 NIV**

He replied, "Because you have so little faith. Truly I tell you, if you have faith as small as a mustard seed, you can say to this mountain, "Move from here to there," and it will move. Nothing will be impossible for you." **Matthew 17:20 NIV**

Consequently, faith comes from hearing the message, and the message is heard through the word about Christ. **Romans 10:17 NIV**

Fixing our eyes on Jesus, the pioneer and perfecter of faith. For the joy set before him he endured the cross, scorning its shame, and sat down at the right hand of the throne of God. **Hebrews 12:2 NIV**

For it is by grace you have been saved, through faith – and this is not from yourselves, it is the gift of God – not by works, so that no one can boast. **Ephesians 2:8-9 NIV**

The life I now live in the body, I live by faith in the Son of God, who loved me and gave himself for me. **Galatians 2:20 NIV**

Therefore, put on the full armor of God, so that when the day of evil comes, you may be able to stand your ground, and after you have done everything, to stand. Stand firm then, with the belt of truth buckled around your waist, with the breastplate of righteousness in place, and with your feet fitted with the readiness that comes from the gospel of peace. In addition to all this, take up the shield of faith, with which you can extinguish all the flaming arrows of the evil one. Take the helmet of salvation and the sword of the spirit, which is the word of God. **Ephesians 6:13-17 NIV**